FREE Test Taking Tips Video/DVD Offer

To better serve you, we created videos covering test taking tips that we want to give you for FREE. **These videos cover world-class tips that will help you succeed on your test.**

We just ask that you send us feedback about this product. Please let us know what you thought about it—whether good, bad, or indifferent.

To get your **FREE videos**, you can use the QR code below or email freevideos@studyguideteam.com with "Free Videos" in the subject line and the following information in the body of the email:

   a. The title of your product

   b. Your product rating on a scale of 1-5, with 5 being the highest

   c. Your feedback about the product

If you have any questions or concerns, please don't hesitate to contact us at info@studyguideteam.com.

Thank you!

AP US History 2023 and 2024 Study Guide

APUSH Review Book with Practice Test Questions for College Board Exam Prep [2nd Edition]

Joshua Rueda

Interested in buying more than 10 copies of our product? Contact us about bulk discounts:
bulkorders@studyguideteam.com

ISBN 13: 9781637755006
ISBN 10: 1637755007

Table of Contents

Quick Overview

As you draw closer to taking your exam, effective preparation becomes more and more important. Thankfully, you have this study guide to help you get ready. Use this guide to help keep your studying on track and refer to it often.

This study guide contains several key sections that will help you be successful on your exam. The guide contains tips for what you should do the night before and the day of the test. Also included are test-taking tips. Knowing the right information is not always enough. Many well-prepared test takers struggle with exams. These tips will help equip you to accurately read, assess, and answer test questions.

A large part of the guide is devoted to showing you what content to expect on the exam and to helping you better understand that content. In this guide are practice test questions so that you can see how well you have grasped the content. Then, answer explanations are provided so that you can understand why you missed certain questions.

Don't try to cram the night before you take your exam. This is not a wise strategy for a few reasons. First, your retention of the information will be low. Your time would be better used by reviewing information you already know rather than trying to learn a lot of new information. Second, you will likely become stressed as you try to gain a large amount of knowledge in a short amount of time. Third, you will be depriving yourself of sleep. So be sure to go to bed at a reasonable time the night before. Being well-rested helps you focus and remain calm.

Be sure to eat a substantial breakfast the morning of the exam. If you are taking the exam in the afternoon, be sure to have a good lunch as well. Being hungry is distracting and can make it difficult to focus. You have hopefully spent lots of time preparing for the exam. Don't let an empty stomach get in the way of success!

When travelling to the testing center, leave earlier than needed. That way, you have a buffer in case you experience any delays. This will help you remain calm and will keep you from missing your appointment time at the testing center.

Be sure to pace yourself during the exam. Don't try to rush through the exam. There is no need to risk performing poorly on the exam just so you can leave the testing center early. Allow yourself to use all of the allotted time if needed.

Remain positive while taking the exam even if you feel like you are performing poorly. Thinking about the content you should have mastered will not help you perform better on the exam.

Once the exam is complete, take some time to relax. Even if you feel that you need to take the exam again, you will be well served by some down time before you begin studying again. It's often easier to convince yourself to study if you know that it will come with a reward!

Test-Taking Strategies

1. Predicting the Answer

When you feel confident in your preparation for a multiple-choice test, try predicting the answer before reading the answer choices. This is especially useful on questions that test objective factual knowledge. By predicting the answer before reading the available choices, you eliminate the possibility that you will be distracted or led astray by an incorrect answer choice. You will feel more confident in your selection if you read the question, predict the answer, and then find your prediction among the answer choices. After using this strategy, be sure to still read all of the answer choices carefully and completely. If you feel unprepared, you should not attempt to predict the answers. This would be a waste of time and an opportunity for your mind to wander in the wrong direction.

2. Reading the Whole Question

Too often, test takers scan a multiple-choice question, recognize a few familiar words, and immediately jump to the answer choices. Test authors are aware of this common impatience, and they will sometimes prey upon it. For instance, a test author might subtly turn the question into a negative, or he or she might redirect the focus of the question right at the end. The only way to avoid falling into these traps is to read the entirety of the question carefully before reading the answer choices.

3. Looking for Wrong Answers

Long and complicated multiple-choice questions can be intimidating. One way to simplify a difficult multiple-choice question is to eliminate all of the answer choices that are clearly wrong. In most sets of answers, there will be at least one selection that can be dismissed right away. If the test is administered on paper, the test taker could draw a line through it to indicate that it may be ignored; otherwise, the test taker will have to perform this operation mentally or on scratch paper. In either case, once the obviously incorrect answers have been eliminated, the remaining choices may be considered. Sometimes identifying the clearly wrong answers will give the test taker some information about the correct answer. For instance, if one of the remaining answer choices is a direct opposite of one of the eliminated answer choices, it may well be the correct answer. The opposite of obviously wrong is obviously right! Of course, this is not always the case. Some answers are obviously incorrect simply because they are irrelevant to the question being asked. Still, identifying and eliminating some incorrect answer choices is a good way to simplify a multiple-choice question.

4. Don't Overanalyze

Anxious test takers often overanalyze questions. When you are nervous, your brain will often run wild, causing you to make associations and discover clues that don't actually exist. If you feel that this may be a problem for you, do whatever you can to slow down during the test. Try taking a deep breath or counting to ten. As you read and consider the question, restrict yourself to the particular words used by the author. Avoid thought tangents about what the author *really* meant, or what he or she was *trying* to say. The only things that matter on a multiple-choice test are the words that are actually in the question. You must avoid reading too much into a multiple-choice question, or supposing that the writer meant something other than what he or she wrote.

2

5. No Need for Panic

It is wise to learn as many strategies as possible before taking a multiple-choice test, but it is likely that you will come across a few questions for which you simply don't know the answer. In this situation, avoid panicking. Because most multiple-choice tests include dozens of questions, the relative value of a single wrong answer is small. As much as possible, you should compartmentalize each question on a multiple-choice test. In other words, you should not allow your feelings about one question to affect your success on the others. When you find a question that you either don't understand or don't know how to answer, just take a deep breath and do your best. Read the entire question slowly and carefully. Try rephrasing the question a couple of different ways. Then, read all of the answer choices carefully. After eliminating obviously wrong answers, make a selection and move on to the next question.

6. Confusing Answer Choices

When working on a difficult multiple-choice question, there may be a tendency to focus on the answer choices that are the easiest to understand. Many people, whether consciously or not, gravitate to the answer choices that require the least concentration, knowledge, and memory. This is a mistake. When you come across an answer choice that is confusing, you should give it extra attention. A question might be confusing because you do not know the subject matter to which it refers. If this is the case, don't eliminate the answer before you have affirmatively settled on another. When you come across an answer choice of this type, set it aside as you look at the remaining choices. If you can confidently assert that one of the other choices is correct, you can leave the confusing answer aside. Otherwise, you will need to take a moment to try to better understand the confusing answer choice. Rephrasing is one way to tease out the sense of a confusing answer choice.

7. Your First Instinct

Many people struggle with multiple-choice tests because they overthink the questions. If you have studied sufficiently for the test, you should be prepared to trust your first instinct once you have carefully and completely read the question and all of the answer choices. There is a great deal of research suggesting that the mind can come to the correct conclusion very quickly once it has obtained all of the relevant information. At times, it may seem to you as if your intuition is working faster even than your reasoning mind. This may in fact be true. The knowledge you obtain while studying may be retrieved from your subconscious before you have a chance to work out the associations that support it. Verify your instinct by working out the reasons that it should be trusted.

8. Key Words

Many test takers struggle with multiple-choice questions because they have poor reading comprehension skills. Quickly reading and understanding a multiple-choice question requires a mixture of skill and experience. To help with this, try jotting down a few key words and phrases on a piece of scrap paper. Doing this concentrates the process of reading and forces the mind to weigh the relative importance of the question's parts. In selecting words and phrases to write down, the test taker thinks about the question more deeply and carefully. This is especially true for multiple-choice questions that are preceded by a long prompt.

9. Subtle Negatives

One of the oldest tricks in the multiple-choice test writer's book is to subtly reverse the meaning of a question with a word like *not* or *except*. If you are not paying attention to each word in the question, you can easily be led astray by this trick. For instance, a common question format is, "Which of the following is...?" Obviously, if the question instead is, "Which of the following is not...?," then the answer will be quite different. Even worse, the test makers are aware of the potential for this mistake and will include one answer choice that would be correct if the question were not negated or reversed. A test taker who misses the reversal will find what he or she believes to be a correct answer and will be so confident that he or she will fail to reread the question and discover the original error. The only way to avoid this is to practice a wide variety of multiple-choice questions and to pay close attention to each and every word.

10. Reading Every Answer Choice

It may seem obvious, but you should always read every one of the answer choices! Too many test takers fall into the habit of scanning the question and assuming that they understand the question because they recognize a few key words. From there, they pick the first answer choice that answers the question they believe they have read. Test takers who read all of the answer choices might discover that one of the latter answer choices is actually *more* correct. Moreover, reading all of the answer choices can remind you of facts related to the question that can help you arrive at the correct answer. Sometimes, a misstatement or incorrect detail in one of the latter answer choices will trigger your memory of the subject and will enable you to find the right answer. Failing to read all of the answer choices is like not reading all of the items on a restaurant menu: you might miss out on the perfect choice.

11. Spot the Hedges

One of the keys to success on multiple-choice tests is paying close attention to every word. This is never truer than with words like almost, most, some, and sometimes. These words are called "hedges" because they indicate that a statement is not totally true or not true in every place and time. An absolute statement will contain no hedges, but in many subjects, the answers are not always straightforward or absolute. There are always exceptions to the rules in these subjects. For this reason, you should favor those multiple-choice questions that contain hedging language. The presence of qualifying words indicates that the author is taking special care with their words, which is certainly important when composing the right answer. After all, there are many ways to be wrong, but there is only one way to be right! For this reason, it is wise to avoid answers that are absolute when taking a multiple-choice test. An absolute answer is one that says things are either all one way or all another. They often include words like *every, always, best,* and *never*. If you are taking a multiple-choice test in a subject that doesn't lend itself to absolute answers, be on your guard if you see any of these words.

12. Long Answers

In many subject areas, the answers are not simple. As already mentioned, the right answer often requires hedges. Another common feature of the answers to a complex or subjective question are qualifying clauses, which are groups of words that subtly modify the meaning of the sentence. If the question or answer choice describes a rule to which there are exceptions or the subject matter is complicated, ambiguous, or confusing, the correct answer will require many words in order to be expressed clearly and accurately. In essence, you should not be deterred by answer choices that seem

4

excessively long. Oftentimes, the author of the text will not be able to write the correct answer without offering some qualifications and modifications. Your job is to read the answer choices thoroughly and completely and to select the one that most accurately and precisely answers the question.

13. Restating to Understand

Sometimes, a question on a multiple-choice test is difficult not because of what it asks but because of how it is written. If this is the case, restate the question or answer choice in different words. This process serves a couple of important purposes. First, it forces you to concentrate on the core of the question. In order to rephrase the question accurately, you have to understand it well. Rephrasing the question will concentrate your mind on the key words and ideas. Second, it will present the information to your mind in a fresh way. This process may trigger your memory and render some useful scrap of information picked up while studying.

14. True Statements

Sometimes an answer choice will be true in itself, but it does not answer the question. This is one of the main reasons why it is essential to read the question carefully and completely before proceeding to the answer choices. Too often, test takers skip ahead to the answer choices and look for true statements. Having found one of these, they are content to select it without reference to the question above. Obviously, this provides an easy way for test makers to play tricks. The savvy test taker will always read the entire question before turning to the answer choices. Then, having settled on a correct answer choice, he or she will refer to the original question and ensure that the selected answer is relevant. The mistake of choosing a correct-but-irrelevant answer choice is especially common on questions related to specific pieces of objective knowledge. A prepared test taker will have a wealth of factual knowledge at their disposal, and should not be careless in its application.

15. No Patterns

One of the more dangerous ideas that circulates about multiple-choice tests is that the correct answers tend to fall into patterns. These erroneous ideas range from a belief that B and C are the most common right answers, to the idea that an unprepared test-taker should answer "A-B-A-C-A-D-A-B-A." It cannot be emphasized enough that pattern-seeking of this type is exactly the WRONG way to approach a multiple-choice test. To begin with, it is highly unlikely that the test maker will plot the correct answers according to some predetermined pattern. The questions are scrambled and delivered in a random order. Furthermore, even if the test maker was following a pattern in the assignation of correct answers, there is no reason why the test taker would know which pattern he or she was using. Any attempt to discern a pattern in the answer choices is a waste of time and a distraction from the real work of taking the test. A test taker would be much better served by extra preparation before the test than by reliance on a pattern in the answers.

FREE Videos/DVD OFFER

Doing well on your exam requires both knowing the test content and understanding how to use that knowledge to do well on the test. We offer completely FREE test taking tip videos. **These videos cover world-class tips that you can use to succeed on your test.**

To get your **FREE videos**, you can use the QR code below or email freevideos@studyguideteam.com with "Free Videos" in the subject line and the following information in the body of the email:

    a. The title of your product

    b. Your product rating on a scale of 1-5, with 5 being the highest

    c. Your feedback about the product

If you have any questions or concerns, please don't hesitate to contact us at info@studyguideteam.com.

Thanks again!

Introduction to the AP U.S. History Exam

Function of the Test

The Advanced Placement (AP) U.S. History Exam, created by the College Board, is an exam designed to offer college placement for high school students. The AP program allows students to earn college credit, advanced placement, or both, through the program's offering of the course and end-of-course exam. Sometimes universities may also look at AP scores to determine college admission. This guide gives an overview of the exam along with a condensed version of what might be taught in the AP U.S. History course, and a practice test.

The AP program creates multiple versions of each AP exam to be administered within various U.S. geographic regions. With these exams, schools can offer late testing and discourage sharing questions across time zones. The AP exam is given in the U.S. nationwide; and outside of Canada and the U.S., credits are only sometimes accepted in other countries. The College Board website has a list of universities outside of the U.S. that recognize AP for credit and admission.

In 2019, 496,573 students took the AP U.S. History exam.

Test Administration

On their website, the College Board provides a specific day that the AP U.S. History exam is given. Because the exam is a culminating exam for a year-long course, the date is usually in mid-May. Coordinators should notify students when and where to report.

Students may take the exam again if they are not happy with their results. However, since the exam is given one day per year, students must wait until the following year to retake the exam. Both scores will be reported unless the student cancels or withholds one of the scores.

A wide range of accommodations are available to students who live with disabilities. Students will work with their school to request accommodations. If students or parents do not request accommodations through their school, disabilities must be appropriately documented and requested in advance via the College Board website.

Test Format

The AP U.S. History exam is three hours and fifteen minutes long and contains a multiple-choice section, a short-answer section, and a free-response section. The multiple-choice section is made up of reading passages from primary and secondary-source historical documents, and has fifty-five questions total. This section comprises 40 percent of the exam score and lasts fifty-five minutes. The questions will mostly appear in sets of 3-4 questions per passage, and students will need to analyze historical texts and evidence, and then interpret that information. Both primary and secondary sources will be included, along with graphics such as maps, tables, and images.

The short-answer section has three questions that the test taker must analyze and answer. This section accounts for 20 percent of the exam score and lasts forty minutes. Students are asked to analyze historical sources and historians' interpretation of sources or topics. Each of the three questions focuses

7

on a different time period and may include a primary source. Four questions are presented, and the first two are required. Test takers can select whether they answer Question 3 or Question 4.

The free-response section has a document-based question and a long essay question. This section contributes 40 percent of the exam score and lasts for one hour and forty minutes, with one hour dedicated to document-based question (25% of the score), and 40 minutes given for the long essay question (15% of the score). In the document-based question, the student must analyze seven documents that offer different perspectives on a historical process, event, or development pertinent to the years of 1754-1980. Students respond with a written argument using the historical evidence and their own insight. The long essay requires students to explain and analyze an important issue pertinent to U.S. history from one of three major time periods: 1491-1800, 1800-1898, or 1890-2001.

Scoring

Scoring on the AP exam is similar to that of a college course. The table below shows an outline of scores and what they mean:

Score	Recommendation	College Grade
5	Extremely well qualified	A
4	Well qualified	A-, B+,B
3	Qualified	B-,C+,C
2	Possibly qualified	n/a
1	No recommendation	n/a

While multiple-choice questions are graded via machine, the short-answer and free-response questions are graded by AP Readers. Scores on the free-response section are weighted and combined with the scores from the multiple-choice questions. The raw score from these two sections is converted into a 1–5 scale, as explained in the table above.

In 2019, 496,573 took the AP U.S. History exam worldwide. In this cohort of test takers, 11.8% earned a 5, 18.4% earned a 4, 23.4% earned a 3, 22.0% earned a 2, and 24.3% of test takers earned a 1. The mean score was 2.71.

Colleges are responsible for setting their own criteria for placement and admissions, so check with specific universities to assess their criteria concerning the AP exam.

Study Prep Plan for the AP U.S. History Exam

1 **Schedule -** Use one of our study schedules below or come up with one of your own.

2 **Relax -** Test anxiety can hurt even the best students. There are many ways to reduce stress. Find the one that works best for you.

3 **Execute -** Once you have a good plan in place, be sure to stick to it.

One Week Study Schedule

Day 1	Period 1: 1491-1607
Day 2	Period 3: 1754-1800
Day 3	Period 4: 1800-1848
Day 4	Period 6: 1865-1898
Day 5	Period 8: 1945-1980
Day 6	Practice Test
Day 7	Take Your Exam!

Two Week Study Schedule

Day 1	Period 1: 1491-1607	Day 8	Period 7: 1890-1945
Day 2	Period 2: 1607-1754	Day 9	Period 8: 1945-1980
Day 3	Period 3: 1754-1800	Day 10	The Civil Rights Movement Expands
Day 4	The Constitution	Day 11	Period 9: 1980-Present
Day 5	Period 4: 1800-1848	Day 12	Practice Test
Day 6	Period 5: 1844-1877	Day 13	Answer Explanations
Day 7	Period 6: 1865-1898	Day 14	Take Your Exam!

This material is provided for exam preparation purposes only and does not indicate an endorsement of any specific scientific, political, or religious point of view. © TPB Publishing. You have been licensed one copy of this document for personal use only. Any other reproduction or redistribution is strictly prohibited. All rights reserved.

One Month Study Schedule					
Day 1	Period 1: 1491-1607	Day 11	Practice Questions	Day 21	Period 8: 1945-1980
Day 2	Practice Questions	Day 12	Period 5: 1844-1877	Day 22	America as a World Power
Day 3	Period 2: 1607-1754	Day 13	Military Conflict in the Civil War	Day 23	The Civil Rights Movement Expands
Day 4	Practice Questions	Day 14	Practice Questions	Day 24	Practice Questions
Day 5	Period 3: 1754-1800	Day 15	Period 6: 1865-1898	Day 25	Period 9: 1980-Present
Day 6	The Influence of Revolutionary Ideals	Day 16	Immigration and Migration in the Gilded Age	Day 26	Migration and Immigration in the 1990s and 2000s
Day 7	Shaping a New Republic	Day 17	Practice Questions	Day 27	Practice Questions
Day 8	Practice Questions	Day 18	Period 7: 1890-1945	Day 28	Practice Test
Day 9	Period 4: 1800-1848	Day 19	1920s: Cultural and Political Controversies	Day 29	Answer Explanations
Day 10	Expanding Democracy	Day 20	Practice Questions	Day 30	Take Your Exam!

Build your own prep plan by visiting:
testprepbooks.com/prep

Native American Societies Before European Contact

Maize Cultivation in the Southwest

Maize (corn) is a cereal grain that played a significant role in the development of American settlements. Indigenous tribes first domesticated maize approximately 10,000 years ago in present-day Mexico. Eventually, human migration and cultural interactions resulted in the spread of maize from Central America and Mexico to the present-day American southwest. Eventually, nearly all North American indigenous agricultural societies relied on maize in some way, either through production or trade.

The cultivation of maize triggered dramatic changes in many indigenous societies. Compared to other crops, maize could be produced at a relatively larger scale with fewer resources. Additionally, maize was rich in calories and dynamic in its application to a wide variety of recipes. As such, the cultivation of maize helped agricultural societies generate a food surplus, facilitating the establishment of permanent settlements and diversification of socioeconomic classes. Furthermore, diversification spurred more dynamic economic development, complex trade patterns, and sophisticated urbanization. For example, the cultivation of maize led to societies discovering advanced irrigation techniques through the pursuit of more consistent and robust production. Lastly, the size of indigenous militaries increased as more males were freed from providing agricultural labor, and the rise of permanent settlements led to more competition over resources.

Mobile Lifestyles in the Great Basin and Great Plains

Indigenous societies living in the Great Basin and Great Plains didn't engage in agricultural development; instead, they developed complex hunter-gatherer societies to adapt to the climate and open space. The **Great Basin** is an enormous watershed with a relatively arid climate primarily located in present-day eastern California, southeastern Oregon, Nevada, and western Utah. Because much of the climate was generally incompatible with permanent large-scale agricultural production, the indigenous societies tended to travel based on the movement of wildlife and freshwater. The **Great Plains** had a more hospitable climate for agriculture, but indigenous societies specialized in hunting buffalo across the Great Plains' unusually flat land located in present-day eastern Wyoming, eastern Colorado, Nebraska, and Kansas.

Spanish expeditions into South America introduced pack animals, such as donkeys and horses, to the Great Basin and Great Plains during the late sixteenth and early seventeenth centuries. The arrival of domesticated horses strongly complemented Great Plain Native Americans' hunter-gatherer societies by enhancing mobility and expediting travel times. Mobile societies living in teepees didn't have the luxury of storing materials, so Great Plains Native Americans learned to use every part of the animals they killed. For example, the fur, skin, and bones of buffaloes provided everything from teepees to cooking tools.

The Development of Permanent Villages in the East

Many indigenous societies blended characteristics of agricultural and hunter-gatherer societies. Within the present-day United States, many indigenous nations with mixed forms of development were

established in the Mississippi River Valley, Atlantic Coastal region, and Northeast due to the temperate climate and availability of plentiful fish, wildlife, and fertile soil. When British and French expeditions arrived in the sixteenth century, they expected to find mines of gold and silver like the Spanish encountered in South America. Instead, much of the eastern portion of the present-day United States had an abundance of natural resources such as waterways, timber, and arable land. In addition, the relatively temperate climate and rich soil allowed for consistent agricultural production. Agriculture provided a consistent source of food, bringing stability and permanence to settlements.

The combination of agricultural productivity and hunter-gatherer lifestyles produced powerful and enduring indigenous confederations across the Mississippi Valley and Atlantic region of the present-day United States and Canada. Indigenous confederations in these areas constructed permanent villages, facilitating the rise of more complex political organizations. As a result, many European colonies in New England and along the Atlantic seaboard struggled mightily to gain a foothold and expand frontier borders in this region throughout the seventeenth century.

Hunter-Gatherer Societies in the West

Indigenous societies in present-day California and the North American Northwest were primarily hunter-gatherer societies with some notable exceptions along the Pacific coastline. As with indigenous nations in the Great Basin region, the climate was mostly incompatible with large-scale agriculture. So, most nations from northern California to the Pacific Northwest favored transient settlement patterns that mirrored the migratory path of natural resources. Permanent settlements in this region were, significantly, built within fertile valleys, especially in present-day southern California, and areas with direct access to the Pacific Ocean.

Pacific Northwest indigenous communities stood apart from the rest of the region. Increased access to waterways facilitated expansion by expediting travel times and reducing the burden of moving supplies across long distances. These settlements were also unique because they established permanence without a stable agricultural system; instead, fishing functioned as the primary method of acquiring food, and fish were plentiful enough to support significant population growth. Pacific Northwest regions especially prized and revered salmon as nature's greatest bounty. For example, many indigenous cultures incorporated the worship of deities tied to salmon. Salmon also had long-distance seasonal migration patterns, which resulted in the natural growth of shared cultural and economic characteristics across the region.

European Exploration in the Americas

European Nations' Motives to Conquer the New World

When examining how Europeans explored what would become the United States of America, one must first examine why Europeans came to explore the New World as a whole. In the fifteenth century, tensions increased between the Eastern and Mediterranean nations of Europe and the expanding Ottoman Empire to the east. As war and piracy spread across the Mediterranean, the once-prosperous trade routes across Asia's Silk Road began to decline, and nations across Europe began to explore alternative routes for trade. Italian explorer Christopher Columbus proposed a westward route. Contrary to popular lore, proving that the world was round was not the main challenge that Columbus faced in finding backers. In fact, much of Europe's educated elite knew that the world was round; the real issue was that they rightly believed that a westward route to Asia, even assuming a lack of obstacles, would

12

be too long to be practical. Nevertheless, Columbus set sail in 1492 after obtaining support from Spain and arrived in the West Indies three months later.

Spain launched further expeditions to the new continents and established **New Spain**. The colony consisted not only of Central America and Mexico, but also the American Southwest and Florida. France claimed much of what would become Canada, along with the Mississippi River region and the Midwest. In addition, the Dutch established colonies that covered New Jersey, New York, and Connecticut. Each nation managed its colonies differently, and thus influenced how they would assimilate into the United States. For instance, Spain strove to establish a system of Christian missions throughout its territory, while France focused on trading networks and had limited infrastructure in regions such as the Midwest. Even in cases of limited colonial growth, the land of America was hardly vacant because a diverse array of Native American nations and groups were already present.

Throughout much of colonial history, European settlers commonly misperceived native peoples as a singular, static entity. In reality, Native Americans had a variety of traditions depending on their history and environment. Additionally, their culture continued to change through the course of interactions with European settlers; for instance, tribes such as the Cheyenne and Comanche used horses, which were introduced by white settlers, to become powerful warrior nations. However, a few generalizations can be made: many, but not all, tribes were matrilineal, which gave women a fair degree of power, and land was commonly seen as belonging to everyone. These differences, particularly European settlers' continual focus on land ownership, contributed to increasing prejudice and violence.

News of success sparked a number of other expeditions and the British, French, Dutch, Spanish, and Portuguese all eventually laid claim to lands in the New World. Columbus himself made three more voyages to the Americas. The French and Dutch focused mostly on the lucrative fur trade in North America. The Spanish and Portuguese sought gold in Central and South America but also tried to convert Native Americans to Christianity. British settlers also sought economic opportunity and created the first British colony at Jamestown, Virginia, in 1607. However, the Puritans, who landed at Plymouth Rock in 1620, left for the New World in order to establish their ideal religious community.

Columbian Exchange, Spanish Exploration, and Conquest

The Columbian Exchange

European exploration in North America dates back to around 1000 AD when Scandinavian Vikings, led by **Leif Eriksson**, first made their way to Greenland and then journeyed on to modern-day Newfoundland. They settled briefly in an area now known as L'Anse Meadows. However, clashes with the Native American people living nearby caused them to return to Greenland a few years later. The first permanent settlements in North America began after Italian sailor Christopher Columbus landed in the Caribbean in 1492. This was a significant breakthrough since most Europeans did not know that this huge landmass even existed. It initiated a period of discovery, conquest, and colonization of the Americas by the Europeans.

Often referred to as the **Columbian Exchange**, this period allowed people who had been cut off from each other for 15,000 years to share knowledge, ideas, culture, food, plants and animals, technology, and religion. This led to significant changes and enhancements for both regions. The population in Europe grew, largely due to the benefits imparted by new crops such as maize, potatoes, and tomatoes, which diversified and enriched the diet over time. Additionally, new sources of mineral wealth,

particularly silver, contributed to the shift in much of Europe from feudalism to capitalism. Various types of livestock, including horses, and crops such as rice, wheat, coffee, and sugarcane were introduced to the New World.

The Columbian Exchange also led to massive cultural changes as Europeans and Africans came to the new world, bringing new religions and moral codes as well as diseases against which the Native Americans had no natural immunity. Slavery was already present among the Native American tribes, but it was practiced on a much larger scale by the arriving Europeans. Desire to control the riches of the New World also led to clashes among European powers.

Maritime Technological Advancements and Joint-Stock Companies

European powers leveraged technological, political, and economic innovations to colonize the Americas. During the fifteenth century, European explorers adopted and improved several types of existing **maritime technologies** including lateen sails, magnetic compasses, and cartography. European engineers created significantly larger versions of Indian dhows, such as galleys, and outfitted the ships with cannons to achieve maritime superiority. Portugal and Spain were the early European maritime powers during this period, but by the late sixteenth century, the Iberian powers faced stiff competition from the Dutch, English, French, and Swiss.

From the late sixteenth century through the seventeenth century, European powers established joint-stock companies to facilitate colonization. **Joint-stock companies** consisted of a public-private partnership in which the government granted property rights and legal authority over colonies to private companies, and the parties shared the necessary capital investments and potential profits in accordance with a formalized agreement. In effect, joint-stock companies allowed governments to mitigate the risk and subsidize the cost of colonization. In the Americas, European settlements experienced exponential expansion due to the injection of capital investments and consolidation of resources. Overall, this expansion led to a colossal transfer of wealth from indigenous to European societies. Wealth transfers especially facilitated the beginning stages of European textile manufacturing and industrialization.

Diseases Spread to Native Americans

Native Americans were vulnerable to diseases to which the Europeans had developed immunity. These diseases included bubonic plague, cholera, chicken pox, pneumonic plague, influenza, measles, scarlet fever, typhus, smallpox, and tuberculosis. These diseases killed millions of Native Americans and were sometimes used as a biological weapon. Historians estimate that as much as 80 percent of the Native American population died through disease and warfare.

Labor, Slavery, and Caste in the Spanish Colonial System

The Encomienda System

Initially, Spain enforced the **encomienda system** in the Americas to meet its labor needs. Under this labor system, the Spanish crown allowed conquistadors to enslave people they conquered, so as to incentivize territorial expansion. More specifically, the Spanish crown sought to expand profitable economic opportunities, such as large-scale plantation (**haciendas**) agriculture and mining precious metals. In theory, enslaving indigenous people was more efficient than importing Africans, but the

14

encomienda system failed spectacularly for two reasons. First, it was ineffective. Indigenous populations resisted enslavement, and the Spanish elites killed indigenous workers at an unsustainable rate. Second, the horrific working conditions and massive death toll shocked the Spanish crown and broader public. Due to these reasons, the Spanish crown implemented the **New Laws of 1542** to abolish the encomienda system in the Americas. This reform didn't quite free indigenous workers from forced labor; instead, the New Laws replaced the encomienda system with a policy known as the *repartimiento system*.

Repartimiento placed indigenous populations under the monarchy's direct authority. As a result, the Spanish crown allotted labor to plantation owners and regulated working conditions. Despite this effort to reduce overt abuses, indigenous populations continued to suffer staggering death tolls until the system collapsed at the end of the seventeenth century.

The Beginnings of the Transatlantic Slave Trade

The **transatlantic slave trade** involved European merchants acquiring slaves from West Africa and transporting them to the Americas. During the early sixteenth century, Portugal and Spain were the dominant powers in West Africa and, as a result, they played an outsized role in shaping the transatlantic slave trade in its early stages. However, by the beginning of the seventeenth century, Dutch, English, and French merchants had become significantly more involved in the slave trade. The competition was fierce due to the immense value of African slaves because they were the most profitable source of labor for plantation-based agriculture and mining in the Americas.

Slavery had been practiced in West Africa for many centuries prior to the arrival of Europeans, and most slaves were prisoners of war. European merchants originally worked within this traditional framework; however, when demand for labor increased in the Americas, European merchants sought to increase the supply of slaves. Consequently, the merchants allied themselves with individual tribes and financed military expeditions for the explicit purpose of enslaving the conquered people. These tribal conflicts also benefited the Europeans by sowing chaos and preventing the consolidation of political power under a united African kingdom.

The Spanish-Imposed Caste System

To increase socioeconomic stability, Spain instituted a highly unique and complex racial caste system in its American colonies. The **caste system** classified the colonial population based on residents' ancestry and purity of blood. These racial classifications functioned as the foundation of a rigid social system that determined residents' legal status, rights, and obligations within the Spanish Empire.

The highest classes had the closest connections to Spain and the most Spanish blood. As such, Spaniards born in Spain (*peninsulares*) occupied the highest tier in the caste system. Slightly below the *peninsulares* were the American-born Spaniards (*criolles*). Mixed-race classes were significantly below these two European classes, but they occupied the middle tiers of the caste system. Examples of mixed-race classes included: Spanish and indigenous (*mestizo*), Spanish and mestizo (*castizos*), Spanish and African (*mulatto*), and Spanish and mulatto (*moriscos*). Despite the severe restrictions Spain placed on mixed-race residents' property and legal rights, they were still above two classes—African slaves (*negros*) and indigenous peoples (*indios*). African slaves effectively had no rights, while indigenous societies enjoyed some very limited protections under the *repartimiento* system. Given the dramatic

15

disparities in class status, people in the Spanish Empire often attempted to forge ancestral histories and pass as a member of a different class.

Cultural Interactions Between Europeans, Native Americans, and Africans

Divergent Worldviews Between Europeans and Native Americans

The conflict between Europeans and Native Americans was largely the product of their different worldviews on major issues including land use, power, land ownership, religion, and family dynamics.

Compared to Native Americans, Europeans were far less likely to consider the long-term sustainability of land use practices. North America is Native Americans' ancestral homeland, but colonization was a for-profit venture for Europeans. Likewise, although Native Americans regularly consolidated power at the expense of their rivals, their conquests were far more regionally based and limited in scope. Europeans held a much more global attitude. European powers were already fighting all over the globe before they arrived in North America. As such, they didn't just want to make a tidy profit; they wanted to monopolize power and conquer as much territory as they possibly could.

Land ownership was another area of significant divergence. While Native Americans did occupy territories, they viewed land as a common resource of the tribe that could, at most, be leased for its use. They had no concept of private land ownership or of exclusive use of the land. Europeans, on the other hand, believed strongly in owning land and, after its purchase, enjoying the exclusive use of that land. This led to frequent misunderstandings and clashes between the two groups.

Europeans were almost universally Christian, and many leaders believed non-Christians were condemned to eternal damnation. So, European colonizers often believed it was their moral duty to convert Native Americans by any means necessary. In contrast, Native American groups rarely proselytized and practiced a diverse array of traditional religions ranging from nature-based monotheism to polytheistic animism. Furthermore, Native American family dynamics were relatively egalitarian, with women and elders assuming key leadership roles in many groups. Europeans were far more hierarchical, with men serving as the head of the household and holding undisputed authority. Native Americans also valued kinship and revered elders, whereas aggressive young men with few family ties dominated European colonial expeditions and early settlements.

Interactions Between Native Americans and Europeans

Native Americans played an important role in the early history of Britain's North American colonies. Some Native American tribes were friendly towards the colonists and traded with them. **Squanto** was an Algonquian Indian who helped English settlers in Massachusetts survive by teaching them how to plant native crops. However, Native Americans and Europeans often came into conflict, frequently over land disputes. The Native Americans and Europeans had very different concepts of land use and ownership. Native Americans did not understand the concept of landownership or sale. When they entered into agreements with the colonists, Native Americans thought they were allowing the settlers to farm the land temporarily, rather than retain it in perpetuity. On the other hand, colonists were frustrated when Native Americans continued to hunt and fish on lands they had "sold." These, and other disagreements, eventually led to bloody conflicts that gradually weakened Native American tribes.

16

Although the early years of their interactions were often marked by mutual misunderstandings, over time Europeans and Native Americans did adopt some aspects of one another's culture that proved useful. For example, European technology such as hatchets, weapons, and kettles were adopted by some Native American tribes. A Native American agricultural technique known as **companion planting** was adopted by Europeans who had settled in New England and the Chesapeake areas for crops such as the **Three Sisters** (maize, winter squash, and climbing beans). Because these three crops, when planted together, benefited one another, Europeans were able to have a reliable food source and stay alive.

Native Americans' Efforts to Preserve Their Way of Life

The arrival of Europeans in the Americas quickly posed an existential challenge to indigenous peoples' ways of life. Europeans seized vast swathes of indigenous territory and violated indigenous peoples' **political sovereignty**, meaning the ability to self-govern without external interference. Similarly, Europeans enslaved indigenous people and disrupted ancient patterns of trade, effectively stunting indigenous economic development. Indigenous cultural values also came under attack through forced conversions to Christianity and limitations placed on the role of women in tribal leadership.

Indigenous peoples adopted a variety of diplomatic and military strategies to resist European colonization between 1491 and 1607. Some indigenous tribes, like those encountered by **Hernando de Soto** during his expedition across the present-day southeastern United States, provided European explorers with gifts and guides as a sign of friendship. Other tribes, like the **Powhatan** in present-day Virginia, initially accepted European colonies' boundaries and graciously traded maize to prevent the newly arrived colonists from starving. However, by 1609 the English and the Powhatan were at war. The Araucanians successfully turned back **Francisco Pizzaro's** forces after he conquered the Inca Empire in the mid-sixteenth century and held out against Spanish colonization for centuries.

Justifications for the Subjugation of Non-Europeans

Europeans propagated a host of arguments to justify and encourage their subjection, persecution, and domination of Africans and Native American populations. The foundation was the idea that Africans and Native American were sub-human "savages" with self-evidently inferior cultures. Some arguments even took it a step further, saying it was not only natural but also the Europeans' duty to spread their more advanced technological and supposedly superior cultural characteristics to Africa and the Americas. Likewise, Christian leaders viewed it as their sacred duty to save the souls of these populations, especially in Catholic Spain and Portugal. Broadly speaking, the "savagery" of Africans and Native Americans was treated as a settled truth across Europe throughout the sixteenth century, with few exceptions.

Due to the overwhelming popular support of these theories, few Europeans publicly called for the abolition of slavery or an end to colonization, and dissidents who did so were relentlessly persecuted. Still, in the aftermath of particularly horrific massacres, some Europeans called for limited reforms. For example, Spanish religious and political leaders pushed for the **New Laws of 1542** to categorize indigenous populations as the monarchy's property; mostly, the leaders hoped to secure some oversight authority over how the colonists exploited the indigenous labor force.

Practice Quiz

Questions 1–5 are based on the following passage:

2. Chap.

Of their departure into Holland and their troubls ther aboute, with some of the many difficulties they found and mete withall.

Being thus constrained to leave their native country, their lands and livings, and all their friends and familiar acquaintance, it was much, and thought marvellous by many. But to go into a country they knew not, but by hearsay, where they must learn a new language, and get their livings they knew not how, it being a dear place, and subject to the miseries of war, it was by many thought an adventure almost desperate, a case intolerable, and a misery worse than death; especially seeing they were not acquainted with trades nor traffic, (by which the country doth subsist) but had only been used to a plain country life and the innocent trade of husbandry. But these things did not dismay them, (although they did sometimes trouble them,) for their desires were set on the ways of God, and to enjoy his ordinances. But they rested on his providence, and knew whom they had believed. Yet this was not all. For although they could not stay, yet were they not suffered to go; but the ports and havens were shut against them, so as they were fain to seek secret means of conveyance, and to fee the mariners, and give extraordinary rates for their passages. And yet were they oftentimes betrayed, many of them, and both they and their goods intercepted and surprised, and thereby put to great trouble and charge; of which I will give an instance or two, and omit the rest."

"There was a great company of them purposed to get passage at Boston, in Lincolnshire; and for that end had hired a ship wholly to themselves, and made agreement with the master to be ready at a certain day, and take them and their goods in, at a convenient place, where they accordingly would all attend in readiness. So after long waiting and large expenses, though he kept not the day with them, yet he came at length, and took them in, in the night. And when he had them and their goods aboard, he betrayed them, having beforehand complotted with the searchers and other officers so to do; who took them and put them into open boats, and there rifled and ransacked them, searching them to their shirts for money, yae, even the women, further than became modesty; and then carried them back into the town, and made them a spectacle and wonderment to the multitude, which came flocking on all sides to behold them. Being thus by the catchpole officers riffled and stripped of their money, books and much other goods, they were presented to the magistrates, and messengers sent to inform the Lords of the Council of them; and so they were committed to ward. Indeed the magistrates used them courteously, and showed them what favor they could; but could not deliver them until order came from the Council table. But the issue was, that after a month's imprisonment the greatest part were dismissed, and sent to the places from whence they came; but seven of the principal men were still kept in prison and bound over to the assizes."

In the spring of 1608 another attempt was made to embark and another Dutch shipmaster engaged. This second party assembled at a point between Grimsby and Hull not far from the mouth of the Humber. The women and children arrived in a small bark which became grounded

at low water and while some of the men on shore were taken off in the ship's boat they were again apprehended. And to quote again:

"But after the first boat-full was got aboard, and she was ready to go for more, the master espied a great company, both horse and foot, with bills and guns and other weapons: for the country was raised to take them."

"But the poor men which were got on board were in great distress for their wives and children, which they saw thus to be taken, and were left distitute of their helps, and themselves also not having a cloth to shift them with, more than they had on their backs, and some scarce a penny about them, all they had being on the bark. It drew tears from their eyes, and anything they had they would have given to have been on shore again. But all in vain; there was no remedy; they must thus sadly part.

Excerpt from *History of Plymouth Plantation* by William Bradford, written between 1630 and 1651

1. Which of the following was NOT a difficulty faced by the group of travelers?
   a. They didn't know the new country's language.
   b. They weren't allowed to bring their wives or children to the new country.
   c. They didn't know how to make a living in the new country.
   d. Ships charged exorbitant rates for the voyage to the new country.

2. What type of passage is this?
   a. Historical memoir or journal
   b. Passage from a textbook
   c. Poem or Epic Poem
   d. An instructional/technical document

3. What went wrong with the ship hired at Boston in Lincoln-shire?
   a. The women got sick due to the rough seas.
   b. The men were separated from their wives and children.
   c. The group couldn't get out of jail in time to board the ship.
   d. The shipmaster betrayed them.

4. Based on the passage, why did the men leave their wives and children?
   a. Armed government officials arrived on the shore.
   b. The government refused to let them out of prison.
   c. The sea was too rough to risk going back for them.
   d. The women were too sick to make the voyage.

5. Ships charged the group of travelers extra fees because:
   a. They were a vulnerable minority group.
   b. The voyage was particularly long and dangerous.
   c. The government outlawed their departure.
   d. They were wealthy enough to afford it.

See answers on next page.

Answer Explanations

1. B: The first paragraph explains the difficulties facing the group of travelers. Language and making a living are listed in the second sentence, so Choices *A* and *C* are both incorrect. Extra fees and exorbitant rates are described in the first paragraph's final sentence; therefore, Choice *D* is incorrect. Although the men were later separated from their wives and children, that separation was due to a problem with logistics. There was no prohibition specifically against bringing their wives and children. The entire group was legally barred from leaving the country.

2. A: We can see that this text records parts of history, so this is most likely a historical memoir or the author's personal journal retelling an event that happened. We see a brief summary of the event before the passage begins.

3. D: The ship hired at Boston in Lincoln-shire is the group's first attempt to flee their homeland, and it's described in the second paragraph. After the group reached an agreement with the shipmaster, he betrayed them to the government, which led to government officials arresting the group. The women didn't become sick or get separated until their second attempt at fleeing, so Choices *A* and *B* are both incorrect. Following the first shipmaster's betrayal, the group did go to jail, but their imprisonment occurred after their first attempt to leave went wrong; therefore, Choice *C* is incorrect. Thus, Choice *D* is the correct answer.

4. A: After the men boarded the ship, armed government officials arrived on the shore. Rather than risk everyone getting caught, the Dutch shipmaster raised the anchor, hoisted the sails, and took off. So, even though the men were moved to tears by the separation, there was nothing they could do. The government refused to let some of the group's member out of prison, but that's not what caused the separation; therefore, Choice *B* is incorrect. Choices *C* and *D* are factually incorrect based on the information contained in the third paragraph. Thus, Choice *A* is the correct answer.

5. C: Ships charged the group of travelers extra fees because the government outlawed their departure. The first paragraph says that the government barred them from the ports and havens, so they needed to find a secret passage out of the country. As helping the group was illegal, ships charged them extra fees in exchange for taking on that risk. The passage doesn't state why the group is being persecuted; therefore, Choice *A* is incorrect. Choice *B* is incorrect because the passage doesn't mention whether the voyage was particularly long or dangerous. While the government did seize property from the group, it's unclear whether the group is particularly wealthy; therefore, Choice *D* is incorrect.

European Colonization

Spanish Colonization Efforts

Spain largely pursued colonization to maintain its status as a European and global power. As a result, once Spain discovered large deposits of precious metals in the Americas, it implemented policies to maximize the extraction of wealth from its colonies. The pursuit of profit necessitated the seizure of strategic and valuable territory and the acquisition of a cheap labor source. So, Spain pressed its military advantages, took advantage of the devastation caused by deadly diseases, and encouraged political infighting to conquer powerful indigenous confederations such as the Inca Empire and Aztec Empire.

The Spanish crown initially allowed **conquistadores** to fully enslave the Native Americans, but over time they sought to better incorporate indigenous populations into colonial society. Religion played a major role in this transformation, including both missionary work and forced large-scale conversions after Spanish conquests. Additionally, reforms introduced through the *repartimiento* system protected some aspects of indigenous societies as well, assuming they fulfilled Spanish demands for labor or tribute. Recall that within territories directly under the colonial system, Spain enforced a strict racial caste system which granted freedoms and opportunities based on blood purity. In a practical sense, the racialization of the caste system served to maintain Spanish superiority in the colonies by formalizing the limitations on mixed-race individuals, Native Americans, and African slaves.

French and Dutch Colonization Efforts

French and Dutch colonization efforts were unique because they relied on maintaining economic relationships with indigenous societies to a far greater degree than Spanish and English colonies. During the sixteenth century, Dutch colonies were generally limited to the northeastern United States, and France mostly colonized eastern Canada. Because these regions couldn't support large-scale mining or agriculture, they mostly extracted wealth through fur trapping and trade with the Native Americans. Oftentimes, a colonial government would control a city or central region, and then joint-stock companies would establish trading posts in the outlying wilderness. Because geographic separation restricted the extent to which French and Dutch colonial governments could protect remote trading posts, they were often motivated to maintain peaceful diplomatic relations with indigenous confederations.

French settlements later developed more permanent structures to support the booming fur trapping trade, which ratcheted up tensions with the Iroquois Confederacy (originally known as the Iroquois League or the Six Nations). The French and Iroquois fought a prolonged series of conflicts, collectively known as the **Beaver Wars**, from 1640 to 1701. The wars began in 1629 when the Iroquois started conquering neighboring tribes as a result of declining beaver populations, but they did not come into conflict with the French until several decades later. The conflict ended in a stalemate with the French consolidating control over present-day eastern Canada and the Iroquois Confederacy establishing itself as the hegemonic power in the Great Lakes region and the wilderness surrounding New England.

English Colonization Efforts

English colonies attracted relatively more European migrants than their competitors for several reasons. England's thirteen colonies in the present-day United States featured a wide array of different climates and ecosystems. As a result, the colonies offered many different types of prosperous economic opportunities such as plantation agriculture, family farming, fur trapping, manufacturing, fishing, and shipping. More broadly, the sheer amount of cheap land offered migrants hope of socioeconomic mobility. Several major groups of Christian dissidents migrated to British North America to establish their own religious communities, which further increased British colonial diversity.

Economies also attracted different European immigrant groups based on different labor demands. For most of the seventeenth century, the southern Atlantic colonies' plantations mostly relied on African slaves, as did the British West Indies. So, the overwhelming bulk of European immigrants, lacking the resources to invest in a plantation, sought to settle further north on the Atlantic Coast where there were more economic opportunities. Northern colonies also attracted more indentured servants compared to other colonial systems. **Indentured servitude** involved colonists paying a European man or woman's immigration and living costs in exchange for a designated future period of free labor. The practice was most cost effective for small-scale farming.

Overall, the English colonies were characterized by their agricultural focus on the lands they had taken from Native Americans.

The Regions of British Colonies

Situated on the Atlantic Coast, the Thirteen Colonies that would become the United States of America constituted only a small portion of North America. Even those colonies had significant differences that stemmed from their different origins. For instance, the Virginia colony under **John Smith** in 1607 started with male bachelors seeking gold, whereas families of Puritans settled Massachusetts. As a result, the Thirteen Colonies—Virginia, Massachusetts, Connecticut, Maryland, New York, New Jersey, Pennsylvania, Delaware, Rhode Island, New Hampshire, Georgia, North Carolina, and South Carolina— had different structures and customs that would each influence the United States.

The Chesapeake and Mid-Atlantic Colonies

Colonial economies in the **mid-Atlantic** (present-day North Carolina and southern Virginia) and **Chesapeake Bay** (present-day Maryland, Delaware, and northern Virginia) regions primarily engaged in tobacco and family farming. Compared to New England, there was less centralization, smaller urban centers, and minimal industrial production. In contrast, North Carolina and Virginia disproportionately relied on producing a single cash crop, **tobacco**, with family farming accounting for the region's only other vibrant economic sector.

Despite their common reliance on agricultural and similar rural settlement patterns, colonial North Carolina and Virginia were strikingly different than the **southern Atlantic colonies** (South Carolina and Georgia). Unlike the southern Atlantic colonies' plantation-based agriculture, farming in North Carolina and Virginia occurred on smaller plots of land. Tobacco was less compatible with large-scale production, and environmental conditions prevented the near-continual production that occurred deeper south.

Chesapeake and mid-Atlantic agriculture also uniquely relied more heavily on European indentured servitude than African slavery for its labor demands from the outset. Consequently, colonies in present-day North Carolina and Virginia had much more ethnic and religious diversity than the more universally British southern Atlantic colonies. However, African slaves gradually overtook indentured servitude as the dominant labor system, largely because the ever-increasing supply of African slaves in the southern Atlantic led to major cost reductions.

The New England Colonies

Connecticut, New Hampshire, Massachusetts, and Rhode Island were considered the **New England colonies**. The settlements in New England were based around an economy focused on fishing and lumber. These colonies maintained puritanical and Congregationalist religious beliefs and developed around family farms situated near small towns. Political power was distributed differently among the colonies. Some colonies, such as New York and Virginia, were royal colonies ruled directly by the king. Pennsylvania was a **proprietary colony**—the king allowed William Penn to appoint officials and govern the colony as he saw fit. **Corporate colonies**, such as Rhode Island and Connecticut, were administered by a group of investors. But, by the early 1700s, the king had revoked the charters of most proprietary and corporate colonies and assumed direct control himself.

The Middle Colonies

While English Puritans mostly settled in New England, a wide variety of colonists settled in the mid-Atlantic region. English, Scottish, Dutch, and Swedish settlers came to Delaware, New York, New Jersey, and Pennsylvania. As a result, the mid-Atlantic colonies were more religiously diverse and tolerant than the settlements in New England. Because the land in the region was so fertile, agriculture was the foundation of the economy in mid-Atlantic colonies. The primary output was **cereal crops** such as wheat, rye, and corn. For this reason, the Middle Colonies were also known as the **Bread Basket colonies**. Shipbuilding and lumbering were also common because of the abundant forests. Settlements were more dispersed, and government and administration were based on counties instead of towns.

Southern Atlantic Coast and the British West Indies Colonies

The Southern Atlantic (South Carolina and Georgia) and British West Indies' tropical climate, long growing seasons, and rich soil supported the development of plantation-based economies. Agricultural production had a sizable effect on these colonies' economic development and demographic makeup. Because land was divided into plantations under the control of societal elites, there was minimal commercial growth and few employment options. As such, the European population of plantation-based economies often consisted only of an elite cadre of ultra-wealthy landlords and a small managerial class to support operational logistics.

Unlike most other English colonies, plantation agriculture primarily relied upon African slaves as a labor force. In many instances, African slaves accounted for the majority of the population in England's plantation-based colonies. Fearing a slave insurrection, plantation owners attempted to enforce slave codes that were designed to be as draconian, dehumanizing, and profitable as possible. To keep the races more firmly separated by skin color, Southern Atlantic and British West Indian slave codes emphasized and sought to preserve the purity of race. The codes enforced prohibitions on interracial relationships and enslaved all descendants of African mothers. Eventually the plantation-based colonies

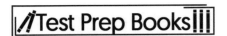
transitioned into using "**one drop**" racial policies, meaning that anyone with any African ancestry was subject to enslavement.

Governing in the Colonies

The thirteen colonies formed when royal charters were granted, either to individuals or corporations, and the colonies were allowed limited **self-rule**. A governor for the colonies was appointed by England, but each colony could rule by its own laws enacted by colonial assemblies. The method in which these men were appointed, and the laws of each colony, differed based on the type of charter each had, if any. In **royal colonies**—Virginia, Massachusetts, New Hampshire, New York, New Jersey, North Carolina, South Carolina, and Georgia—the king of England was the direct authority of the colony and chose the governor, among other things. **Proprietary colonies**, which included Pennsylvania, Delaware, and Maryland, were under the authority of the owner of the colony, while Rhode Island and Connecticut were self-governing and had no direct authority. They elected members to their legislatures.

Transatlantic Trade

The Triangular Trade

European exploration and colonization laid the foundation for a truly global trade network. The transatlantic portion of this network, commonly referred to as the **triangular trade**, consisted of interconnected and economic relationships between Europe (mainly England), Africa, and the Americas.

All of the major European powers adhered to **mercantilist** economic policies which prioritized extracting wealth from colonies and developing domestic industries through the erection of strategic trade barriers. Aside from securing access to valuable commodities and cheap labor, American colonies and African trading posts functioned as markets for European consumer goods and manufactured products. African nations typically exchanged enslaved captives for European goods such as guns and cloth. Likewise, Europeans sought American colonies to extract commodities such as sugar, cotton, and tobacco, and to exploit labor to an unprecedented degree.

Mercantilism was inarguably transformative. Within a relatively short time span, Europeans depleted South American mines, seized stockpiles of commodities, decimated animal populations, and installed large-scale agriculture of cash crops. Colonial domestic economies benefited from the run-off of the staggering production of wealth, but European political and economic power centers were the clear-cut victors, as intended. Consequently, European powers were able to maintain a firm grip on the fledgling global trade network, ensuring they had a consistent supply of cheap labor and access to raw materials.

Impact of Trading with Europeans on Native Americans

Extended contact with Europeans produced many transformative cultural, economic, and political changes across indigenous societies. Horses enhanced indigenous societies' mobility and cavalry tactics. Likewise, steel and gunpowder revolutionized warfare. Commerce led to more cultural exchanges including Christian proselytizing and the evolution of syncretic blends of Christianity, African Vodun, and traditional indigenous beliefs.

At the same time, European contact ultimately devastated and nearly eradicated most indigenous communities and confederations due to the spread of disease. Indigenous populations suffered

staggering population loss in massive waves due to the lightning-fast spread of epidemics, many of which struck communities shortly before Europeans made formal contact. Europeans had developed genetic immunities to diseases like smallpox, plague, and flu varieties for many centuries prior to their arrival in the Americas. On the other hand, indigenous populations had no genetic resistance to the diseases, and they had a genocide-like effect on indigenous societies.

The destabilizing impact unchecked epidemics had on indigenous political structures cannot be overstated. Indigenous militaries were certainly terrified by cavalry and gunpowder, but more importantly, Europeans were attacking societies suffering an apocalyptic crisis. Some previously powerful indigenous tribes didn't have the male labor to gather food, let alone the military strength and resiliency to fend off an invasion.

British Mercantilist Efforts in the Colonies

Like the other major European powers, Britain pursued mercantilist goals in terms of economic development. **Mercantilism** aims to maximize resource extraction, develop domestic industries, and centralize the state's authority. European powers sought to implement mercantilist policies through the establishment of a relatively centralized imperial government based on a top-down, hierarchical command structure with the monarchy at the very top. European powers had tremendous success at destabilizing Native American confederations, subjugating indigenous populations, and exercising absolute authority over colonial governments. The only slight exception to this general trend was British North America.

As a multinational representative government, Britain was uniquely flexible in granting some autonomy and authority to popularly elected colonial governments. British leaders viewed local autonomy as an advantage because it improved how colonial governments responded to immediate threats; rather than waiting for specific instructions from across the Atlantic, British colonial governments could adjust to, leverage, and exploit current happenings. However, conditions on the ground also forced Britain to go further than they otherwise would have preferred. Unlike most other colonial systems, Britain struggled in subduing their strongest indigenous military rivals like the Powhatan, Algonquin, and Iroquois confederations. As a result, Britain couldn't always defend frontiers or enforce imperial laws, which granted legitimacy to colonial power structures.

Interactions Between American Indians and Europeans

Conflicts and Alliances Between Europeans and American Indians

Indigenous groups regularly sought and secured military alliances with European groups to gain an advantage in regional conflicts with other indigenous nations. Naturally, Native Americans adjusted to the initial stages of colonization by incorporating European groups into their traditional diplomatic and military systems, treating them like ascendant and powerful indigenous nations. Europeans routinely exploited this opportunity to carry out a divide-and-conquer strategy. Overall, European powers and indigenous groups acted in their self-interest, resulting in a fluid system of shifting military alliances.

Given the deep and complex regional rivalries within indigenous communities, it was common for colonial conflicts to have alliances of Native American groups aligned on both sides. The rise of the Iroquois Confederacy during the seventeenth century is indicative of European and indigenous alliances. During the **Beaver Wars**, the French established alliances with numerous Algonquian societies including

the Erie, Huron, and Mohican (also spelled Mahican). The Algonquians believed they would be rewarded for their support of the rising French power and that any losses suffered by the Iroquois would automatically be their gain. On the other side, the Dutch and English supported the Iroquois to undermine the French. However, once the Iroquois emerged as the clear-cut indigenous power, they began to threaten the British North American frontier.

Military Conflicts Between the British and American Indians

British colonies' aggressive territorial expansion, broad consolidation of resources, and wanton violation of treaties naturally resulted in near-constant conflicts with many Native American nations.

By the late seventeenth century, most British colonies had survived starvation-like conditions, established a consistent agricultural food supply, and commanded well-armed and robust military units featuring a strong mix of imperial troops and more informal citizen militia-type forces. At this point, most indigenous leaders viewed Europeans as rising regional competitors, not as an existential threat to indigenous societies. Although Britain was generally less successful than its European rivals at decimating local indigenous power centers, the British fiercely protected their territory and engaged in incremental expansion.

King Philip's War (1675–1678, also called Metacom's War) was one of the most influential conflicts with an indigenous confederation in British colonial history. **King Philip, or Metacom,** was a Wampanoag chief who formed an alliance with New England-based indigenous tribes such as the Narragansetts and Podunks. The New England colonies barely survived King Philip's War. Approximately half of New England colonial villages were attacked during the conflict, and more than a dozen towns totally collapsed. Despite the heavy losses, King Philip's War forged an American identity because it marked the first time the colonists fought without any imperial support.

American Indians' Resistance to Spanish Colonizing Efforts

Prior to the arrival of Europeans, the **Pueblo** confederation had a large population, centralized urban centers, and influence across much of present-day northern Mexico and the southwestern United States. During the late sixteenth and early seventeenth centuries, Spanish Franciscans sought to subjugate indigenous populations under a totalitarian and coercive theocracy. Successive poor harvests and famines increased tensions, which reached a boiling point in 1675 when a Pueblo religious leader named **Popé** was arrested along with forty-seven others. He was rescued from prison and spent the next five years building alliances and organizing a covert insurrection to rid New Mexico of the Spanish. The rebellion came to be known as the **Pueblo Revolt**.

The revolt began on August 10, 1680, and swept through the Spanish settlements. The Pueblo experienced little resistance until they besieged Santa Fe. The remaining Spaniards, in desperation, broke the siege on August 21, and by September 6 the Spaniards were gone from New Mexico. Following this decisive victory, Popé assumed leadership over the Pueblo people. Despite several attempts, the Spanish were not able to reclaim Pueblo territory until 1692. Although it didn't secure long-term freedom, the Pueblo Revolt led to meaningful cultural accommodations such as tolerance for traditional religions and access to legal assistance while navigating the colonial legal system.

Slavery in the British Colonies

Slavery in the British Colonies

Slavery was pervasive across British North America. The New England economies attracted religiously and ethnically diverse groups of Europeans. Because the dominant economic sector was commerce, New England's African slave population never reached southern levels due to slavery's limited application and associated costs. New England areas with the highest concentration of slaves were the ports because transporting and processing cargo was labor intensive.

The Chesapeake colonies' slave populations steadily increased throughout the seventeenth and early eighteenth centuries. These colonies primarily developed around small family and tobacco farms. Such types of small-scale agriculture primarily relied on indentured servitude and cheap labor contracts with landless immigrants. However, as the scales of these operations increased and labor shortages arose, Chesapeake farmers purchased larger quantities of African slaves.

The Southern Atlantic colonies were most similar to European colonies in South America. The tropical climate and longer growing seasons supported the development of a plantation-based agricultural system designed for large-scale agricultural production.

Because the British West Indies had the highest concentration of plantations, it also had the largest cumulative and per capita slave population. The slaves condemned to the West Indies suffered a staggering, genocidal-like death rate due to the physical labor demands and abominable working conditions.

Slave Codes and Racial Laws

During the latter half of the seventeenth and early eighteenth centuries, southern Atlantic plantation-based economies began to resemble the British West Indies more strongly in their utter dependence on **chattel slavery**, wherein slaves were considered the owner's personal property to be bought and sold. Under this system, even the children of the purchased slave were automatically inherited by the owner as property. Southern colonial government also went much further than nearly all other historical systems of slavery. Because the population of African slaves exceeded the white population, southern governments developed a particularly totalitarian system of chattel slavery.

The British West Indies and Southern Atlantic colonies enacted brutal slave codes to enforce white supremacy and purity of blood through prohibitions on interracial relationships. Some codes even went so far as to classify anyone with one drop of African ancestry as a slave. Overall, the British colonies' hyper-racial and generational enslavement of Africans actively sought to beat down, physically and emotionally, the humanity of the people it ensnared.

British colonial slave codes were especially dehumanizing because African slaves had dramatically different cultural, linguistic, and historical backgrounds. During the sixteenth and seventeenth centuries, the West African political system was incredibly decentralized with dozens of regional rival nations, making it relatively easier for European powers to manipulate. Consequently, African slaves struggled to communicate and navigate cultural differences among themselves, greatly undermining the establishment of an Afro-American community.

Africans' Resistance to Slavery

Despite their physical isolation and the persecution of chattel slavery, Africans still found ways to overtly and covertly resist chattel slavery's most dehumanizing and domineering effects.

African slaves developed a complex Afro-American culture that relied on numerous resistance strategies to survive. One tactic involved incorporating aspects of European culture under a **syncretic model**. For example, the ancient religious practice of Vodun influenced myriad syncretic religions with regional differences including British West Indian Obeah, Haitian Vodou, and Hoodoo folk magic systems. All of these syncretic religions adapted to Christianity in order to survive forced conversions and blanket prohibitions. For example, many Afro-American religions characterized the worship of saints in the same way as traditional African deities. Other private cultural practices remained mostly intact, like the traditional leadership role African women played within families.

Some acts of cultural preservation appealed to Europeans' desire for profits, like African slaves being allowed to cultivate traditional food crops such as yams and okra. Covert actions against labor exploitation were also incredibly common, including work slowdowns and intentional sabotage. In some instances, slaves overtly rebelled, most commonly by fleeing. One of the strongest motivations behind the desire for escape was to reunite with loved ones.

Colonial Society and Culture

Pluralism and Intellectual Exchange

British colonies had significant religious and ethnic diversity. Unlike the Catholic French and Spanish monarchies, Britain's state-sanctioned Anglican Church tolerated the presence of minority Protestant denominations to varying degrees. When the Anglican Church began persecuting and expelling some of these denominations during the seventeenth century, they typically migrated to the Americas. British colonies' ethnic diversity was the product of Britain's rise as a truly global empire and its rising status as the undisputed global maritime power. As such, British merchants and manufacturing leaders maintained close commercial relationships throughout Europe. Finally, the British colonies' climate, geography, and economic development influenced the establishment of sprawling large-scale permanent settlements. As a result, Britain was much more aggressive in attracting mainland European indentured servants.

Enlightenment philosophy and the First Great Awakening stimulated intellectual exchange and cultural interactions across British North America. **The Enlightenment** (1687–1789) argued the importance of civil liberties, including the free exercise of religion and some separation of church and state. British colonists seized on these arguments to preserve their religious freedom in the Americas. **The First Great Awakening** (1730–1750) was a grassroots evangelical movement that swept across British North America. Unlike more establishment Christian denominations, **evangelicalism** emphasized an individualized, active, and spiritual relationship with the divine.

Despite their relatively dynamic ethnic and religious diversity—as compared to other American colonial systems—the British colonies still underwent extensive **Anglicization** during the sixteenth and seventeenth centuries. Specifically, the British colonies adopted their home country's political and legal systems. The common law legal society increased the British colonies' uniformity, while representative government fueled colonists' demands for the right to more autonomy and self-government.

Commercial ties between the British colonies also played a unifying role, especially as their economic differences strongly complemented each other. For example, southern Atlantic agricultural products were often shipped to New England where they were exchanged for timber and manufactured goods.

The First Great Awakening further unified British North America through a uniquely American cultural and religious experience. **Colonial evangelicalism** differed from British-based Protestantism, including dissident sects, because it prioritized individualism and the power of direct revelations. Religious and political movements were able to rapidly spread across the Americas due to the growth of **print culture**, including the publication of pamphlets and newsletters. The American-based print culture also established ties across the Atlantic. So, British colonists generally kept abreast of major European events and cultural movements despite the vast physical separation from their ruler's seat of power.

Colonists' Dissatisfaction with European Leaders

The most influential and powerful American-based economic groups generally strove for more autonomy. In Spanish colonies, plantation owners and mine operators deeply resented the Spanish crown's role in the acquisition of indigenous labor. Likewise, Dutch and French merchants objected to profit sharing and their limited involvement in high-level decision making in colonial policies. Wealthy British colonists resisted numerous imperial policies concerning political boundaries, frontier protection, self-government, and mercantilist trade policies.

Many factors contributed to British colonists being uniquely dissatisfied and mistrustful of the imperial government. Perhaps the greatest challenge was the proximity and resistance of North American indigenous confederations. Other European colonial systems thoroughly dismantled regional indigenous rivals, such as Spain's strangling of the Aztec and Inca confederations. In contrast, the Iroquois regularly and successfully challenged British North America's territorial integrity and resisted expansionist military expeditions. As a result, British colonies struggled to expand and protect their frontier regions.

Widespread insecurity also contributed to the legitimization of colonial self-government in British North America. Oftentimes, Britain would be unable or unwilling to reinforce frontier areas, placing territorial matters squarely within the purview of colonial governments. Over time, colonial desire for self-rule spread from military decision making to economic development.

British North America's Resistance to Imperial Control

British North America had a uniquely independent and dynamic political culture for four major reasons.

First, the British constitutional monarchy and parliamentary system drew a sharp contrast with European absolute monarchies. Out of all the European powers, the British system was by far the most flexible in delegating political authority because they viewed the flexibility as a developmental advantage.

Second, Enlightenment philosophers popularized concepts of universal equality among men and the model of popular sovereignty in which the people legitimize government authority. So, Enlightenment thought directly provided colonial authorities legal and ethical arguments for independence, fanning the flames of an ascending independence movement.

Third, the British colonies had partially been settled to secure the free exercise of religion, so they were naturally more independent-minded and hostile to British meddling in domestic affairs. The lack of a

29

majority religion also helped preserve religious freedom because there was no central religious authority to ally with state actors.

Fourth, the British colonists condemned the actual and perceived corruption within the colonial system. While corruption undoubtedly hampered the governance of British North America, colonists took a radical approach to taxation. Even when British taxes specifically funded frontier defenses, colonists regularly characterized the practice as imperial coercion.

Slavery in the English Colonies

Slavery is believed to be as old as civilization itself, likely beginning during the First Agricultural Revolution nearly ten thousand years ago. The enslavement of human beings was integral to such early civilizations as Egypt, China, the Mayan Empire, Greece, and Rome. Nevertheless, race did not become the primary driving force behind human captivity and forced labor until the so-called Age of Exploration. Previously, slaves were held captive as prisoners of war. In the case of Egypt, the Jews were enslaved because of their ethnic origins and religious beliefs, but not their "race." **Race** is a construct that did not develop fully until the Early Modern period of world history.

Once the Europeans made contact with the New World, they developed a new system of slavery in the Atlantic World that categorized black and indigenous persons as naturally inferior. The Transatlantic Slave Trade was built upon the foundations of the need for cheap labor. Slavery in the Americas became a hereditary phenomenon during the peak centuries of the Transatlantic Slave Trade. This slave trade was also economic in origin: The sugar and tobacco plantations of the Americas demanded an excess of cheap or free labor. Initially, European Americans looked to Native Americans as their enslaved labor supply. Quickly, however, millions of Native Americans died because of the spread of unfamiliar diseases. By the 18th century, the slave trade industry grew because of the higher labor demands. This slave trade lasted from the 1400s well into the late nineteenth century.

Practice Quiz

Questions 1–3 refer to the passage below:

I come now to the Pyrates that have rose since the Peace of Utrecht; in War Time there is no room for any, because all those of a roving advent'rous Disposition find Employment in Privateers, so there is no Opportunity for Pyrates; like our Mobs in London, when they come to any Height, our Superiors order out the Train Bands, and when once they are raised, the others are suppressed of Course; I take the Reason of it to be, that the Mob go into the tame Army, and immediately from notorious Breakers of the Peace, become, by being put into order, solemn Preservers of it. And should our Legislators put some of the Pyrates into Authority, it would not only lessen their Number, but, I imagine, set them upon the rest, and they would be the likeliest People to find them out, according to the Proverb, set a Thief to catch a Thief. To bring this about, there needs no other Encouragement, but to give all the Effects taken aboard a Pyrate Vessel to the Captors; for in Case of Plunder and Gain, they like it as well from Friends, as Enemies, but are not fond, as Things are carry'd, of ruining poor Fellowes, say the Creoleans, with no Advantage to themselves.

Excerpt from *A General History of the Pyrates* by Charles Johnson, 1724

1. According to the historian, which of the following groups of people would be the most effective at capturing pirates?
    a. Creolans
    b. Mobs
    c. Pirates
    d. Privateers

2. Which of the following did the historian propose as an incentive for capturing pirates?
    a. Crews that captured pirates received a military promotion.
    b. Crews that captured pirates were allotted territory in the Caribbean.
    c. Crews that captured pirates were given legal permission to plunder merchant ships.
    d. Crews that captured pirates were allowed to keep the treasure they found onboard.

3. According to the historian, what caused the rise in piracy?
    a. The Mobs in London funded piracy to increase their profits.
    b. The government refused to prohibit privateering.
    c. Many sailors were left unemployed after the Peace of Utrecht.
    d. The English Royal Navy stopped patrolling in the Caribbean.

Questions 4 and 5 refer to the diagram below.

Patterns of Diffusion, circa 1600

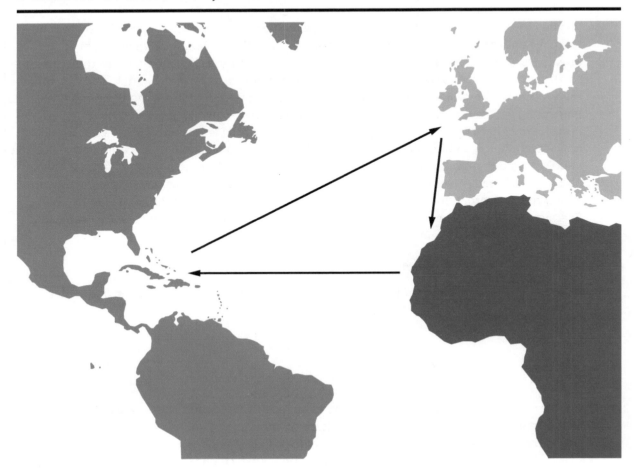

4. The diagram most likely illustrates which of the following patterns of diffusion?
   a. Columbian Exchange
   b. Contemporary global supply chain
   c. Free-trade network
   d. Green Revolution

5. Which of the following most accurately describes the consequence of this pattern of diffusion?
   a. The pattern of diffusion led to the corporatization of agricultural production, resulting in economic catastrophe for small family farms.
   b. The pattern of diffusion resulted in the spread of the Norfolk crop rotation techniques and new iron swing ploughs.
   c. The pattern of diffusion generated new employment opportunities, disproportionately benefiting low-income communities.
   d. The pattern of diffusion triggered groundbreaking global diffusion of agricultural products.

See answers on next page.

Answer Explanations

1. C: The historian argues for granting pirates legal authority to capture their fellow pirates because it takes a "Thief to catch a Thief." Thus, Choice *C* is the correct answer. Creolans are mentioned as people pirates would only rob when it was financially advantageous to do so; therefore, Choice *A* is incorrect. The historian only references the Mobs in London in a metaphor to support enlisting pirates as law enforcement officers, so Choice *B* is incorrect. Choice *D* is the second-best answer choice. During the seventeenth and eighteenth centuries, governments occasionally enlisted former pirates as privateers, which were essentially state-sanctioned pirates. However, Choice *C* more directly addresses this phenomenon, so Choice *D* is incorrect.

2. D: The historian argued that pirates would be motivated to capture fellow pirates if they were allowed to keep what they found aboard. The relevant line appears at the end of the passage: "To bring this about, there needs no other Encouragement, but to give all the Effects taken aboard a Pyrate Vessel to the Captors; for in Case of Plunder and Gain, they like it as well from Friends, as Enemies." Thus, Choice *D* is the correct answer. Military promotions and territorial allotments are not mentioned anywhere in the passage, so Choices *A* and *B* are both incorrect. Choice *C* is the second-best answer. Governments often tasked privateers with capturing pirates, and privateers were also generally allowed to attack enemy merchant ships. However, Choice *C* is too broad because it doesn't specify what types of merchant ships could be plundered. In addition, attacking merchant ships isn't mentioned in the passage. So, Choice *C* is incorrect.

3. C: In the first sentence, the historian mentions that piracy increased after the Peace of Utrecht because sailors could no longer find employment as privateers. Thus, Choice *C* is the correct answer. During the seventeenth and eighteenth centuries, European criminal syndicates funded piracy and shared in the profits, but the historian doesn't claim that the Mobs in London are funding piracy. So, Choice *A* is incorrect. Choice *B* is incorrect because the historian doesn't describe or support a prohibition on privateering; in fact, the historian is arguing for the government to hire pirates as privateers. The Royal Navy is not mentioned in the passage, so Choice *D* is incorrect.

4. A: The diagram has a series of arrows pointing from the Americas to Europe, Europe to Africa, and Africa to the Americas. This pattern is consistent with the Columbian Exchange. During the colonization of the Americas, Europeans transported African slaves to the Americas, extracted raw resources from the Americas, and exported manufactured goods to Africa. Choice *B* is incorrect because the title of the map says it represents a pattern of diffusion that was active in the seventeenth century, and the contemporary global supply chain includes Asia and Australia. Similarly, Choice *C* is incorrect because free-trade networks weren't active in the seventeenth century. Choice *D* is incorrect because the Green Revolution involved the diffusion of high-yield crops and technological innovations during the mid-twentieth century.

5. D: The pattern of diffusion can be identified as the Columbian Exchange due to the time period and emphasis on Europe, Africa, and the Americas. The Columbian Exchange included a significant diffusion of agricultural products. For example, merchants exported the American potato to Europe, where it quickly became a staple crop. Choice *A* is incorrect because small family farms thrived during the Columbian Exchange, and the corporatization of agricultural production didn't occur until the latter half of the twentieth century. Choice *B* is incorrect because the Norfolk crop rotation and iron swing plough spread from England to the Americas during the Second Agricultural Revolution in the eighteenth

33

century. Choice *C* is incorrect because although the Columbian Exchange did generate new employment opportunities in international commerce, the economic activity enriched states and wealthy investors.

The Seven Years' War (The French and Indian War)

The Beginnings of the Seven Years' War

In the mid-eighteenth century, conflict between the French and British North American colonial systems intensified within the broad historical context of a decades-long rivalry between the global superpowers. Tensions between France and Britain erupted in the **Seven Years' War** (1756–1763), and both superpowers marshaled powerful coalitions in a contest for economic and military superiority. The Seven Years' War had an unprecedented global scope with military theaters in the Americas, Europe, West Africa, India, and Southeast Asia. In North America, the conflict was referred to as the **French and Indian War** because British colonists were pitted against French Canada and its indigenous allies, including the Algonquin, Ojibwe, and Shawnee tribes and the Huron confederacy.

Colonial rivalries over land, resources, and trade networks ratcheted up tensions prior to the outbreak of the Seven Years' War. Both French Canadians and the Iroquois leaders, who were initially neutral but eventually sided with the British, categorically opposed British settlers creeping north toward Nova Scotia and westward over the Appalachian Mountains, which threated both the autonomy of American Indian populations and the French-Indian trade networks. With the fate of the colonies on the line, much of present-day eastern Canada and northeastern United States quickly became engulfed in war. The French and Indian War was a transformative experience for the British colonists. Despite living in proximity to active frontlines, the conflict was relatively popular because the colonists assumed they would be able to seize northern and western lands.

Britain's Territorial Expansion

Britain's victory in the Seven Years' War was a transformative achievement. Under the terms of the **Treaty of Paris** (1763), British gained control over the entirety of French territory in present-day Canada and the fortress of Minorca.

On the losing side, the Seven Years' War grievously injured the French economy and national pride. While Britain had overextended itself financially, France had risked triggering a complete financial meltdown in leveraging itself to fund the conflict. Afterward, France chose to keep its more profitable Caribbean colonies at the cost of all its Canadian territory. Furthermore, Spain annexed French Louisiana. As a result, Britain established itself as the undisputed colonial power in northern North America with Spain remaining as its only major competition to the south.

Although Britain certainly fared much better than France in the late 1760s, it still needed to service its own significant debts. From the British perspective, it was more than reasonable to expect the British colonists to repay some of those debts because Britain's global empire had enriched and protected the colonies. However, British colonists viewed the new restrictions and imperial taxes as a slap in the face given what they'd sacrificed and contributed to the French and Indian War. The financial expense of the war served as the root of Britain's subsequent imperial efforts to raise increased revenue from the colonies.

Imperial Efforts to Prevent Westward Expansion in the Colonies

Following its decisive victory in the Seven Years' War, Britain struggled to balance conflicting promises it had made to indigenous allies and colonists. Britain had not formally promised to back the colonists' expansion, but the British military had heavily relied on colonial militias during the conflict. One of the shining stars of the British officer corps was **George Washington**, who standardized colonial military units to fight alongside citizen militias. Given their invaluable role in Britain's victory, many colonists naturally assumed they'd be allowed to take share in the spoils. Unfortunately, all of the above directly contradicted British agreements with its indigenous allies, like the Iroquois.

The **Royal Proclamation of 1763** forbade British colonization west of the Appalachian Mountains, and it reserved all western lands for the Iroquois and associated indigenous allies. While the indigenous people gained the short-term benefit of legal protection for tribal lands and continued access to colonial markets, the Proclamation was a major factor in the American independence movement. Believing they were betrayed, the colonists exploded in anger and widespread organized protests occurred for the first time across many of the colonies. Combined with the new imperial taxes, the Proclamation served as the breaking point and rallying cry for the **American Independence Movement**.

Taxation Without Representation

Competition among several imperial powers in eastern areas of North America led to conflicts that would later bring about the independence of the United States. The **French and Indian War** from 1754 to 1763, which was a subsidiary war of the **Seven Years' War**, ended with Great Britain claiming France's Canadian territories as well as the Ohio Valley. The war was costly for all the powers involved, which led to increased taxes on the Thirteen Colonies. In addition, the new lands to the west of the colonies attracted new settlers, and they came into conflict with Native Americans and British troops that were trying to maintain the boundaries laid out by treaties between Great Britain and the Native American tribes. These growing tensions with Great Britain, as well as other issues, eventually led to the American Revolution, which ended with Britain relinquishing its control of the colonies.

As the colonies grew in population, they began to develop local institutions and a separate sense of identity. For example, it became common for ministers to receive their education at seminaries in North America rather than Britain. Newspapers began to focus on printing more local news as well. Perhaps most importantly, the colonies began to exercise more control over their own political affairs. The British government retained control over international issues, such as war and trade, but the colonists controlled their own domestic affairs. Colonies began to form their own political assemblies and elect landowners who represented local districts. In addition, communications between the colonies and Britain were very slow because it took months for a ship to cross the Atlantic and return with a response.

Taxes were imposed in an effort to help reduce the debt Britain amassed during the French and Indian War. In 1764, Parliament passed the **Sugar Act**, which reduced the tax on molasses but also provided for greater enforcement powers. Some colonists protested by organizing boycotts on British goods. One year later, in 1765, Parliament passed the **Quartering Act**, which required colonists to provide housing and food to British troops. This law was also very unpopular and led to protests in the North American colonies.

36

The **Stamp Act** of 1765 required the colonists to pay a tax on legal documents, newspapers, magazines, and other printed materials. Colonial assemblies protested the tax and petitioned the British government in order to have it repealed. Merchants also organized boycotts and established correspondence committees in order to share information. Eventually, Parliament repealed the Stamp Act but simultaneously reaffirmed the Crown's right to tax the colonies.

In 1767, Parliament introduced the **Townshend Acts**, which imposed a tax on goods the colonies imported from Britain, such as tea, lead, paint, glass, and paper. The colonies protested again and British imperial officials were assaulted in some cases. The British government sent additional troops to North America to restore order. The arrival of troops in Boston only led to more tension that eventually culminated in the **Boston Massacre** in 1770, where five colonists were killed and eight were wounded. Except for the duty on tea, all of the Townshend Act taxes were repealed after the Boston Massacre.

Parliament passed the **Tea Act** in 1773 and, although it actually reduced the price of tea, it was another unpopular piece of legislation. The Tea Act made the British East India Company the sole legal seller of tea in the colonies in North America and allowed the Company to ship its products directly to the colonies without stopping in England and paying import taxes, effectively cutting out colonial merchants and stirring more Anglo-American anger and resentment. This resulted in the **Boston Tea Party** in 1773, an incident in which colonial tea merchants disguised themselves as Indians before storming several British ships that were anchored in Boston harbor. Once aboard, the disguised colonists dumped more than 300 chests of tea into the water.

Because the British government was unable to identify the perpetrators, Parliament passed a series of laws that punished the entire colony of Massachusetts. These acts were known as the **Coercive** or **Intolerable Acts**. The first law closed the port of Boston until the tea had been paid for (an estimated $1.7 million in today's currency). The second act curtailed the authority of Massachusetts' colonial government. Instead of being elected by colonists, most government officials were now appointed by the king. In addition, the act restricted town meetings, the basic form of government in Massachusetts, and limited most villages to one meeting per year. This act angered colonists throughout the thirteen colonies because they feared their rights could be stripped away as well. A third act allowed for British soldiers to be tried in Britain if they were accused of a crime. The fourth act once again required colonists to provide food and shelter to British soldiers.

Colonists responded by forming the **First Continental Congress** in 1774, and all the colonies except for Georgia sent delegates. The delegates sought a compromise with the British government instead of launching an armed revolt. The First Continental Congress sent a petition to King George III affirming their loyalty but demanding the repeal of the Intolerable Acts. The delegates organized a boycott of imports from and exports to Britain until their demands were met.

The colonists began to form militias and gather weapons and ammunition. The first battle of the revolution began at Lexington and Concord in April 1775 when British troops tried to seize a supply of gunpowder and were confronted by about eighty Minutemen. A brief skirmish left eight colonists dead and ten wounded. Colonial reinforcements poured in and harassed the British force as they retreated to Boston. Although the battle did not result in many casualties, it marked the beginning of war.

A month later, the Second Continental Congress convened in Philadelphia. The delegates formed an army and appointed George Washington as commander in chief. Delegates were still reluctant to repudiate their allegiance to King George III and did not do so until they issued the **Declaration of**

Independence on July 4, 1776. The Declaration drew on the ideas of the Enlightenment and declared that the colonists had the right to life, liberty, and the pursuit of happiness. The Declaration stated that the colonists had to break away from Britain because King George III had violated their rights.

After the Battle of Lexington and Concord, British troops retreated to Boston and the colonial militias laid siege to the city. Colonists built fortifications on Bunker Hill outside the city and British troops attacked the position in June 1775. The colonists inflicted heavy casualties on the British and killed a number of officers. However, the defenders ran out of ammunition and British troops captured Bunker Hill on the third assault. Although it was a defeat for the colonists, the Battle of Bunker Hill demonstrated that they could stand and fight against the disciplined and professional British army.

The British army initially had the upper hand and defeated colonial forces in a number of engagements. The Americans did not achieve a victory until the **Battle of Trenton** in December 1776. Washington famously crossed the Delaware River on Christmas Day and launched a surprise attack against Hessian mercenaries. They captured more than 1,000 soldiers and suffered minimal casualties. The victory at Trenton bolstered American morale and showed that they could defeat professional European soldiers.

The **Battle of Saratoga** in New York in the fall of 1777 was an important turning point in the American War for Independence. American troops surrounded and captured more than 6,000 British soldiers. This victory convinced the French king to support the revolutionaries by sending troops, money, weapons, and ships to the American continent. French officers who fought alongside the Patriots brought back many ideas with them that eventually sparked a revolution in France in 1789.

Unification of Colonists

The aftermath of the Seven Years' War triggered renewed calls for more political representation and autonomy from colonial patriot groups. With Britain weighed down fighting and financing a global conflict, the colonies provided the manpower and resources to defend British North America, so colonists naturally assumed they would share in the spoils of victory. In contrast, Britain expected the colonists to help repay the imperial wartime debt through nominal tax increases on consumer goods.

Many American Patriots rejected the tax increases, arguing that Britain's denial of political representation meant the colonists hadn't consented to imperial authority. In addition, the **Royal Proclamation of 1763** sparked intense anger all across the American colonies for its prohibitions on westward expansion. The Patriots responded by rallying public support for independence, organizing boycotts, and carrying out public demonstrations of anger, like the **Boston Tea Party** (1774). Britain refused to be cowed and passed a series of punitive measures widely referred to as the **Intolerable Acts** (1774). The **Quebec Act** of 1774 was especially provocative because it allowed the Province of Quebec to annex territory previously reserved for indigenous populations under the Royal Proclamation of 1763. By early 1775, the American colonists were fed up and prepared to escalate.

The concept of colonial unity originated with the famous publisher and political leader Benjamin Franklin's **Albany Plan of Union** (1754). The Albany Plan proposed a unified colonial government that would work with the British Crown to increase cooperation and coordination. Although it was ultimately rejected, the Albany Plan marked the beginning of a larger discussion about unity and self-government in the colonies.

Following the French and Indian War, colonial unity increased out of shared opposition to perceived and real issues with British rule. The British government claimed the colonies cost approximately four times

38

as much to defend and govern than they generated in tax revenue. Consequently, the British Parliament passed the **Stamp Act** of 1765, its first direct tax on the colonies, to help repay wartime debts. Colonial leaders admitted the tax was relatively minor, but they objected to being taxed without representation. In response, an anonymous separatist group, the **Sons of Liberty**, organized mass protests, acts of vigilante violence, and boycotts of British goods. Parliament refused to be bullied and passed the **Townshend Acts** (1767) and the **Tea Act** (1773) to implement more aggressive mercantilist economic policies. This only hardened the resolve of American Patriots, and requests for more political rights quickly became demands for independence.

Colonial Arguments to Resist British Rule

The **American Independence Movement** was predicated on a revolutionary ideology steeped in Enlightenment ideals about equality, and American Patriots developed a series of arguments to rally resistance to British policies and support for American independence.

Americans Patriots claimed that because the colonists paid taxes as British subjects, they should be entitled to the same rights as citizens living in the British homeland. When Britain not only rejected those demands but also increased taxes as a punishment for civil unrest, the American Patriots asserted that it was their natural right to revoke the social contract with Britain and revolt against tyranny. The American Independence Movement also greatly benefited from the colonies' tradition of self-rule, particularly the political infrastructure and a large class of experienced public servants. The colonies' experience navigating and winning the chaotic French and Indian War was also critical because it arguably demonstrated that the colonies could survive and prosper as an independent state.

Historians continue to debate the American Patriots' intentions, especially in regard to the meaning of universal human rights, civic liberties, and popular sovereignty. Regardless of intent, the **American Revolution** ultimately ushered in a new era for the historical development of secular and representative government.

Leaders in the American Independence Movement

The American Independence movement enjoyed strong support across a diverse cross-section of the colonial population. At the top of the rebel hierarchy were societal and economic elites. Among other professions, this class of patriots generally owned plantations, farms, shipping companies, and law firms. Colonial elites developed Enlightenment-based and common law arguments to justify their rebellion. Some of the more influential elite colonial leaders were the military officer George Washington, writer Thomas Paine, and lawyers John Adams and Thomas Jefferson.

During the initial stages of the American Revolution, these colonial elites leveraged their local influence to energize and organize the independence movement. **Benjamin Franklin** was especially prolific at disseminating revolutionary works, and he continued in this role as the inaugural United States Postmaster General during the war.

The groundswell of support for independence also came from various grassroots movements. Laborers and artisans deeply resented British taxes on consumer goods and the Crown's mercantilist restrictions on trade. The lower classes were also the people most devastated by the Proclamation of 1763 because they viewed western expansion as their chance to own land and secure the American dream. Colonial women also contributed in diverse ways to the war effort, ranging from nurses to seamstresses.

 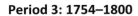

Popular Support for the Independence Movement

Obtaining and maintaining widespread popular support was essential to the American Independence movement. Armed conflict resulted in widespread economic shortages due to the British naval blockade, and British forces seized and stockpiled resources in regions they occupied. Additionally, the newly created States lacked a political system capable of levying taxes and distributing resources along the front lines. As a result, the American army depended on the financial support of private citizens.

The American military strategy similarly relied on leveraging popular support amongst the broader public. American armies and militias required a steady flow of volunteers to stay afloat in the struggle against a military and economic superpower. Furthermore, the militias often carried out irregular, asymmetric strikes against British forces and adopted guerillas tactics like launching surprise strikes on nontraditional military targets and blending into the civilian population. British generals viewed the Americans as terrorists because American militias refused to "honorably" fight battles on open battlefields where their weaker forces surely would've been annihilated. As such, maintaining popular support was essential to the American tactic of asymmetric warfare, particularly in the context of taking active measures against high-value targets behind enemy lines.

Philosophical Foundations of the American Revolution

Enlightenment Ideals Influenced the Patriot Movement

The Enlightenment was far and away the greatest intellectual, philosophical, and political influence on the movement for American independence. Enlightenment philosophers like Thomas Hobbes and Jean-Jacques Rousseau popularized the concept of social contract theory, which later developed into the political model of popular sovereignty. Under **social contract theory** and **popular sovereignty**, citizens collectively grant legitimacy and authority to the government, and that delegation could all be withdrawn at the public's will. Likewise, the Enlightenment popularized theories about universal rights and liberty, which later became the revolutionaries' rallying cry. Consequently, Enlightenment ideals inspired Americans to push for even more civil liberties, religious protections, and property rights. Overall, colonial rebel leaders wielded Enlightenment philosophy to legally justify and inspire their rebellion.

Religion also increased national unity and the public's desire for independence. Many of the British colonies, such as Rhode Island and Maryland, had been founded for the explicit purpose of protecting the free exercise of religion. As a result, these colonies were predisposed to support the independence movement to further cement their freedom. In addition, the First Great Awakening created a shared spiritual connection across the colonies, and evangelicalism combined with the Enlightenment to create a more individualistic colonial culture.

Documents that Shaped American Ideals

The majority of colonists believed that republican forms of government were ideal. Several groundbreaking documents played an outsized role in popularizing the concepts of universal natural rights and representative government. These documents served as the foundations for what became generalized American ideals.

40

The dissemination of democratic documents was facilitated through the colonial **printing press** culture, which mass-produced revolutionary leaflets and newsletters in the run-up to the conflict. Some of the most important revolutionary pamphlets were Thomas Paine's *Common Sense* (1776) and *The American Crisis* (1776). Both pamphlets popularized and inspired the independence movement with its emphasis on civic virtue, the natural rights of people, and denunciations of King George III.

Based on its legal, moral, and rhetorical arguments, the **Declaration of Independence** is widely regarded as one of the most influential political documents in modern history. Mostly written by **Thomas Jefferson**, the Declaration of Independence stated the colonists' grievances against Britain, such as taxation without representation, and argued that Britain had violated Americans' unalienable rights of "life, liberty, and the pursuit of happiness." On July 4, 1776, the **Second Continental Congress** adopted and signed the Declaration of Independence, marking the official establishment of an independent United States.

Without a long national history, liberty and independence functioned as the American identity. This foundational legacy has endured to the present day, especially in many Americans' hostility to government intervention in the economy, society, and daily life.

The American Revolution

Colonial Upset in the American Revolution

The American Independence movement suffered several glaring and large-scale disadvantages at the outset of the **American Revolutionary War** (1775–1783). Britain was the undisputed European superpower due to its hegemonic naval superiority and influence over global trade. Furthermore, Britain enjoyed a significant amount of loyalist support within the colonies. While the rebel forces worked to present the struggle as a united, patriotic effort, the colonies remained divided throughout the war. Thousands of colonists, known as **Loyalists** or **Tories**, supported Britain. Even the revolutionaries proved to be significantly fragmented, and many militias only served in their home states. The **Continental Congress** was also divided over whether to reconcile with Britain or push for full separation. These issues hindered the ability of the revolutionary armies to resist the British, who had superior training and resources at their disposal. Despite these difficulties, the Americans stunned the world and won the war with their ideological strength, asymmetric warfare, brilliant military leadership, and foreign assistance.

The ideological emphasis on liberty helped generate a steady supply of volunteers and popular support for the American war effort. American militias terrorized British supply lines and defense positions throughout the conflict. The militias refused to wear uniforms and violated traditional norms of warfare like conducting surprise attacks on lightly defended targets and targeting British officers in battle. This asymmetric warfare stretched the British military's resources to the breaking point, and the **Continental Army**, under General **George Washington**, gradually built up a force that utilized Prussian military training and backwoods guerrilla tactics to make up for their limited resources.

Although the British forces continued to win significant battles, the Continental Army gradually reduced Britain's will to fight as the years passed. Furthermore, Americans appealed to the rivalry that other European nations had with the British Empire. The support was initially limited to indirect assistance, but aid gradually increased. For example, French loans and training also helped transform the Continental Army into a modern military, and Dutch and Spanish merchants broke the British blockade

41

to provide the Americans with supplies and weapons. After the American victory at the **Battle of Saratoga** in 1777, France and other nations began to actively support the American cause by providing much-needed troops and equipment.

In 1781, the primary British army under **General Cornwallis** was defeated by an American and French coalition at Yorktown, Virginia, which paved the way for peace negotiations. The **Treaty of Paris** (1783) ended the war, recognized the former colonies' independence from Great Britain, and gave America control over territory between the Appalachian Mountains and Mississippi River. However, the state of the new nation was still uncertain.

The Influence of Revolutionary Ideals

Revolutionary Ideals of Equality and Slavery

The American Revolution's elaborate intellectual justifications for what amounted to an armed insurrection raised questions about the true meaning of equality, liberty, and representative government. Compared to Britain and other European states, the American Revolution was dramatic in terms of enhancing the political rights and economic freedom of common citizens, particularly by genuinely seeking to form a more meritocratic and representative government rather than a traditional aristocracy. However, concepts like equality were only ever intended for male Europeans, especially those wealthy enough to own land.

During the latter half of the eighteenth century, people of color faced enslavement in southern states. While most northern states abolished slavery between 1780 and 1804, racial discrimination was rampant. African Americans regularly faced economic barriers, and slave traders routinely kidnapped and enslaved free people of color. Indigenous populations fared little better under the American legal system due to lax and/or nonexistent enforcement of treaty rights. Women were also politically disenfranchised and subjugated under a patriarchal socioeconomic system. However, there were some limited calls for more direct democracy in the state and federal political systems. In particular, property qualifications for white male suffrage were abolished during the late eighteenth century, beginning with Kentucky in 1792.

Republican Motherhood

American women gained newfound influence during and after the American Revolution, though the bulk of the revolution's victories didn't extend across gender lines. Women played an indispensable role during the American Revolutionary War. Without the widespread and unshakeable support of women, the revolutionaries would have had an impossible time turning American households into shelters for clandestine troops and centers of economic production. Following the American Revolution, the American home retained its status as the cradle of democracy, and women continued to function as the embodiment of **republican motherhood**. This motherhood sought to entrust women with the role of teaching their families republican values. As a result, women held considerable political power due to their informal role as civic teachers and patriotic leaders.

At the same time, women were systematically disenfranchised and generally barred from participating in the system they championed. The **Confederation Congress** and its successor, the United States Congress, restricted women's property rights and economic opportunities. Consequently, women were often dependent on their fathers and husbands for material support. As a result, early American

societies typically upheld traditional gender norms with women serving as housewives and men as breadwinners. Gender roles were more fluid on the frontier out of necessity due to these areas' smaller and less dense populations.

The American Revolution Inspired Other Independence Movements

Putting aside the American Revolution's historical impact as the birth of an economic and military superpower, the American Revolution was an earth-shattering historical moment. The American Revolution marked the first time a colony successfully overthrew a European power and gained the right to self-government. Although far from perfect, the American political system protected an unprecedented number of political rights and civil liberties. As a result, the American victory inspired a variety of revolutionary movements in France, Haiti, and Latin America.

Along with Enlightenment thought, the American Revolution served as a major catalyst for the **French Revolution** (1789–1799). Inspired by the Americans' victory over the British imperial constitutional monarchy, revolutionaries overthrew the French absolute monarchy and installed a republican system of government. In August 1789, the National Constituent Assembly, a democratic assembly formed during the French Revolution, passed the Declaration of the Rights of Man and of the Citizen, which defined the natural right of men to be free and equal under the law. Unlike the American Revolution, however, the French Revolution led to the brutal murders of French aristocrats and other political leaders and the French government was eventually overthrown by Napoleon Bonaparte in 1799, effectively ending the French Revolution. Napoleon declared himself emperor of France in 1804 and then attempted to conquer Europe.

Fueled by the successful American and French Revolutions and the writings of the Enlightenment, a spirit of revolution swept across the Americas. The French colony in Haiti was the first major revolution occurring in 1791. The **Haitian Revolution** was the largest slave uprising since the Roman Empire, and it holds a unique place in history because it is the only slave uprising to establish a slave-free nation ruled by nonwhites and former slaves. In 1804, the Haitians achieved independence from France and became the first independent nation in Latin America.

When Napoleon conquered Spain in 1808, Latin American colonies refused to recognize his elder brother, Joseph Bonaparte, as the new Spanish monarch and advocated for their own independence. Known as the **Latin American Wars of Independence**, Venezuela, Colombia, Ecuador, Argentina, Uruguay, Paraguay, Chile, Peru, and Bolivia all achieved independence between 1810 and 1830. In 1824, Mexico declared itself a republic when, after several attempts by the lower classes of Mexico to revolt against Spain, the wealthier classes joined and launched a final and successful revolt. When Napoleon overtook Portugal in 1807, King John VI fled to Brazil and set up court. John VI returned to Portugal in 1821 and left his son Pedro behind to rule Brazil. In 1822 Pedro launched a revolution against Portugal that saw him crowned emperor of Brazil.

By the mid-1800s, the revolutions of Latin America ceased, and only a few areas remained under European rule. The U.S. President James Monroe issued the **Monroe Doctrine**, which stated that the Americas could no longer be colonized. It was an attempt to stop European nations, especially Spain, from colonizing or attempting to recapture territory within the Americas. England's navy contributed to the success of the doctrine, as they were eager to increase trade with the Americas and establish an alliance with the United States.

The Articles of Confederation

State Constitutions

Following the American Revolutionary War, the newly freed British colonies each adopted state constitutions to establish a government and delineate its powers. Like the Declaration of Independence, the state constitutions were steeped in Enlightenment thought. As such, state constitutions provided for extensive civil liberties, legal rights, and private property protections. Shared historical and cultural experiences also shaped how state constitutions implemented relatively limited governments with exceptionally weak executive branches. While governors and courts enjoyed some influence, state legislatures generally wielded the overwhelming majority of political power because they were theoretically more representative of the people and responsive to their needs.

At the same time, early state constitutions were oppressive documents and essentially functioned as a means of maintaining elite power structures. Early state constitutions placed limits on both voting rights and citizenship, typically in the form of property qualifications. So, the state government generally represented the views of an elite class of landowners, merchants, and religious leaders. Over time, low-income Europeans gained political equality, but people of color suffered systemic discrimination until at least the **Civil War** (1861–1865). For indigenous populations, the development and centralization of state power historically came at their expense, and state constitutions were no different.

The Articles of Confederation

The thirteen States ratified the **Articles of Confederation**, adopted by the Continental Congress on November 15, 1777, on March 1, 1781. The Articles broadly sought to maintain some degree of unity between the former British colonies and avoid destructive European-like regional rivalries.

The Articles of Confederation established a formal agreement or confederation between the original thirteen states. The Articles of Confederation established a central government composed of a unicameral legislative assembly, called the **Confederation Congress**, in which each state had a single representative. Passing a bill required votes from nine of the thirteen representatives. Under the Articles of Confederation, the Confederation Congress was granted very limited powers, rendering it largely ineffective. Those powers included:

- Borrowing money from states or foreign governments
- Creating post offices
- Appointing military offices
- Declaring war
- Signing treaties with foreign states

Due to the colonial experience with a centralized constitutional monarchy, the central government under the Articles of Confederation was comically weak. Right from the outset, the Confederation Congress was severely undermined by states' reservation of robust powers. For example, states held the power to print currency, assume debt, and pursue independent foreign trade deals; the central government couldn't implement a uniform economic agenda under this power-sharing scheme. In addition, states enjoyed veto power over the central government, effectively allowing minority opinions to override the entire confederation. The central government also lacked an executive branch because

44

political leaders believed it would lead to tyrannical rule. As a result, even when the Confederation Congress passed laws, enforcement was close to impossible.

The early American political system deteriorated rapidly. Domestic unrest and border conflicts sapped the central government of its legitimacy and forced American political leaders to realize they needed to revamp the entire system.

The Northwest Ordinance

A driving force behind the American Revolution was overwhelming opposition to British restrictions on westward expansion. Once Americans gained independence, settlers streamed across the Appalachian Mountains and settled in land between the Ohio River and Great Lakes. During the nineteenth century, the Northwest Territories became the states of Ohio (1803), Indiana (1816), Illinois (1818), Michigan (1837), Wisconsin (1848), and Minnesota (1858).

The Confederation Congress passed a series of land ordinances to disentangle states' claims to the land and directly oversee its development during the transition to statehood.

The **Northwest Ordinance** of 1787 was arguably the Confederation Congress's most impactful piece of legislation passed, marking one of the few times they successfully centralized political power. This legislation established federal conservatorship over territories as public domain until they qualified for statehood, effectively denying states the power to expand their individual boundaries. As such, the federal government enjoyed the power to enforce property rights and direct the development of civic institutions, such as a public education system, in the territories. Additionally, the Northwest Ordinance enacted one of the few federal prohibitions on slavery, and the area between the Appalachian Mountains and Mississippi River became an extension of the **Mason-Dixon Line**, which later divided free and slave states.

The Constitutional Convention and Debates over Ratification

The Constitutional Convention

The **Constitutional Convention** met in Philadelphia in May 1787 after the new country was rocked by economic troubles and Shays' Rebellion, an uprising in Massachusetts due to the debt crisis from the Revolutionary War, with the goal of creating a stronger federal government. However, delegates disagreed over how to structure the new system. The **Virginia Plan** was one proposal that included a bicameral legislature where states were awarded representation based on their population size. This would benefit more populous states at the expense of smaller states.

The other main proposal was the **New Jersey Plan**, which retained many elements of the Articles of Confederation including a unicameral legislature with one vote per state. This plan would put states on an equal footing regardless of population. Eventually, delegates agreed to support the **Connecticut Compromise** (also known as the **Great Compromise**), which incorporated elements from both the Virginia and New Jersey Plans and embodied federalism. Under the new Constitution, Congress would be a bicameral body. In the House of Representatives, states would be allocated seats based on population, but in the Senate each state would have two votes. The Constitution also included a president and judiciary that would each serve to check the power of other branches of government. In addition, Congress had the power to tax and had more enforcement powers.

Slavery and the Constitutional Convention

Even more than political representation and separation of powers, disputes over slavery threatened the Constitutional Convention. From the very beginning, overt limitations on chattel slavery were a political nonstarter, carrying the risk of a complete withdrawal of the southern Atlantic state delegations from the Constitutional Convention. With the continuation of slavery being a foregone conclusion, the founding fathers eventually reached two pivotal compromises over slavery.

The first compromise was the **Three-Fifths Compromise**, which determined that three-fifths of the slave population of each state would be counted for both taxes and representation. This was an effort to appease both the Southern states, who wanted slaves to be counted as part of the population for the purpose of representation but not counted for the purpose of taxes, and the Northern states, who demanded slaves be counted for taxes but not representation. This generally worked to the benefit of large slave-holding states because it inflated their populations by counting nonvoters while still giving a massive tax cut to slave owners who treated Africans purely as a commodity.

Second, the southern states agreed to a future federal prohibition on the international slave trade. The prohibition, called the **Commerce and Slave Trade Compromise**, would take effect in 1808, so southern states knew they had thirty years to safeguard slavery. This eased Southerners' fears that the Northern states would control the federal government and enforce antislavery policies. Shortly after ratification, the importation of African slaves increased exponentially, partially due to the booming cotton industry. So, by 1808, domestic slave populations had become self-sustainable, and the domestic slave trade easily kept pace with demand. The southern states also accepted the future prohibition because they, correctly, assumed it would be impossible to enforce.

Debates Over Ratifying the Constitution

Once the Constitution had been drafted, nine of the thirteen states had to ratify it for it to take effect. Vigorous debate erupted over whether or not the Constitution should be approved. Two different political factions emerged. The **Federalists** supported the Constitution because they felt a stronger central government was necessary in order to promote economic growth and improve national security. Several leading federalists, including Alexander Hamilton, John Jay, and James Madison, published a series of articles collectively called the Federalist Papers urging voters to support the Constitution. However, the **Anti-Federalists**, including Thomas Jefferson and Patrick Henry, felt that the Constitution took too much power away from the states and gave it to the national government. They also thought there weren't enough protections for individual rights and lobbied for the addition of a **Bill of Rights** that guaranteed basic liberties.

The debates between these two parties continued for two years and inspired two series of essays known as the **Federalist Papers** and the **Anti-Federalist Papers** that debated various topics surrounding the ratification of the Constitution. The essays were authored anonymously by leaders of the respective parties. Scholars are fairly confident of the authorship of the Federalist Papers, but the authorship of many of the Anti-Federalist Papers is still uncertain.

Notable Federalists include:

- **Alexander Hamilton**: founder of the Federalist Party, advocate for a centralized financial system, and author of 51 of the Federalist Papers

- **James Madison**: one of the primary drafters of the Constitution, the future fourth president of the United States, and author of 29 of the Federalist Papers

- **John Jay**: president of the Continental Congress, future first chief justice of the United States, and author of 5 of the Federalist Papers

- **John Adams**: future second president of the United States

- **George Washington**: commander-in-chief of the Continental Army and future first president of the United States (Washington never officially joined the Federalist party, but he was a strong supporter of ratifying the Constitution)

Notable anti-Federalists include:

- **Thomas Jefferson**: primary author of the Declaration of Independence and future third president of the United States

- **Patrick Henry**: governor of Virginia (1776–1779, 1784–1786) and author of works frequently included in the Anti-Federalist Papers

- **Samuel Adams**: governor of Massachusetts (1794–1797), lieutenant governor of Massachusetts (1789–1794), and president of the Massachusetts Senate (1782–1785, 1787–1788)

- **George Mason**: one of only three delegates who did not sign the Constitution at the Constitutional Convention and author of Objections to This Constitution of Government (1787) and the Virginia Declaration of Rights of 1776, which served as the basis for the Bill of Rights

- Possible authors of the Anti-Federalist Papers include Robert Yates, George Clinton, Samuel Bryan, Melancton Smith, Richard Henry Lee, and Patrick Henry

The first state to ratify the Constitution was Delaware in a unanimous vote on December 7, 1787. Pennsylvania, New Jersey, Georgia, Connecticut, Massachusetts, Maryland, and South Carolina followed and, after six months, New Hampshire became the ninth state to ratify the Constitution in June 1788. However, some states still remained divided between Federalist and anti-Federalist sentiments and had yet to approve the document, including the two most populous states, Virginia and New York. To reconcile their differing views, the Federalists agreed to include a bill of rights if anti-Federalists supported the new Constitution. Federalist sentiment prevailed, and the remaining states approved the document. On May 29, 1790, the last holdout, Rhode Island, ratified the Constitution by two votes. As promised, the **Bill of Rights**—the first 10 amendments to the Constitution—was added in 1791, providing expanded civil liberty protection and due process of law.

47

The Constitution

Separation of Powers in the Constitution

To strengthen the central government, while still appeasing the individual states who preferred to remain sovereign over their territories, the framers of the Constitution based the new government upon the principle of **Federalism**—a compound government system that divides powers between a central government and various regional governments. The Constitution clearly defined the roles of both the state governments and the new federal government, specifying the limited power of the federal government and reserving all other powers not specifically granted by the Constitution to the federal government to the states in the Tenth Amendment to the Constitution, commonly referred to as the **Reservation Clause**.

The Constitution establishes the specific powers granted to the federal and state governments.

- **Delegated powers**: the specific powers granted to the federal government by the Constitution

- **Implied powers**: the unstated powers of the federal government that can be reasonably inferred from the Constitution

- **Inherent powers**: the reasonable powers required by the federal government to manage the nation's affairs and maintain sovereignty

- **Reserved powers**: the unspecified powers belonging to the states that are not expressly granted to the federal government or denied to the state governments by the Constitution

- **Concurrent powers**: the powers shared between the federal and state governments

The Constitution delegated the following expanded powers to the federal government:

- Coin money
- Declare war
- Establish federal courts
- Sign foreign treaties
- Expand the territories of the United States and admit new states into the union
- Regulate immigration
- Regulate interstate commerce

The following powers were reserved for the states:

- Establish local governments
- Hold elections
- Implement welfare and benefit programs
- Create public school systems
- Establish licensing standards and requirements
- Regulate state corporations
- Regulate commerce within the state

The **concurrent powers** granted to both the federal and state governments in the Constitution include:

- The power to levy taxes
- The power to borrow money
- The power to charter corporations

The Constitution established a federal government divided into three branches: legislative, executive, and judicial.

The Three Branches of the U.S. Government

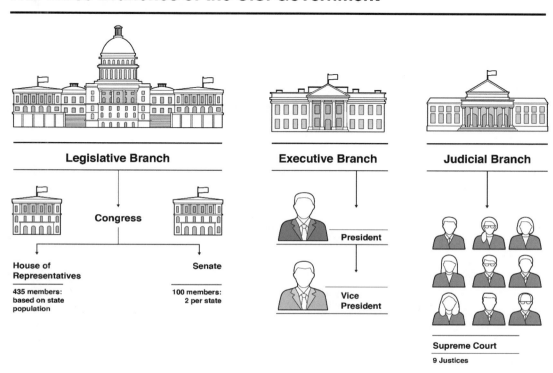

Executive Branch
The **executive branch** is responsible for enforcing the laws. The executive branch consists of the president, the vice president, the president's cabinet, and federal agencies created by Congress to execute some delegated task or authority.

The **president** of the United States:

- Serves a four-year term and is limited to two terms in office
- Is the chief executive officer of the United States and commander-in-chief of the armed forces
- Is elected by the Electoral College
- Appoints cabinet members, federal judges, and the heads of federal agencies
- Vetoes or signs bills into law

- Handles foreign affairs, including appointing diplomats and negotiating treaties
- Must be at least thirty-five years old, a natural-born U.S. citizen, and have lived in the United States for at least fourteen years

The **vice president**:

- Serves four-year terms alongside and at the will of the president
- Acts as president of the Senate
- Assumes the presidency if the president is incapacitated
- Assumes any additional duties assigned by the president

The **cabinet members**:

- Are appointed by the president
- Act as heads for the fifteen executive departments
- Advise the president in matters relating to their departments and carry out delegated power

Note that the president can only sign and veto laws and cannot initiate them himself. As head of the executive branch, it is the responsibility of the president to execute and enforce the laws passed by the legislative branch.

Although Congress delegates their legislative authority to agencies in an enabling statute, they are located in the executive branch because they are tasked with executing their delegated authority. The president enjoys the power of appointment and removal over all federal agency workers, except those tasked with quasi-legislative or quasi-judicial powers.

Legislative Branch

The **legislative branch** is responsible for enacting federal laws. This branch possesses the power to declare war, regulate interstate commerce, approve or reject presidential appointments, and investigate the other branches. The legislative branch is **bicameral**, meaning it consists of two houses: the lower house, called the **House of Representatives**, and the upper house, known as the **Senate**. Both houses are elected by popular vote.

Members of both houses are intended to represent the interests of the constituents in their home states and to bring their concerns to a national level while also being consistent with the interests of the nation as a whole. Drafts of laws, called **bills**, are proposed in one chamber and then are voted upon according to that chamber's rules; should the bill pass the vote in the first house of Congress, the other legislative chamber must approve it before it can be sent to the president.

The two houses (or **chambers**) are similar though they differ on some procedures such as how debates on bills take place.

House of Representatives

The **House of Representatives** is responsible for enacting bills relating to revenue; impeaching federal officers, including the president and Supreme Court justices; and electing the president in the case of no candidate reaching a majority in the Electoral College.

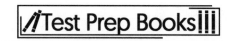

In the House of Representatives:

- Each state's representation in the House of Representatives is determined proportionally by population, with the total number of voting seats limited to 435.

- There are six nonvoting members in the House, one each from Washington, D.C.; Puerto Rico; American Samoa; Guam; the Northern Mariana Islands; and the U.S. Virgin Islands.

- The **Speaker of the House** is elected by the other representatives and is responsible for presiding over the House. In the event that the president and vice president are unable to fulfill their duties, the Speaker of the House will succeed to the presidency.

- The representatives of the House serve two-year terms.

- The requirements for eligibility in the House include:

  o Must be twenty-five years of age
  o Must have been a U.S. citizen for at least seven years
  o Must be a resident of the state they are representing by the time of the election

Senate

The **Senate** has the exclusive powers to confirm or reject all presidential appointments, ratify treaties, and try impeachment cases initiated by the House of Representatives.

In the Senate:

- The number of representatives is one hundred, with two representatives from each state.
- The vice president presides over the Senate and breaks a tied vote, if necessary.
- The representatives serve six-year terms.
- The requirements for eligibility in the Senate include:
  o Must be thirty years of age
  o Must have been a U.S. citizen for the past nine years
  o Must be a resident of the state they are representing at the time of their election

Legislative Process

Although all members of the houses vote on whether or not bills should become laws, the senators and representatives also serve on committees and subcommittees dedicated to specific areas of policy. These committees are responsible for debating the merit of bills, revising bills, and passing or killing bills that are assigned to their committee. If it passes, they then present the bill to the entire Senate or House of Representatives (depending on which they are a part of). In most cases, a bill can be introduced in either the Senate or the House, but a majority vote of both houses is required to approve a new bill before the President may sign the bill into law.

Judicial Branch

The **judicial branch**, though it cannot pass laws itself, is tasked with interpreting the law and ensuring citizens receive due process under the law. The judicial branch consists of the **Supreme Court**, the highest court in the country, overseeing all federal and state courts. Lower federal courts are the district courts and the courts of appeals.

In the Supreme Court:

- Judges are appointed by the president and confirmed by the Senate.
- Judges serve until retirement, death, or impeachment.
- Judges possess sole power to judge the constitutionality of a law.
- Judges set precedents for lower courts based on their decisions.
- Judges try appeals that have proceeded from the lower courts.

Checks and Balances

A system of deliberate **checks and balances** between the branches exists to ensure that no branch oversteps its authority. They include:

- Checks on the Legislative Branch:

  o The president can veto bills passed by Congress.

  o The president can call special sessions of Congress.

  o The judicial branch can rule legislation unconstitutional.

- Checks on the Executive Branch:

  o Congress has the power to override presidential vetoes by a two-thirds majority vote.

  o Congress can impeach or remove a president, and the chief justice of the Supreme Court presides over impeachment proceedings.

  o Congress can refuse to approve presidential appointments or ratify treaties.

  o Congress, particularly the House of Representatives, has the **power of the purse** (the ability to tax and spend money for the federal government). All bills concerning revenue must be introduced in the House of Representatives.

- Checks on the Judicial Branch:

  o The president appoints justices to the Supreme Court, as well as district courts and courts of appeals.

  o The president can pardon federal prisoners.

  o The executive branch can refuse to enforce court decisions.

  o Congress can create federal courts below the Supreme Court.

  o Congress can determine the number of Supreme Court justices.

  o Congress can set the salaries of federal judges.

  o Congress can refuse to approve presidential appointments of judges.

  o Congress can impeach and convict federal judges.

52

The three branches of government operate separately, but they must rely on each other to create, enforce, and interpret the laws of the United States.

Checks and Balances

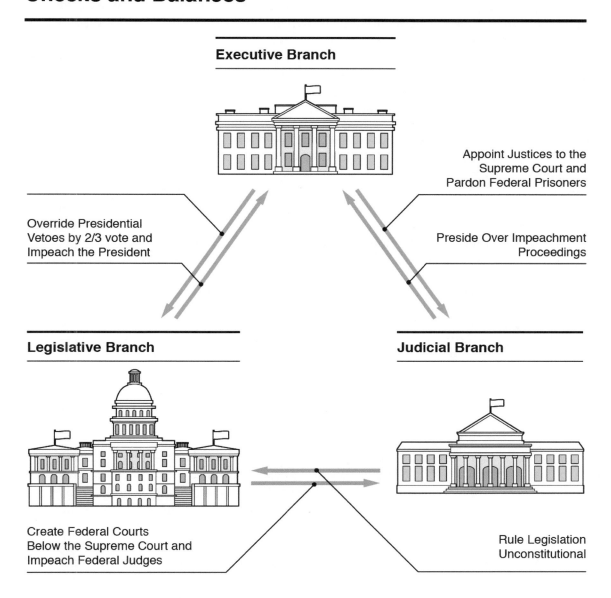

Shaping a New Republic

Initiatives Addressing Continued European Colonial Powers

The United States took a variety of actions to mollify and usurp European colonial powers during the late eighteenth century.

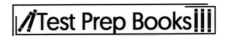

British Canada had remained loyal during the American Revolutionary War and even taken up arms against the Americans when they invaded Quebec in 1775. Consequently, Britain continued to be a major force in the Americas even after America gained independence. American expansion across the Appalachian Mountains poured fuel on the fire, igniting frontier conflicts all across the Great Lakes region. The federal government negotiated numerous ceasefires, but the border skirmishes continued until Washington signed the **Jay Treaty** in 1794. The treaty's aim was to settle issues that had lingered between Britain and the United States since the Revolutionary War. It provided for the British evacuation of the Northwest Territory, compensation to the United States for British attacks on American shipping, payment of American debts to British merchants, trade agreements between Britain and the United States, equal use of the Mississippi river by both nations, and plans to determine the borders between the United States and the British Canadian colonies. The treaty was very unpopular, but it did succeed in preserving peace between the United States and Britain.

Spain held some of the most strategically valuable territory in North America, but most of it was lightly populated and underdeveloped. American settlers regularly violated the Spanish territorial border in northern Florida, which was a haven for escaped slaves and indigenous military units. Angered by the Americans' encroachment, Spain revoked American merchants' access to the port city of New Orleans in 1798. This was unacceptable for the Americans, who used the port to send supplies up the Mississippi River to territories west of the Appalachian Mountains. So, once Spain secretly ceded much of its American territory to France, the Jefferson administration purchased the entire Louisiana territory from Napoleon in 1803 in an act called the **Louisiana Purchase**.

The Impact of War Between France and Britain on the United States

The **French Revolution** created a pressing challenge for the United States. France had been the United States' first and most important European benefactor. Without French loans, training, supplies, and troops, the Americans likely would have lost the fight for independence. Furthermore, the American Revolution partially inspired the French Revolution, which overthrew King Louis XVI and established a revolutionary representative government. Thus, when Britain formed a coalition of European powers to oust the French revolutionaries, many Americans demanded it was their moral obligation to support their ally and repay the revolutionary debt they owed.

Other Americans viewed the conflict through clear eyes and realized an intervention was squarely against their national self-interest. The Constitution had been written, but not ratified, when the French Revolution began. Consequently, the United States lacked the political strength, financial resources, and military power to wage war on foreign soil against multiple world powers. The British Royal Navy also occupied the status of a global hegemonic naval power, and American foreign policy experts understood that supporting France would come at the cost of British blockades. Given its precarious political and economic situation at the end of the eighteenth century, a steep decline in international trade posed a direct threat to the long-term stability of the United States. As a result, President George Washington declared the neutrality of the United States in his **Proclamation of Neutrality** on April 22, 1793.

Spanish Colonization in California

Spanish colonization in California expanded throughout the eighteenth century. Franciscan friars migrated from Spanish colonies further south in present-day Mexico and western South America, founding **mission settlements** in coastal California. Mission settlements often began with a group of

friars backed by a small retinue of laborers and/or soldiers, and the friars led a theocratic colonial system.

The mission settlements implemented the same policies toward indigenous populations as other Spanish colonies. The friars used forced conversions and persuasive proselytizing to gain some degree of cultural and societal control over the local population and actively pursued alliances with influential groups and leaders. Once they were in a position to carry out enforcement, the friars instituted the *repartimiento* **labor system**, which required indigenous populations to provide free labor in exchange for some limited legal rights and protections.

Combined with a massive amount of undeveloped land and an abundance of natural resources, the region's relatively small population of Spanish soldiers and migrants enjoyed more social mobility than nearly anywhere else in the world. Greater accommodation of indigenous culture and Europeans led to considerable cross-cultural interactions, including the development of syncretic religious beliefs and interracial family blending.

Struggles Between the Federal Government and American Indian Tribes

The United States had a contentious and, in some cases, ambiguous relationship with Native American tribes. Frontier groups actively pressed into tribal lands, so westward expansion was a continual source of conflict due to the resulting displacement of indigenous populations. In many instances, the federal government was forced into the role of mediator between tribes, states, and settlers.

The federal government signed dozens of agreements with Native American tribes during the late eighteenth century, but the **Treaty of Harmar** (1789) illustrates what ultimately occurred under almost all the agreements. The Americans had agreed to limit settlers and reduce violence in the Great Lakes territories, but even if it desperately wanted to, the federal government lacked the authority and power to enforce the treaty on frontier communities. In response, indigenous regional powers, including the Huron and Delaware tribes, formed the **Western Confederation**. The West Confederation inflicted some of the worst defeats in American military history, but the Americans ultimately recovered and achieved a decisive victory at the **Battle of Fallen Timbers** (1794). Capitalizing on this victory, the federal government agreed to split the Northwest Territories with the Western Confederation under the **Treaty of Greenville** (1795), which was similarly violated in short order.

George Washington and John Adams' Presidential Terms

The first several presidential administrations developed political institutions and precedents to legitimize the Constitution.

George Washington was unanimously elected as America's first president in 1789, and he reluctantly agreed to serve two terms to stabilize the constitutional regime. Consequently, two terms served as an informal precedent for future presidential administrations. Washington's Treasury Secretary, **Alexander Hamilton**, established the **United States Mint** to print and regulate the new national currency and oversaw the passage of an excise tax on liquor to raise revenue. When distillers launched the **Whiskey Rebellion** (1791–1794), Washington personally led a militia to shut it down, setting a precedent for the enforcement of federal laws.

John Adams won the presidential election of 1796, establishing the precedent of peaceful and democratic regime change, and he was the first president to govern from the permanent capital city of

55

Washington, D.C. Unlike Washington, Adams wasn't a war hero with widespread popular support. Thus, to protect federal authority, Adams passed the controversial **Alien and Sedition Acts (1798).** This series of acts allowed the federal government to deport noncitizens, raised the citizen residency requirement for immigrants from five years to 14 years, and criminalized slanderous criticism of the federal government. Adams also spearheaded the formation of a large standing army and navy to defend against French warships harassing American merchants.

The Formation of Political Parties

American political leaders held conflicting views on numerous critical issues. Following the ratification of the Constitution, **Federalists** dominated the Washington administration and enacted policies designed to centralize political power. Washington's Treasury Secretary Alexander Hamilton was an especially fierce advocate for free trade, central banking, federal taxes, and economic interventions. More broadly, the Federalists valued an organized and efficient government more than maximizing the protection of personal freedoms.

Organized opposition to the Federalists increased during Washington's second term through the formation of the **Democratic Republican Party** during the early 1790s. The Democratic Republicans favored limited government, civil liberty protections, and decentralized banking. In addition, the Democratic Republicans were less committed to free trade and an isolationist foreign policy. Many Democratic Republican leaders, including Thomas Jefferson and James Madison, viewed the **Jay Treaty** as a betrayal of Republican values for its concessions to Britain in exchange for reduced tensions on the frontier.

The Democratic Republicans nominated a presidential candidate, **Thomas Jefferson**, for the first time in 1796. Although Jefferson lost to the Federalist John Adams, he was victorious in the presidential election of 1800. Democratic Republicans then proceeded to control the executive branch until Andrew Jackson won the presidential election of 1828.

George Washington's Farewell Address

George Washington's **Farewell Address** is one of the most famous speeches in American history. While Washington reluctantly served as president, he had near-unanimous popular support. Washington realized that future American presidents would not enjoy that luxury, and he hoped the country wouldn't fracture when divisive issues arose. The revolutionary hero turned first president felt it was his duty to impart some words of wisdom to the country as it embarked on its first regime change.

Washington primarily warned of the dangers of **factionalism**. He argued that the United States would be safe and prosperous as long as it was a cohesive entity and then proceeded to give a number of warnings about factionalism. He believed political factionalism would grind the new constitutional system to a halt and possibly lead to state disintegration. To prevent partisan bickering, Washington cautioned against the establishment of political parties, believing that they would consolidate power and dissolve the core tenets of representative government. The Farewell Address is also famous for Washington cautioning America against getting entangled in European rivalries, foreign disputes, and permanent foreign alliances. Washington pointed to the benefits of America's geographic location and urged the government to continue developing prosperous and peaceful relations with foreign powers whenever possible.

Developing an American Identity

New Forms of National and Regional Culture

The development of a national culture transformed the United States over the latter half of the eighteenth century. A cohesive national culture first formed in the aftermath of the French and Indian War (1754–1763) as American colonists increasingly established militias and self-governing political institutions to defend their land. During the 1770s and 1780s, Enlightenment philosophies popularized the concepts of civil liberties, private property rights, and limited government. A robust publishing industry helped disseminate these ideas across the country, which led to the inclusion of **Enlightenment ideas** in the U.S. Constitution (1789) and Bill of Rights (1791). These ideas laid the foundation for a capitalist economic system and shaped government policies, especially in terms of promoting individual liberties.

The new national culture was relatively diverse for its time. Although British culture played an outsized role in American culture, the presence of other European immigrants and a wide variety of Christian denominations resulted in considerable multiculturalism. However, white Europeans dominated the national identity by forcibly excluding African slaves and American Indians from mainstream society.

Early American culture also had significant regional variance. Northern states tended to place greater emphasis on economic and social freedom due to their larger urban centers of trade, technological investments, and immigrant populations. In contrast, Southern states were more conservative and hierarchical, largely due to their greater reliance on slavery and a plantation-based agricultural system. After Eli Whitney invented the **cotton gin** in 1793, the cultural and economic divide deepened as Southern states invested more heavily in large-scale agricultural production.

The Depiction of National Identity in Art

Given its relatively short and disjointed history, American-based artistic movements inspired and expressed the development of a uniquely American identity. American architects, artists, and writers all supported the revolutionary cause with works highlighting the twin virtues of patriotism and independence.

Americans tweaked the traditional British colonial architectural style after gaining independence. The new Federalist architectural style retained some colonial elements, like Georgian columns, but it added Classical Greek and Roman elements to link America with ancient democracies.

The American art movement primarily produced patriotic portraits of founding fathers and military triumphs. Artists also depicted the everyday life of merchants and farmers, such as John Singleton Copley's famous *Paul Revere* (1768). Additionally, American artists created British-style landscape paintings that depicted nature's abundance, open land, and frontier life to emphasize America's divine blessing and unlimited opportunities.

American literature grew out of political writings, incorporating themes from the Declaration of Independence, *Common Sense*, and *The Federalist Papers*. At the tail end of the eighteenth century, American literary writers adopted the modern novel as a form of patriotic expression. Many early American novels were sentimental and idealistic, underscoring the importance and values of the

American experiment. Other novels were satirical, such as Philip Freneau's mockery of British colonization.

Movement in the Early Republic

The Dynamic Relationships Between Native Americans and Others

Native American tribes responded with dynamic and ever-changing efforts to maintain political autonomy and economic prosperity against a creeping tide of European colonization. Both European settlers and Native American tribes pursued the same divide-and-conquer strategy of military alliances to isolate key rivals. Smaller indigenous tribes pursued alliances to establish more unified confederations, and regional powers sought alliances with other powerful indigenous confederations and European groups. For example, the Iroquois Confederacy incorporated smaller indigenous societies and allied with the British first against the French and then later to push back the American frontier.

Wars were common between indigenous and European societies, especially in frontier areas that were outside the control of central governing authority. The **Northwest Indian War** (1785–1795) was the United States' first prolonged conflict with indigenous societies. With the support of British forts in the present-day American Midwest, the Delaware and Miami tribes led the Western Confederacy to decisive victories over the United States before the **Jay Treaty** (1794) temporarily stopped the bloodshed. Britain's continued support of indigenous confederations not only undermined the United States' foreign policy ambitions but also bred political controversy as more Americans pushed for aggressive actions to be taken against Britain during the **French Revolutionary Wars** (1792–1802).

Westward Migration

Westward expansion across the Appalachian Mountains attracted a diverse group of migrants. The British colonies had rapidly increased in population density over the late seventeenth century and into the eighteenth century, and migrants hoped to settle what they viewed as unclaimed lands. British colonists accounted for the vast majority of migrants, but there was considerable religious diversity as minority Christian sects sought even greater levels of independence. French, Spanish, and Dutch merchants also joined westward expeditions in the hopes of establishing a commercial presence in the early development of frontier settlements. Indigenous populations also had significantly more commercial and cultural interactions with frontier settlements, and it wasn't uncommon for indigenous people to live alongside frontier groups. Similarly, people of color often fled to the frontier due to the Northwest Territory's prohibitions on slavery, economic opportunities, and less traditional social institutions.

The clashing of cultures on the frontier often resulted in seething tensions and chilling violence. The diverse groups were interacting in a mostly lawless geographic area, and they often held conflicting values, beliefs, and economic interests. So, when political, social, and economic disputes arose, groups were quick to violence because they knew there was little hope of a central authority providing assistance or enforcing consequences.

Differing Regional Attitudes Toward Slavery

In the early 1800s, political and economic differences between the North and South became more apparent. Politically, a small but vocal group of abolitionists emerged in the North who demanded a

complete end to slavery throughout the United States. **William Lloyd Garrison** edited the abolitionist newspaper *The Liberator* and vehemently denounced the brutality of slavery. His criticism was so vicious that the legislature of Georgia offered a $5,000 bounty to anyone who could capture Garrison and deliver him to state authorities. Other activists participated in the **Underground Railroad**—a network that helped fugitive slaves escape to the Northern United States or Canada.

Economic differences emerged as the North began to industrialize, especially in the textile industry where factories increased productivity. However, the Southern economy remained largely agricultural and focused on labor-intensive crops such as tobacco and cotton. This meant that slavery remained an essential part of the Southern economy. In addition, the North built more roads, railroads, and canals, while the Southern transportation system lagged behind. The Northern economy was also based on cash, while many Southerners still bartered for goods and services. This led to growing sectional tension between the North and South as their economies began to diverge.

These economic differences led to political tension as well, especially over the debate about the expansion of slavery. This debate became more important as the United States expanded westward into the Louisiana Purchase and acquired more land after the Mexican-American War. Most Northerners were not abolitionists. However, many opposed the expansion of slavery into the western territories because it would limit their economic opportunities. If a territory was open to slavery, it would be more attractive to wealthy slave owners who could afford to buy up the best land. In addition, the presence of slave labor would make it hard for independent farmers, artisans, and craftsman to make a living because they would have to compete against slaves who did not earn any wages. For their part, Southerners felt it was essential to continue expanding in order to strengthen the southern economy and ensure that the Southern way of life survived. As intensive farming depleted the soil of nutrients, Southern slave owners sought more fertile land in the west.

Practice Quiz

Questions 1–3 refer to the passage below:

"The problem is to find a form of association which will defend and protect with the whole common force the person and goods of each associate, and in which each, while uniting himself with all, may still obey himself alone, and remain as free as before." This is the fundamental problem of which the *Social Contract* provides the solution.

The clauses of this contract are so determined by the nature of the act that the slightest modification would make them vain and ineffective; so that, although they have perhaps never been formally set forth, they are everywhere the same and everywhere tacitly admitted and recognised, until, on the violation of the social compact, each regains his original rights and resumes his natural liberty, while losing the conventional liberty in favour of which he renounced it.

Excerpt from The Social Contract by Jean-Jacques Rousseau, 1762

1. According to the passage, what happens after a "violation of the social compact"?
    a.   The social compact resumes protecting rights and liberty as soon as possible.
    b.   The social compact institutes reforms to serve the common good.
    c.   The social compact dissolves and releases its constituent parties.
    d.   The social compact reverts to the Social Contract between the state and citizens.

2. Social contract theory developed in which one of the following intellectual contexts?
    a.   The Enlightenment
    b.   Humanism
    c.   Modernism
    d.   The Renaissance

3. Which one of the following most accurately describes a consequence of social contract theory?
    a.   Social contract theory incentivized imperial conquests and colonization.
    b.   Social contract theory contributed to an intense period of revolutions.
    c.   Social contract theory incentivized an expansion of international trade networks.
    d.   Social contract theory led to the growth of state power.

4. Which of the following was NOT one of the compromises made in the Connecticut Compromise?
    a.   A lower House of Representatives that is to be selected based on population size
    b.   An Electoral College to give delegates a chance to intervene in the event of a wrong choice by the electorate
    c.   A Senate consisting of two representatives from each state
    d.   A Supreme Court with nine justices to prevent any ties during voting

5. Federalism is described as the relationship between the federal government and which of the following?

    a. The people
    b. State governments
    c. The branches of government
    d. The Constitution

See answers on next page.

Answer Explanations

1. C: Social contract theory essentially involved a compromise where people sacrifice some individual freedom in exchange for mutual legal protection. If the social contract is violated, then people return to a state of complete natural freedom. This is not ideal because natural freedom encompasses the ability to inflict harm. After mentioning the "violation of the social compact," the passage describes how people regain original rights and natural liberty. This is referencing people returning to a state of complete natural freedom, meaning they are released from the dissolved social contract. Thus, Choice *C* is the correct answer. The social contract doesn't resume after a violation; in fact, the opposite happens. So, Choice *A* is incorrect. Choice *B* is incorrect because the passage doesn't mention reform. Choice *D* is a red herring. Although the passage refers to a social contract and social compact, contract and compact carry the same meaning—a mutual agreement. Nothing in the passage indicates otherwise, so Choice *D* is incorrect.

2. A: Social contract theory developed during the Enlightenment in the eighteenth and nineteenth centuries. Along with John Locke and Thomas Hobbes, Jean-Jacques Rousseau was a prominent Enlightenment philosopher and social contract theorist. Thus, Choice *A* is the correct answer. Choice *B* is the second-best answer. Humanism is a philosophy that emphasizes individualism, human freedom, critical thinking, and rationalism, and Jean-Jacques Rousseau was heavily influenced by the humanist tradition. However, the Enlightenment better describes the intellectual context of the eighteenth and nineteenth centuries because humanism dates back to ancient times. So, Choice *B* is incorrect. Modernism is a philosophical and artistic movement that developed in the late nineteenth century based on the rejection of traditionalism, so Choice *C* is incorrect. The Renaissance was a cultural movement that revived humanism; however, the Renaissance lasted from the fourteenth century to the seventeenth century, and social contract theory did not develop until the Enlightenment. So, Choice *D* is incorrect.

3. B: Social contract theory directly contributed to an intense period of revolution. According to social contract theory, if the state fails to fulfill its obligations, then the contract is broken. Because the contract is broken, people are released and free to form a new state. For example, French revolutionaries claimed the monarchy had broken the social contract by denying citizens basic liberties and legal protections. In addition, in the Americas, more than a dozen new nation-states gained independence in the nineteenth century. Thus, Choice *B* is the correct answer. Social contract theory didn't incentivize imperialism or colonization; if anything, it did the opposite. So, Choice *A* is incorrect. International trade isn't directly related to social contract theory, so Choice *C* is incorrect. Although a firm social contract would theoretically strengthen the state, social contract theory didn't directly lead to the growth of power. So, Choice *D* is incorrect.

4. D: The Connecticut Compromise finally eased the tensions of the Constitutional Convention enough to get a deal on the table. Combining the better parts of all of the proposed deals, the compromise was able to get through to become the frame of the new Constitution. Choice *A* (a House of Representatives fixed to population size for representation), Choice *B* (an Electoral College), and Choice *C* (a Senate where each state has exactly two representatives) were all part of the Connecticut Compromise. Choice *D*, the number of justices that currently sit on the court, is not mandated by the Constitution. There can be as many or as few as Congress wants.

5. B: Federalism, at least as it was put forth by the Founders, describes the relationship between the federal and state governments wherein the powers of government are divided between the two. Choice *A* is incorrect because Federalism does not refer to a relationship between the federal government and the people. Instead, the federal government interacts with the people through their state governments. Choice *C* is incorrect because the relationship between the branches of the federal government is defined by a system of checks and balances, not federalism. Choice *D* is incorrect because the Constitution lays out the system of federalism, but federalism does not describe the relationship between the federal government and the Constitution.

The Rise of Political Parties and the Era of Jefferson

Debates Between Political Parties in the Early 1800s

As American political parties developed during the early nineteenth century, partisanship and rancor over hotly debated issues increased dramatically. Most broadly, politicians fiercely debated the extent of federal powers, particularly when those powers conflicted with the states' autonomy. Federalists advocated for a robust federal government to oversee nationwide policies such as a centralized banking system, heavy tariffs, and national infrastructure projects. In contrast, the **Democratic Republicans**— members of the Democratic Republican Party—prioritized civil liberties, local government, and state autonomy. Aside from their distrust of the federal government, Democratic Republicans aggressively condemned tariffs intended to protect American agricultural exports.

However, at times, some Democratic Republican leaders strayed away from their ideals about limited government, such as when Thomas Jefferson dramatically expanded federal powers to facilitate the **Louisiana Purchase** (1803). For $15 million, Jefferson bought French territory west of the Mississippi River that doubled the size of the United States. He then appointed Meriwether Lewis and William Clark to lead an expedition to explore the vast new territory and study its geography, vegetation, and plant life. Clark also brought his African American slave, York, on the journey. York helped hunt and even saved Clark's life during a flood. The expedition was also aided by Sacagawea, a Shoshone woman who acted as a guide and interpreter. The explorers established relations with Native American tribes and set the stage for further western expansion in the 1800s.

Relations with European powers were another sharply contested political issue. George Washington and the leading Federalists wanted to remain neutral and consolidate American resources. In contrast, the Democratic Republicans advocated for defending France, America's first meaningful ally, against Britain during the French Revolutionary wars (1792–1802). Hostilities between the United States and Britain boiled over during the **Napoleonic Wars** (1803–1815) largely as a result of British blockades and limitations on trade impacting American commerce, the British Royal Navy boarding American ships and impressing American seamen, and continued clashes between American settlers, British Canada, and Native American tribes supported by Britain on the frontier.

War between the United States and Britain broke out in 1812 because the United States was drawn into a conflict between Britain and France. Britain refused to stop interfering with American ships bound for France and had begun forcibly recruiting American citizens into the British navy. Furthermore, the British still occupied several forts near the Great Lakes and continued to encourage Indians to attack American settlements in the Northwest Territories. The resulting **War of 1812** was a military stalemate, and hostilities concluded with the **Treaty of Ghent** (1815), which returned Anglo-American relations to the status quo.

Supreme Court Decisions in the Early 1800s

The Supreme Court spent much of the early nineteenth century attempting to gain formal constitutional authority and expand federal power. Legislative powers were found in Article I. The sweeping authority

granted to the executive branch was found under Article II. Article III created a Supreme Court and delegated control and oversight over the development of a judiciary system to Congress.

Marbury v. Madison (1803) was an important case for the Supreme Court. Chief Justice John Marshall's decision legitimized the power of judicial review, meaning that that the Supreme Court enjoyed the power to review and possibly overturn any American law if the court deemed the law contradicted the Constitution of the United States. This was a power far beyond anything explicitly provided under the Constitution, though Marshall persuasively argued that it was implied.

McCulloch v. Maryland (1819) similarly stands out as an unprecedented change to American law. Marshall again wrote the majority decision and ruled that the **Supremacy Clause** of the Constitution (Article IV, Clause 2) elevated federal law above any conflicting state law. Furthermore, Marshall cited the **Necessary and Proper Clause** of the Constitution (Article I, Section 8) to justify the existence of implied legislative powers. As a result, Congress gained broad power to pass laws necessary for the implementation of an express power, such as regulating interstate commerce.

Governmental Efforts to Control North America

Constant immigration meant that land prices in the eastern United States rose and people sought new economic opportunities on the frontier where land was cheaper. The United States government tried purchasing land from Native Americans, but most refused to relinquish their territories. Native Americans continued to defend their land until the Shawnee chief Tecumseh, who had formed a confederacy of Native American tribes to establish a self-governing Indian nation and oppose U.S. expansion into the Northwest Territory, was defeated and killed in the **War of 1812**. This defeat helped secure the **Northwest Territory**, and more settlers began pouring in. After the Louisiana Purchase, Lewis and Clark paved the way for expansion into the Great Plains and further west.

By the mid-1800s, the revolutions of Latin America ceased and only a few areas remained under European rule. The U.S. President James Monroe issued the **Monroe Doctrine** (1823), which stated that the Americas could no longer be colonized. It was an attempt to stop European nations, especially Spain, from colonizing areas or attempting to recapture areas they had previously colonized. England's navy contributed to the success of the doctrine, as they were eager to increase trade with the Americas and establish an alliance with the United States.

The concept of **Manifest Destiny** emerged during the 1800s and introduced the idea that God wanted Americans to civilize and control the entire North American continent. This led to conflict when the province of Texas declared its independence from Mexico and asked to be annexed by the United States. President James K. Polk tried to buy Texas, but when Mexico refused, he sent troops into the disputed territory. Mexican troops responding by attacking an American unit, which led to the **Mexican-American War** (1846–1848). Manifest Destiny also sparked a desire to expand American influence into Central and South America. Adventurers launched several unsuccessful attempts to invade Nicaragua and Cuba.

Politics and Regional Interests

Leaders' Responses to Regional v. National Concerns

Regional interests heavily influenced politicians' economic policies and approach to the looming controversy over slavery. The economies of Southern states were highly dependent on slave labor. Without an immense supply of African slaves, plantations would face exponentially higher costs and lost profits. Given their disproportionate wealth and power, plantation owners dominated Southern state governments and their federal representatives and were able to leverage political power to undermine attempts at reforming slavery and regulating agriculture. Many Southern political leaders, like John Calhoun of South Carolina, claimed the right to nullify federal laws and secede from the union.

Northern states industrialized during the nineteenth century, and they relied on cheap immigrant labor rather than slaves. Therefore, Northern states were relatively quick to abolish slavery, and their state governments willingly permitted, if not outright encouraged, the **abolitionist movement**.

Politicians on the frontier were sometimes pro-slavery and sometimes anti-slavery depending on location. The American Midwest generally opposed slavery and pushed for the federal government to support industrialization efforts. In contrast, the southern portion of the frontier hoped to recreate the plantation-based economies as practiced in the American South and therefore supported the expansion of slavery into the territories.

The American System

The **American System** was a series of economic policies designed to unite and strengthen the United States stemming directly from the grand economic vision of **Alexander Hamilton**, who was treasury secretary under President George Washington. During the first half of the nineteenth century, congressmen **Daniel Webster** and **Henry Clay** led the charge to unify America's regional economies. More specifically, Webster and Clay championed heavy tariffs to protect domestic industries, a unified banking system to stabilize the country's fledgling financial system, and major infrastructure investments to develop the western frontier. The American System was highly ambitious in its attempt to unify the United States and integrate regional economies.

Despite its undeniable effectiveness in binding the states together and generating economic growth, the American System was extraordinarily controversial. The **Whig Party**, who asserted Congress' supremacy over the president and primarily focused on economic concerns, easily convinced Northern businessmen of the financial benefits related to unification, and Western frontiersmen reluctantly supported the federal government's consolidation of power in order to finance large-scale infrastructure projects. However, the reaction of Southern states ranged from seething hostility to vocal resistance. They viewed the American System as a handout to northern industrialists at the expense of agricultural production. In particular, Southern states balked at tariffs because it was far more profitable to ship cotton and foodstuffs to European markets than to the Northern states.

Congressional Attempts at Political Compromise

Both the North and South also feared losing political power as more states were admitted to the nation. For example, neither side wanted to lose influence in the United States senate if the careful balance of free and slave state representation was disrupted. Several compromises were negotiated in Congress,

but they only temporarily quieted the debate. The first such effort, called the **Missouri Compromise**, was passed in 1820, and it maintained political parity in the U.S. Senate by admitting Missouri as a slave state and Maine as a free state. The Missouri Compromise banned slavery in the portion of the Louisiana Purchase that was north of the 36°30' parallel (the **Mason-Dixon Line**), excluding Missouri, and permitted slavery in the portion south of that line.

However, the slavery debate erupted again after the acquisition of new territory during the Mexican-American War. The **Compromise of 1850** admitted California as a free state and ended the slave trade in Washington, D.C., but not slavery itself, in order to please Northern politicians. In return, Southern politicians were able to pass a stronger fugitive slave law and demanded that New Mexico and Utah be allowed to vote on whether or not slavery would be permitted in their state constitutions. This introduced the idea of popular sovereignty where the residents of each new territory, and not the federal government, could decide whether or not they would become a slave state or a free state. This essentially negated the Missouri Compromise of 1820. The enhanced fugitive slave law also angered many Northerners because it empowered federal marshals to deputize anyone, even residents of a free state, and force them to help recapture escaped slaves. Anyone who refused would be subject to a $1,000 fine (equivalent to more than $28,000 in 2015).

America on the World Stage

United States' Efforts to Create an Independent Global Presence

The United States encountered significant difficulties in competing with European powers on the world stage during the first half of the nineteenth century. As a result, the United States sharpened its focus on increasing foreign trade and expanding its North American territories, which were far more achievable goals.

The United States relied on foreign trade to stimulate economic growth and gain global influence. During the early nineteenth century, the United States primarily traded with Europe, and cotton represented its most valuable export. In particular, the United States leveraged its commercial power to navigate the Anglo-French rivalry. After fighting Great Britain to a stalemate in the War of 1812, the United States quickly established itself as an important ally and trade partner with its former colonizer. Furthermore, the United States sought and gained export markets for its manufactured goods in Latin America and China.

The United States greatly benefited from the tumultuous conditions of the **Napoleonic Era** (1799–1815). With incessant warfare drowning French finances, Napoleon decided to abandon much of his North American colonial project and sell France's vast Louisiana Territory to the United States. The Louisiana Purchase (1803) nearly doubled American territory, and over the next several decades, the United States subsidized exploratory missions, commercial enterprises, and pioneer settlements to populate its new territory. As the United States expanded, Americans increasingly claimed Manifest Destiny to justify further conquests as a divine right.

Governmental Efforts to Gain Control over the Western Hemisphere

The United States combined skillful diplomacy and military might to dominate the Western hemisphere during the first half of the nineteenth century.

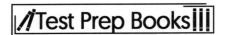

Several presidential administrations skillfully deployed diplomacy to mitigate the threat posed by European powers operating in the Western hemisphere. President Thomas Jefferson exploited Napoleon's precarious financial and military situation when negotiating the Louisiana Purchase, and France's departure from continental North America shored up the United States' western border. President James Monroe similarly acquired Florida for cash in the **Adams-Onis Treaty** of 1819 and also issued the highly influential Monroe Doctrine (1823) to threaten retaliation against European interventions in the newly independent Latin American states. The United States likely couldn't have prevented such an intervention, but this public declaration resulted in the United States developing a near-exclusive sphere of influence in Central and South America. The United States also signed a multitude of border treaties with Great Britain. For example, the **Oregon Treaty** (1846) established the 49th parallel of north latitude as the American-Canadian border from present-day Minnesota to Washington.

In its dealings with competing regional powers, the United States heavily favored military action. Congress worked to pass the **Indian Removal Act** of 1830 to increase the land available for settlement, and President Andrew Jackson enforced it by relocating more than sixty thousand American Indians from their ancestral homelands in the southeastern United States to lands west of the Mississippi River. When the Cherokee tribe was moved, about four thousand people died out of the sixteen thousand removed from their ancestral lands. This event is commonly referred to as the **Trail of Tears**. Additionally, President James K. Polk secured nearly all of the present-day American Southwest by annexing Texas (1845) and instigating the Mexican-American War (1846–1848).

Market Revolution: Industrialization

The Industrial Revolution

The **Industrial Revolution** transformed the relationship between producers and consumers in the marketplace. Prior to the development of large-scale industrial manufacturing, economies depended on specialized tradesmen to produce goods for trade. Following the creation of interchangeable parts and mechanized tools, industrial production output soared. American entrepreneurs were early adopters of these British innovations, and they spearheaded the establishment of novel forms of economic organization such as company mills and factories.

Samuel Slater is generally recognized as the father of the American Industrial Revolution. During the late eighteenth century, Slater toured British textile mills, memorized their designs, and then emigrated to the United States, where he adapted British innovations to American conditions. Slater built the first textile mills and factory towns in the United States, with most of his commercial empire located in Massachusetts and Rhode Island. Like Slater, **Francis Cabot Lowell** famously financed an innovative company town in the present-day city of Lowell, Massachusetts. Lowell pioneered new methods of corporate financing to raise capital investments, and his Boston Manufacturing Company was one of the first to employ women as factory workers. Lowell had a lasting impact on American manufacturing due to the Waltham-Lowell system's application of textile machinery to boost production.

Industrial Revolution Innovations

The American Industrial Revolution was powered and accelerated by technological innovations. Of all the innovations, the concept of using interchangeable parts was arguably the most influential in its impact on myriad industries. With interchangeable parts, workers could be assigned specific and

isolated tasks, rather than bearing responsibility for an entire finished product. This more efficient model of production both reduced the skill requirements for workers and increased total industrial output as factories implemented increasingly complex assembly lines.

Similar groundbreaking innovations occurred in agriculture, such as advancements to Eli Whitney's cotton gin and the invention of mechanized farming equipment. The resulting increase in cotton production directly supported the deployment of textile machinery, such as the spinning jenny and the water frame, in order to mass produce garments.

Other inventions increased the efficiency of transportation and communication, which contributed to more economic integration and unification. The steam engine increased the reliability and speed of maritime travel on the Atlantic Ocean as well as critical domestic waterways like the Mississippi River. Likewise, the telegraph provided an unprecedented form of expedited communication across vast distances. As a result, interrelated networks of commercial relationships between consumers, producers, and investors sprang up all across the United States and even extended overseas.

Transportation Advancements and Networks

Several important laws also stimulated western expansion during the second half of the nineteenth century. Congress passed the **Homestead Act** in 1862, which allowed citizens to claim 160 acres for only $1.25 per acre. The settler also had to live on the land for five years and make improvements. That same year, Congress also passed the **Pacific Railroad Act**, which supported the construction of a transcontinental railroad. The United States government provided land and financial support to railroad companies and the first transcontinental link was established in 1869. This facilitated trade and communication between the eastern and western United States.

The government also supported the development of additional roads and canals throughout the country, which helped build further-reaching transportation networks. However, not all regions were equally connected; the North and Midwest regions were more closely linked together than either region was linked to the South. Transportation networks and advancements enhanced the mobility of goods and people.

The Development of National Commercial Ties

National commercial ties were predicated on intertwined economic growth and specialization. Northern states functioned as the engine for ramping up economic growth. Industrialization resulted in a skyrocketing supply of consumer goods at unprecedentedly low prices. Furthermore, the establishment of the First Bank of the United States (1791–1811) and the Second Bank of the United States (1816–1836) provided the necessary capital for aggressive and ambitious industrial efforts.

Southern states were nearly as indispensable to the development of a capitalist economic system. Aside from generating a considerable amount of staple foods, cotton fed industrialization efforts in the Northern states. For example, textile mills turned cotton into a variety of finished products ranging from clothes to household items. Northern shipping companies facilitated these commercial exchanges up and down the Atlantic seaboard; however, the Southern states sometimes resisted political pressure to engage in domestic trade due to the increased profitability of foreign markets.

Western frontier areas were a combination of Northern and Southern economies. Given the surplus of land they seized from indigenous populations, frontier communities were able to engage in large-scale

agriculture as well as hunting and fishing. However, as their populations increased and territories were admitted as states, the former frontier regions slowly transitioned toward industrialization.

Market Revolution: Society and Culture

Immigration and Internal Migration

Immigration to the United States grew exponentially during the early nineteenth century. The bulk of early immigrants came from Britain and Ireland, especially in the wake of the deadly **Great Famine** (1845–1849). However, diverse ethnic and religious groups also set sail for American shores to obtain civil liberties, economic opportunities, and religious freedom. Germans constituted one of the largest immigrant groups that settled outside of the original British colonies on the western frontier, located in the present-day Midwestern United States.

Frontier communities located near the Appalachian Mountains, the Ohio River Valley, and the Mississippi River were amongst the most diverse in the world. Given the British colonial history in the formally recognized states, the federal territories attracted international migrants at elevated rates. Appalachian communities especially experienced tremendous growth in the early nineteenth century due to their proximity to the states. Irish and German immigrants arrived en masse and established rural settlements, which strongly resembled urban immigrant communities except on a far wider territorial scale. American Indian and African cultural beliefs were also more likely to be incorporated within the Western frontier due to the general lack of manpower and resources. This desire for sustained growth is also why the frontier generally supported unification plans, such as the infrastructure promised under the American System.

Diverging Socioeconomic Classes

Manufacturing led to more intense class stratification in the United States. At the top of the hierarchy, manufacturing magnates and business elites joined plantation owners as the dominant powers in American socioeconomic life. The rise of manufacturing spurred industrialization and urbanization in a virtuous cycle. A **virtuous cycle** is a chain of events in a feedback loop where each step achieves favorable results for the next. As the cost of production plummeted and supplies of goods increased, commercial interactions rose significantly and drove general improvements in the standard of living. For example, many American cities were built with sanitation systems and large marketplaces to support entrepreneurial economic growth.

During the early nineteenth century, the American middle class largely consisted of skilled professionals, factory managers, and investors. The expanded middle class functioned as the consumer class, especially in regard to the purchase of new manufactured products.

The new class of urbanized industrial and unskilled laborers occupied the very bottom position in American society, lower than just about everyone except for slaves. The laboring poor tangentially benefited from rising prosperity, but they worked for twelve to fifteen hours per day under extreme work conditions with nearly no days off and minimal pay. Additionally, a significant portion of the laboring poor had less access to food than subsistence farmers.

The Shift from Semi-Subsistence Agriculture to Manufacturing

American employment opportunities largely shifted from agriculture to the industrial sector as a result of the Industrial Revolution. Prior to the Industrial Revolution, most Americans engaged in **semi-subsistence agriculture**, meaning they grew a sizable percentage of the food they consumed. Therefore, industrialization involved a major change since factory workers depended on wages for food. The type of work was also different in the sense that workers produced goods destined for distant marketplaces.

Northern factory workers produced a variety of goods. The use of interchangeable parts and mass assembly was originally applied to firearms during the American Revolution, and arms manufacturing continued to be big business in the decades afterward. Many of these guns were shipped to the frontier for conflicts against indigenous populations, but they were also a significant export to Europe. Factories also produced mechanized agricultural equipment for farms and plantations across the country, especially the Southern states. Manufactured textiles, including clothing and household items, were another major manufactured product. Tariffs resulted in most of these goods remaining in the United States, but there was also a significant export market to Europe and Latin America. Southern plantations often shipped cotton to northern states in exchange for manufactured textiles and mechanized agricultural tools.

Changes in Gender and Family Roles

Industrialization facilitated incredible diversification in the workforce. Assembly lines and interchangeable parts greatly reduced businesses' reliance on skilled labor. Therefore, fresh opportunities and coercive economic pressure drove women and children to join the market revolution. Overall, women and children worked the most dangerous and least desirable jobs in exchange for inferior compensation relative to adult male peers.

The introduction of women to the workforce had a mixed effect on traditional gender and family norms. On the one hand, women had slightly more independence within the public sphere due to their new source of income and commercial interactions. However, at the same time, American society definitively kept the public and private spheres separate. Women were still expected to bear full responsibility over child rearing and myriad household obligations.

Given pervasive pay inequality and lack of political rights, American society remained firmly within the grasp of patriarchal power structures during the nineteenth century. Many women, including the feminist heroes **Elizabeth Cady Stanton** and **Susan B. Anthony**, helped lead the abolitionist movement during the 1830s and 1840s to not only condemn the injustices of slavery, but also to demand numerous legal reforms for women related to childcare, divorce, property rights, education, and medical access.

Expanding Democracy

The Transition to a More Participatory Democracy

The franchise, or the ability to vote, was significantly expanded in the United States in the early nineteenth century. States originally restricted the franchise to adult white males who owned some minimum amount of property. Between 1800 and 1830, nearly all states eliminated property ownership requirements, although some states continued to allow only taxpayers to vote. This electoral expansion received incredible popular support, despite occasional resistance. For example, in Rhode Island a small

ruling class of rural elites continued to restrict the franchise to property owners. In response, landless laborers and small farmers revolted in the **Dorr Rebellion** (1841–1842) which resulted in the property requirement being replaced with a poll tax for all native-born male citizens regardless of race.

Democratization occurred alongside the development of **factionalism**. The **First Party System** (1792–1824) involved two political parties—the Federalist Party and Democratic-Republican Party—but it was an extremely one-sided contest, with the Democratic-Republicans winning every presidential election between 1800 and 1824. The mobilization of newly enfranchised white males, along with reduced international tensions after the War of 1812, industrialization, and an increasingly national economy, ushered in the **Second Party System** (1828–1854), and it was dominated by the Democratic Party and the Whig Party. Democrats adopted the Democratic-Republican principles about limited government and focused on individual liberty, and Congressman Henry Clay formed the Whig Party to champion Congressional power over Presidential power, protect against majority tyranny, and advocate for federally funded modernization programs.

Compared to its predecessor, the Second Party System featured significantly higher levels of vitriolic partisanship. For example, President Jackson vetoed the Whig-backed Second Bank of the United States, alongside a fiery statement that accused Congress of selling out Americans to financial elites. The debate over slavery eventually broke the Second Party System; however, factionalism has remained a defining characteristic of American democracy ever since.

Jackson and Federal Power

Democrats and Whigs

The Founding Fathers of the United States opposed the divisiveness they associated with political parties, and President George Washington cautioned against political parties in his Farewell Address. However, the ratification of the Constitution led to the creation of the first two American political parties, the **Federalists** and the anti-Federalist **Democratic-Republican Party**. In the 1824 Presidential election, Andrew Jackson won more of the popular vote and the electoral vote than any other candidate.

However, because no candidate had a majority of all the electoral votes, the House of Representatives chose the President by ballot from the top three candidates: Andrew Jackson, John Quincy Adams, and William H. Crawford. The Speaker of the House, Henry Clay, had the fourth most electoral votes, but only the top three candidates were allowed on the ballot. The House elected John Quincy Adams, who then appointed Henry Clay as his Secretary of State. Andrew Jackson believed that Adams and Clay conspired to beat him in a "**corrupt bargain**." In disgust, Jackson and his supporters founded the **Democratic Party**. When Andrew Jackson became the seventh president of the United States as a Democrat, his opposition organized under the **Whig Party**, led by Henry Clay and Daniel Webster among others. The Whigs asserted Congress' supremacy over the president and primarily focused on economic concerns like a national bank and infrastructure projects.

These political parties disagreed about various issues such as the national bank, federal government powers, and federally funded improvement projects.

Federal Power

Andrew Jackson gained national fame as a war hero by defeating the British at the 1815 Battle of New Orleans during the War of 1812. Jackson viewed himself as a representative of the common man against a corrupt aristocracy and fought fiercely for his vision of the United States, particularly by asserting Executive power against Congress.

One of Jackson's most effective weapons against Congress was the **veto**. He vetoed more bills than all previous Presidents put together. He was also the first President to use the pocket veto, an indirect veto that occurs when the President does not sign a bill within ten days and Congress adjourns during that time period (normally an unsigned bill becomes law, but if Congress adjourns during the ten days the bill is vetoed because it cannot be returned to Congress).

One of the most important bills Jackson vetoed was a bill renewing the charter for the Second Bank of the United States. The Bank was a private institution with exclusive national banking privileges granted by the U.S. government, and Jackson viewed it as an elite institution that acted against the interests of the common people. After vetoing the charter renewal, Jackson removed the Bank's federal deposits and redistributed them to state banks. Henry Clay and others saw this as a gross abuse of Executive power and formed the Whig Party to oppose him. This fight became known as the **Bank War**.

Andrew Jackson faced the potential destruction of the Union in the 1832 **Nullification Crisis** when South Carolina passed the **Ordinance of Nullification** in response to the Tariff of 1828, or the **Tariff of Abominations**, and the Tariff Act of 1832. The Tariff of Abominations was a series of tariffs on imported goods designed to protect Northern manufacturing. Although it included tariffs on items primarily imported by the North as well as items imported by the South, it disproportionately affected the Southern economy. The Tariff Act of 1832 only slightly modified the original Act. In response to what it viewed as an abuse of Congressional power, South Carolina passed the Ordinance of Nullification in 1832 declaring both Tariff Acts null and void within the state.

The Ordinance further proclaimed that any act on the part of the federal government to force South Carolina to cooperate would be grounds for the state to secede from the Union. In response, Jackson declared that states did not have the legal right to nullify federal laws and argued for the supremacy of the federal government. Congress passed the **Force Bill** (1833) allowing Jackson to use armed forces to enforce collection of tariffs and passed a bill lowering tariffs, called the **Compromise Tariff**, the same day, mitigating the crisis. South Carolina rescinded the Ordinance of Nullification but proceeded to nullify the Force Bill, maintaining the principle of nullification and state sovereignty that later came to a head in the Civil War.

Indian Removal Act and the Trail of Tears

Despite multiple treaties guaranteeing the land rights of Native American tribes in the Eastern United States, tensions continued to grow between the tribes and white settlers. Andrew Jackson was the first President to initiate a policy of Indian Removal – relocating tribes from the Eastern United States to lands beyond the Mississippi. In 1830 Congress passed the **Indian Removal Act**, which gave the President the authority to negotiate removal with the Native American tribes. While the removal was supposed to be voluntary, threats, bribes, and outright war were all used to convince the tribes to move. In 1833 President Martin van Buren, Jackson's successor, ordered the U.S. Army to force the removal of

the remaining Cherokee people. Out of approximately sixteen thousand Cherokee, an estimated four thousand died on what became known as the **Trail of Tears**.

The Development of an American Culture

A New National Culture

A new national culture developed in the United States combining European identities, Christian beliefs, and regional diversity. Once the United States began expanding westward and industrializing, European immigration diversified considerably with large groups coming from Germany, Ireland, and Scandinavia during the first half of the nineteenth century. Immigration rates also skyrocketed in this period. For example, compared to the rates between 1790 and 1820, immigration increased tenfold by the 1840s. As a result, American culture developed as a melting pot where cultural values and traditions fused together.

Likewise, the promise of religious freedom resulted in more Christian sects taking root in the United States than anywhere else in the world. Christian revivalist movements also contributed to the growth of uniquely American religious beliefs, such as the importance of personal spiritual connections to the divine.

Unlike other countries, an American national culture was heavily influenced by regional economic development. Northern economies featured large-scale industrialization, urbanization, and immigration, which resulted in a greater emphasis on commerce and more frequent interactions among people of different cultures. Wealthy owners of plantations and slaves dominated the Southern economy, resulting in a hierarchical society and culture. In the Western territories, the regional culture was optimistic and adventurous as frontiersmen sought prosperity in the wilderness.

Influences on Art

The **Enlightenment** and the **Romantic movement** both had a transformative impact on early American culture. Beginning in the late seventeenth century, European philosophers embraced Enlightenment thought to strive for societal perfection in terms of liberty, equality, and rule of law. The Enlightenment began in Europe during the late seventeenth century and made its way to America as a period dedicated to scientific reasoning in areas such as science, politics, and religion. Unlike much monarchical rule in Europe, the Enlightenment encouraged public discourse and valued how the public felt about critical issues. For example, the American publishing industry emerged prior to the American Revolution and exploded in its aftermath, a process that gave the public broad access to political and religious texts.

The European Romantic movement directly led to the United States' first homegrown artistic movement, the **American Romantic movement**. Like their European contemporaries, American artists broke with the Enlightenment to inject emotion and spirituality back into philosophical and artistic endeavors. While the Enlightenment sought to perfect government, Romanticism concerned itself with human perfectibility.

The American Romantic movement birthed other artistic movements. **Gothic Revival architecture** popularized medieval European architectural styles with an American twist, such as incorporating chimneys and stained glass in the construction of neoclassical homes. Similarly, **New England Transcendentalism** merged Enlightenment and Romantic philosophy to create art based on spirituality,

74

morality, nature, individualism, and independence. Famous examples of New England Transcendentalism include Ralph Waldo Emerson, Henry David Thoreau, and Louisa May Alcott.

The Second Great Awakening

The Second Great Awakening

The **Second Great Awakening** occurred in the early 1800s in response to the increases in democratic and individualistic beliefs, rationalism, and the social and economic changes brought on by the Industrial Revolution. It urged Protestants to work not only for their own salvation but for the salvation of others as well. This helped fuel a social reform movement that promoted the abolition of slavery, temperance, and prison reform. The question of slavery caused schisms in the Baptist and Methodist churches during the 1840s. The Second Great Awakening, much like the First Great Awakening, inaugurated the creation of several **New Religious Movements** (NRMs) in the United States, especially in the southern states.

An Age of Reform

The Progressive Era

In the late 1800s and early 1900s, the forces of urbanization and industrialization combined to create rampant urban plight across the metropolitan centers of the United States. During this era, many progressive political leaders and groups rose to power, opening the door to urban-based reforms in labor, health care, education, women's rights, and temperance. These reforms coalesced in what is now referred to by historians as the **Progressive Era**. This period included activists in both the Democratic and Republican parties. The Progressives wanted to use scientific methods and government regulation to improve society. For example, they advocated the use of direct democracy procedures such as the ballot initiative (citizens changing a law directly rather than through their legislatures), the referendum (a direct vote on a law passed by Congress), and recall (voters removing public officials from office) to make government more responsive to its citizens. Progressives also argued that it was necessary to breakup large monopolies (known as trust busting) in order to promote equal economic competition.

Abolitionist and Antislavery Movements

The **abolitionist movement**—which was driven by antislavery sentiment—gained steam in the early to mid-1800s as the United States became increasingly sectionalized in character. The abolitionist movement was not a monolithic, static phenomenon, but rather changed over time as different groups created different visions for solving the United States' slave issue. The American Colonization Society (founded 1816), for instance, helped create the African colony of Liberia as a refuge for freed and enslaved blacks living in the United States. Even within this movement, reformers held different visions. Some simply wanted to send black residents back to Africa for the benefit of creating a less diverse and conflicted society; others saw Liberia as a way to help blacks regain their cultures overseas.

Other movements included the American Anti-Slavery Society, the Philadelphia Female Anti-Slavery Society, the Anti-Slavery Convention of American Women, and the Female Vigilant Society. Led and motivated by women, these organizations brought the abolitionist and women's rights movements closer together, planting the seeds of a coalition that would once again join together in American history during the heart of the civil rights movement of the 1950s and 1960s. Abolition was achieved in part

through President Lincoln's Emancipation Proclamation (1863), which freed slave in Confederate states during the Civil War, and fully through the Thirteenth Amendment to the Constitution (1865), thanks in part to the efforts of these reformers.

Overall, the abolitionist movement was more successful in the North, and as a result, even though the rights of African Americans were restricted by many state governments, there was a marked increase in the free African American population. In the South, however, relatively unsuccessful slave rebellions characterized the antislavery efforts.

Antislavery Movements in the North and the Southern Response

Public support for and opposition to slavery exhibited dramatic regional variation. Anti-slavery movements and literature were present in American from the late seventeenth century on, and by 1804 all states north of Maryland had passed laws that abolished slavery. Anti-slavery sentiment spread in the North partly due to the Second Great Awakening, and tension grew between the North and the South as a result of the Northwest Ordinance of 1787, the Missouri Compromise of 1820, the Compromise of 1850, and the Kansas-Nebraska Act of 1854. The abolitionist movement was formed in 1831 when **William Lloyd Garrison** began publishing his abolitionist newspaper, *The Liberator*. In conjunction with African American abolitionists, William Lloyd Garrison established the influential **American Anti-Slavery Society** in 1833 and organized collective actions to protest the institution's continuation.

As anti-slavery sentiment grew in the North, the South responded with stronger and stronger defenses of slavery as an institution. Southerners strenuously objected to all limitations on slavery under the belief that any change threatened their economy and their way of life. The overwhelming majority of Southerners owned few, if any, slaves due to the significant costs. However, most Southerners worked in areas tangentially related to plantation-based agricultures. Some worked at the wholesale purchase of agricultural products, while others worked as field hands and overseers. Therefore, these workers had a vested economic interest in the continuation of slavery. Southerners also strongly believed in the sovereignty of the states versus the federal government and argued that the federal government did not have the right to dictate internal state policies, particularly the issue of slavery. Southern politicians characterized slavery and plantations as a critical part of the region's culture. As a result, Southerners generally viewed abolitionism as "Northern aggression," a constitutional violation of states' rights, and a direct attack on the Southern culture and way of life.

The Women's Rights Movement

The **Women's Rights Movement** in the U.S. ranged from 1848 to 1920. While the goals of the movement changed over time, at the beginning it called for a woman's right to vote (**suffrage**), the right to bodily autonomy, the right to divorce and custody of children, the right to work, the right to fair wages and equal pay, the right to own property, the right to obtain an education, and the right to equality in religion and morals. Famous early women's rights activists include **Susan B. Anthony**, **Lucretia Mott**, **Lucy Stone**, and **Elizabeth Cady Stanton**, who authored the Declaration of Rights and Sentiments, which demanded access to the civil liberties granted to all men.

In July 1848, the **Seneca Falls Convention** met for two days to discuss the current conditions and rights of women in the social, civil, and religious realms. Elizabeth Cady Stanton presented the Seneca Falls Declaration, also known as the **Declaration of Rights and Sentiments**, based on the Declaration of Independence and outlining the rights of women. About one third of the attendees signed the

Declaration. This convention was the first of several women's right conventions in the following few years.

The Fourteenth Amendment specified equal treatment for all citizens; however, it did not establish women's right to vote in elections. Although landowning women were allowed to vote in New Jersey in the late eighteenth century, the right was removed in 1807. The fight for women's suffrage continued in the middle of the nineteenth century and gained momentum in the early twentieth century due to the increased participation of women in the economy during World War I when much of the male workforce went overseas to fight. The National Women's Party picketed outside the White House and led a series of protests in Washington, resulting in the imprisonment of the party's leader, Alice Paul. In 1918, Woodrow Wilson declared his support for women's suffrage despite earlier opposition, and in 1920 Congress passed the Nineteenth Amendment, which made it illegal for states to withhold voting rights based on gender.

Women continue to demand change during the twenty-first century for reasons such as the gender wage gap, better resources for women's health, female reproductive rights, and protection of basic human rights, such as bringing greater awareness to rape culture, violence against women, and protection against female sex trafficking.

African Americans in the Early Republic

African American Communities

Enslaved African Americans collectively struggled to preserve their humanity against the horrors of slavery. Although slaves were descended from different and culturally diverse West African tribes, they crafted unique Afro-American languages to foster and strengthen interpersonal relationships. Likewise, slaves maintained cultural traditions and family structures even when slave owners prohibited such activities. When faced with separation, slaves often escaped to reunite with loved ones, and former slaves established independently governed communities.

Free African Americans similarly established tight-knit communities in the North to collectively thwart kidnappers, and these communities often strongly supported the abolitionist movement. **Frederick Douglass** pushed for equality of all people regardless of race and gender, and his *Narrative of the Life of Frederick Douglass, an American Slave* (1845) was an international bestseller. The brothers Charles Henry Langston and John Mercer Langston formed the **Ohio Anti-Slave Society** to protest the westward expansion of slavery. African Americans' personal anecdotes had the most remarkable impact in terms of persuading the public. For example, former slaves injected the deplorable conditions and sexual abuse of enslaved women into the public consciousness when such topics were flatly denied and widely considered taboo.

The Society of the South in the Early Republic

Southern Agricultural Economy

The Southern regional identity was steeped in agriculture. To maximize the profit potential of large-scale production, plantations primarily grew cash crops such as sugar, tobacco, and, most importantly, cotton. However, less wealthy family farms continued to produce traditional agricultural staple foods such as rice, citrus fruits, wheat, and legumes. Southern plantation owners regularly struggled with the decision

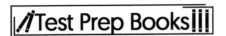

of where to export crops. While Northern markets were closer and had less onerous shipping costs, European markets generally offered higher prices.

Aside from protecting slavery, Southern politicians were most adamant about protecting their agricultural exports. For example, during the **Nullification Crisis** (1832–1833), South Carolina passed legislation to nullify the so-called **Tariff of Abominations**, a high protective tariff from 1828 designed to protect Northern industry, and the **Tariff of 1832**, which lowered the protectionist measures but still did not satisfy Southern concerns. South Carolina attempted to nullify the tariffs because of their negative effect on the Southern economy. The crisis only ended in 1833 when Congress passed the **Force Bill**, which authorized President Andrew Jackson to use the army to enforce federal law in South Carolina, and also passed the Compromise Tariff, which satisfied South Carolina's concerns. South Carolina nullified the Force Bill three days later as a symbolic gesture.

The impact of agriculture on the Southern regional identity cannot be overstated. Southern lands were almost exclusively devoted to agricultural production, which curbed the development of major urban centers. Without alternatives, Southerners either worked in agriculture or migrated outside the region. People lived and died with each successive harvest, and they were united in opposition to anything that threatened their way of life.

Westward Expansion of Plantations

Early settlers in the Southeast had established sprawling plantations, leaving less open land than in other regions. In addition, plantation-based production methods were unsustainable because they extensively extracted nutrients from the soil, resulting in decreased agricultural output. As a result, many plantation owners sought to shift operations westward to western Georgia and Mississippi. This type of economic production was only possible due to a source of cheap labor, namely, slavery. As in the Southeast, plantation owners west of the Appalachians sought to legalize and protect the institution of slavery to sustain their agricultural economy.

The legality of slavery on the western frontier represents one of the most controversial political issues in the history of American politics, requiring numerous compromises. For example, the **Missouri Compromise** of 1820 admitted Maine as a free state, Missouri as a slave state, and prohibited slavery in westward lands above the 36° 30' parallel (the Mason-Dixon Line). The Compromise of 1850 admitted California as a free state and allowed slavery the Territory of New Mexico, gained during the Mexican-American War. It also outlawed the slave trade in Washington, D.C., and created a new, harsher Fugitive Slave Law. The Kansas-Nebraska Act was perhaps the most devastating compromise of all. It allowed the residents of the Kansas and Nebraska territories to vote on whether or not the territories would allow slavery, resulting in fighting and bloodshed as pro- and anti-slavery factions both tried to gain supremacy. Many abolitionists and Northern politicians condemned these compromises because they legitimized and safeguarded slavery. All the compromises eventually unraveled, and the issue of western slavery resulted in mass bloodshed during the run-up to the American **Civil War** (1861–1865).

Practice Quiz

1. What is the term for the ability of a ruling body to influence the actions, behavior, and attitude of a person or group of people?
    a. Politics
    b. Power
    c. Authority
    d. Legitimacy

2. Which of the following is a function of a nation AFTER it has been formed rather than a shared characteristic that would be helpful in the formation of a nation?
    a. Culture and traditions
    b. History
    c. Sovereignty
    d. Beliefs and religion

3. How did the outcome of the French and Indian War impact the life of American colonists?
    a. The colonies expanded west of the Allegheny Mountains.
    b. Great Britain imposed taxes on the colonies to pay off the British war debt.
    c. A lasting peace developed between the colonists and Native Americans.
    d. The power of self-government increased in the colonies.

Question 4 is based on the following passage:

> We hold these Truths to be self-evident: that all Men are created equal; that they are endowed by their creator with certain inalienable rights; that among these are life, liberty, and the pursuit of happiness: that to secure these rights, governments are instituted among men, deriving their just powers from the consent of the governed; that whenever any form of government becomes destructive of these ends, it is the right of the people to alter or abolish it, and to institute new government, laying its foundation on such principles, and organizing its powers in such form, as to them shall seem most likely to effect their safety and happiness.
>
> Prudence indeed will dictate that governments long established should not be changed for light and transient causes; and accordingly all experience hath shown that mankind are more disposed to suffer while evils are sufferable, than to right themselves by abolishing the forms to which they are accustomed. But when a long train of abuses and usurpations begun at a distinguished period and pursuing invariably the same object, evinces a design to reduce them under absolute despotism, it is their right, it is their duty to throw off such government, and to provide new guards for their future security.

Declaration of Independence, adopted July 4, 1776

4. What is the main purpose of the excerpt?
    a. Provide a justification for revolution when the government infringes on "certain inalienable rights"
    b. Provide specific evidence of the "train of abuses"
    c. Provide an argument why "all Men are created equal"
    d. Provide an analysis of the importance of "life, liberty, and the pursuit of happiness"

79

Question 5 is based on the following diagram:

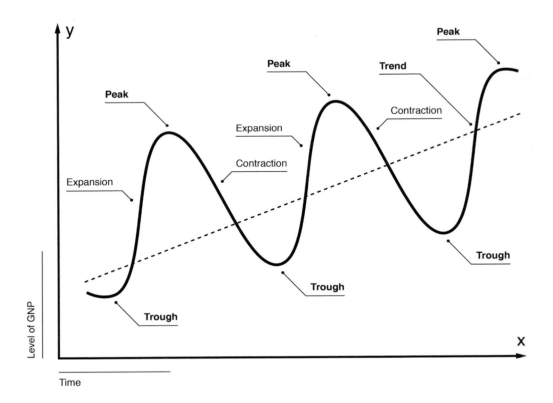

5. Which of the following phases of a business cycle occurs when there is continual growth?
   a. Expansion
   b. Peak
   c. Contraction
   d. Trough

See answers on next page.

Answer Explanations

1. B: Choice *B* is correct, as power is the ability of a ruling body to influence the actions, behavior, and attitude of a person or group of people. Choice *A* is incorrect, as politics is the process of governance typically exercised through the enactment and enforcement of laws over a community, such as a state. Although closely related to power, Choice *C* is incorrect, because authority refers to a political entity's justification to exercise power. Legitimacy is synonymous with authority, so Choice *D* is also incorrect.

2. C: Choice *C* is correct. Sovereignty is a characteristic of a nation that is self-governing, which can only happen after the nation has been formed. Choices *A*, *B*, and *D* are incorrect because, while there are no definitive requirements to form a nation, they typically begin with a group of people bound by some shared characteristic. Examples include language, culture and traditions, history, beliefs and religion, homeland or geography, and ethnicity.

3. B: Choice *B* is correct. Following the French and Indian War, the British government amassed an enormous war debt, and Great Britain imposed taxes on the colonists to generate more revenue. King George III argued that British resources had defended the colonists from French and Native American forces, so the colonists should share in the expenses. Choice *A* is incorrect because the Royal Proclamation of 1763 prevented the colonies from expanding west of the Allegheny Mountains. Choice *C* is incorrect because no lasting peace ever occurred between the colonists and Native Americans. Choice *D* is incorrect because self-government decreased in the colonies after the French and Indian War.

4. A: Choice *A* is correct. Heavily influenced by the Enlightenment, the Declaration of Independence repudiated the colonies' allegiance to Great Britain. The main purpose of the excerpt is to justify the colonists' revolutionary stance due to Great Britain's tyranny and the role of consent in government to protect the natural rights of citizens. Choice *B* is incorrect because, although the excerpt alludes to abuses, the purpose isn't to list specific evidence. This occurs later in the Declaration of Independence. Choices *C* and *D* are supporting evidence for the main purpose.

5. A: Choice *A* is correct. A business cycle is when the gross domestic product (GDP) moves downward and upward over a long-term growth trend, and the four phases are expansion, peak, contraction, and trough. An expansion is the only phase where employment rates and economic growth continually grow. Choice *C* is incorrect because contraction is the opposite of expansion. Choices *B* and *D* are incorrect because the peaks and troughs are the extreme points on the graph.

Manifest Destiny

Westward Migration

In the mid-nineteenth century, people increasingly traveled west to pursue economic prosperity, natural resources, and religious freedom.

Americans and newly arrived immigrants traveled westward where there were more economic opportunities and more land. Innovations like steamships and railways expedited travel times, but travel by caravans of covered wagons was also commonplace. The sudden influx of people and resources led to explosive urban population growth in western cities. For example, Chicago was officially established in 1833 with a population of 200, and by 1870 its population had reached nearly 300,000.

Many migrants sought to acquire and consolidate control over natural resources, with gold being the most prominent example. The **California Gold Rush** (1848–1855) attracted nearly 300,000 migrants and sped up California's path to statehood. The acquisition of natural resources generated tremendous economic growth, but it devastated indigenous communities as settlers violently seized the land.

Several religious groups also traveled westward to proselytize and secure more religious independence. The Mormons were amongst the most organized and prolific migrant groups. **Mormonism** originated in upstate New York during the 1820s and the movement quickly spread to the American Midwest. Following a series of conflicts in Illinois, Brigham Young led Mormon pioneers on a final migratory journey to the Utah Territory in the late 1840s.

Manifest Destiny and Expansion to the Pacific Ocean

The U.S. continued to seek out and acquire new lands, a tactic often based on the idea of **Manifest Destiny,** or the belief that the U.S. was destined to continue its territorial expansion from the Atlantic Ocean to the Pacific Ocean and, eventually, beyond. This practice led to the purchase of Alaska from Russia in 1867 and the annexation of Hawaii in 1898. The Spanish-American War in 1898 lasted just a few months but helped Cuba gain its independence from Spain and the U.S. gain a strategic foothold in many distant locales that were formerly Spanish territories, including Guam and the Philippines. Future president Theodore Roosevelt became a hero when his troops defeated the Spanish fleet at the Battle of San Juan Hill.

Alfred Thayer Mahan was a U.S. naval officer and historian who became famous after publishing a book titled *The Influence of Sea Power Upon History, 1600–1783* (1890). Mahan is famous for extending America's "Manifest Destiny" beyond its coasts and into the seas. Mahan believed that the future of world dominance and democratic hegemony rested upon the creation of a strong navy. He thus encouraged the United States to carry out its imperial dreams on the high seas, paving the way for the aggressive expansionist initiatives of the U.S. government in the late 1800s.

Legislation that Boosted Westward Migration

During the Civil War era, the federal government passed several laws to incentivize westward migration. During the early 1850s, Congress granted a charter for a national railway system and ordered a series of surveys to find a feasible and optimal route for a railroad line connecting the eastern rail system with the Pacific coast. After six years of construction, the **First Transcontinental Railroad** began its official operation in 1869. The national railroad revolutionized the American economy, particularly in facilitating the movement of goods and settlers from coast to coast.

To incentivize the settlement and economic development of western lands, the federal government passed a series of **homestead acts** during the latter half of the nineteenth century. The Donation Land Claim Act of 1850 offered large parcels of land to citizens who relocated to the Pacific Northwest. During the Civil War, President Lincoln oversaw the passage of the Homestead Act of 1862. The law provided plots of western land to citizens who promised to personally settle and develop the area. Citizens above the age of 21 were eligible to apply, including women, except for people who had waged war against the federal government. After the end of the Civil War, Congress passed additional homestead acts to enact land reform in the Southeast, plant forests, and support agriculture.

Increasing Ties with Asia

The United States sought closer ties and stronger commercial relationships with Asian nations during the latter half of the nineteenth century. The **Siamese-American Treaty of Amity and Commerce** of 1833 (Roberts Treaty) was the first treaty between the United States and an Asian state. This treaty was mostly a symbolic victory to showcase American diplomacy, but it also increased commercial exchanges between the United States and Siam (Thailand). Following the Roberts Treaty, the United States attempted to develop a commercial network in China to gain access to the lucrative opium trade; however, Britain's monopoly on the Chinese market largely prevented American merchants from sustaining long-term commercial ties. During the latter half of the nineteenth century, the United States strengthened diplomatic ties to Japan, and San Francisco served as the cultural, diplomatic, and economic center for exchanges.

The United States' most successful initiative in Asia was missionary work. British missionaries had originally popularized Christianity in mainland China, and American evangelicals seized on this opportunity. While the American missionaries were not particularly successful at mass conversions, they did expand American influence in China by teaching English and introducing Western medicine. Back home, missionaries published novels and captivated audiences with stories about Chinese culture.

The Mexican–American War

The Mexican–American War

The **Mexican-American War** (1846–1848) began over a border dispute. The Republic of Texas declared its independence from Mexico in 1836 and applied to join the United States. However, in a desire to avoid war with Mexico, the administration of President Martin van Buren decided not to annex Texas. Two administrations later, President John Tyler, with the support of President-Elect James K. Polk, was able to pass a bill to annex Texas right before he left office in 1845, which Polk then signed. The Texas and Mexican governments disagreed on where the Texas border ended. Polk sent in the U.S. Army under Zachary Taylor to occupy the disputed territory.

After a failed attempt to purchase the disputed territory from Mexico, the United States declared war on Mexico in 1846. The American troops won several battles although the Mexican army usually outnumbered them. The Mexican troops were poorly armed and trained, and the Americans made use of their highly skilled artillery force. The Americans eventually captured Mexico City in 1847 and forced the Mexican government to sign the **Treaty of Guadalupe-Hidalgo** in 1848. The treaty recognized American control over Texas and also ceded territory that would become the states of California, Utah, Colorado, Arizona, New Mexico, and Nevada in exchange for $15 million. Tens of thousands of prospectors flooded into California when gold was discovered in 1849. The prospectors often encroached on Native American lands, which led to further conflict. In 1854, the United States also acquired additional territories in what would become Arizona and New Mexico as part of the **Gadsden Purchase**, which was part of the Treaty of Mesilla between Mexico and the United States. The acquisition of so much new territory sparked a debate over whether the land would be open or closed to slavery.

Governmental Conflict with Mexican Americans and American Indians

The United States' victory in the Mexican-American War (1846–1848) had a devastating effect on Mexican and indigenous culture. When the United States took control, the territory was home to approximately 75,000 Mexicans and several powerful indigenous nations including the Apache, Navajo, and Pueblo. The division of territory between the U.S. and Mexico, as well as the mass arrival of American settlers, proved highly disruptive to both Native American and Mexican communities.

Although the **Treaty of Guadalupe-Hidalgo** had promised citizenship to the territories' current residents, there were significant obstacles and restrictions to citizenship. The United States refused to extend citizenship to indigenous people, even though some had been citizens under Mexican law. The United States also did not follow through with provisions of the Treaty mandating the recognition of indigenous land rights. Mexicans living in the territories were offered American citizenship, but they also faced systematic discrimination. For example, California passed a series of laws including the **Anti-Vagrancy Acts**, which discriminated against people of Mexican and indigenous descent, the Act for the Government and Protection of Indians, which forced indigenous people into indentured servitude, and the Foreign Miner's Tax to exact exorbitant mining taxes from people who were not U.S. citizens.

American settlers' economic activities, such as ranching and mining, frequently triggered conflicts due to settlers encroaching on indigenous nations' ancestral lands. Therefore, the United States military regularly intervened in the region. For example, the American military built permanent forts and coerced indigenous populations into reservations during the **Apache Wars** (1849–1886).

The Compromise of 1850

The Mexican Cession and Slavery

The Republic of Texas declared its independence from Mexico in 1836 and applied for entry into the United States in the same year; this request was denied. However, right before he left office in March 1845, President John Tyler initiated an annexation bill, which President James K. Polk officially signed in December 1845. The Republic of Texas officially revoked its sovereignty, lawfully agreeing to become the 28th state of the Union, in February 1846. The Mexican-American War (1846–1848), in many ways, was a direct response to President Polk's annexation of Texas. The war ended in the Treaty of Guadalupe-Hidalgo, which resulted in the **Mexican Cession** of half of its territory, nearly doubled the

84

size of the United States, and officially brought parts of what would become Texas, New Mexico, Arizona, and California within the territory of the United States. One social impact of U.S. annexation and the Mexican-American War was increased political tensions over the role of slavery, and whether it was to be permitted, in new territories.

Attempts to Resolve the Issue of Slavery in the Territories

As mentioned, the **Compromise of 1850** admitted California as a free state and ended the slave trade, but not slavery itself, in Washington, D.C., in order to please Northern politicians. In return, Southern politicians were able to pass a stronger fugitive slave law and demanded that New Mexico and Utah be allowed to vote on whether or not slavery would be permitted in their state constitutions. This introduced the idea of popular sovereignty where the residents of each new territory, and not the federal government, could decide whether or not states entering the union would become a slave state or a free state. This essentially negated the **Missouri Compromise** of 1820. The enhanced fugitive slave law also angered many Northerners because it empowered federal marshals to deputize anyone, even residents of a free state, and force them to help recapture escaped slaves. Anyone who refused would be subject to a $1,000 fine (equivalent to more than $28,000 in 2015).

The debate over slavery erupted again only a few years later when the territories of Kansas and Nebraska were created by the **Kansas-Nebraska Act** in 1854. The application of popular sovereignty meant that pro- and anti-slavery settlers flooded into these two territories to ensure that their faction would have a majority when it came time to vote on the state constitution. Tension between pro- and anti-slavery forces in Kansas led to an armed conflict known as **Bleeding Kansas**.

John Brown was a militant abolitionist who fought in Bleeding Kansas and murdered five pro-slavery settlers there in 1856 in response to a pro-slavery attack on Lawrence, Kansas, that resulted in widespread looting and destruction. He returned to the eastern United States and attacked the federal arsenal at Harper's Ferry, Virginia, in 1859. He hoped to seize the weapons there and launch a slave rebellion, but federal troops killed or captured most of Brown's accomplices and Brown himself was executed. The attack terrified Southerners and reflected the increasing hostility between North and South.

The growing divide was highlighted in the **Dred Scott** decision. In this 1857 case, the Supreme Court ruled that Dred Scott, who had been born into slavery but had lived with his master for a period of time in a "free" territory, was not a free man, but rather still the property of his master. Moreover, the Supreme Court essentially nullified the Missouri Compromise, stating that it was unconstitutional because it denied citizens the use of their property (as slaves were legally considered property). The most devastating effect, however, was the Court's declaration that no person of African descent, free or enslaved, could be a citizen of the United States and therefore had no right to sue in U.S. federal courts.

The sectional differences that emerged in the last several decades culminated in the presidential election of 1860. Abraham Lincoln led the new Republican Party, which opposed slavery on moral and economic grounds. The question of how best to expand slavery into new territories split the Democratic Party into two different factions that each nominated a presidential candidate. A fourth candidate also ran on a platform of preserving the union by trying to ignore the slavery controversy.

Sectional Conflict: Regional Differences

Irish and German Immigration

Soaring immigration rates led to the development of ethnic communities across the United States. Between 1844 and 1877, German and Irish migrants were the largest migrant group, marking the first time Britain didn't account for the overwhelming majority of immigrants. German immigrants primarily came to the United States due to the economic and political turmoil in Germany prior to its unification in 1871. The **Great Famine** (1845–1849) prompted millions of Irish people to emigrate to the United States during the latter half of the nineteenth century and the early twentieth century.

German and Irish immigrants typically arrived in port cities on the Atlantic seaboard. Most of these immigrants initially settled in cities due to the superior economic opportunities offered in urban and industrial centers like New York City and Boston. Urban ethnic communities helped assimilate newly arrived immigrants. In addition, the communities successfully preserved cultural traditions including language, religious practices, and food. For example, German immigrants are widely credited with introducing kindergartens, Christmas trees, hamburgers, and hot dogs to the United States. When Northeastern urban environments became more crowded and expensive, immigrant communities often ventured westward, settling in the developing cities and often establishing exclusive settlements that protected their culture and history.

The Anti-Catholic Nativist Movement

Although Catholics were a minority during the colonial period of American history, Catholicism had become the largest religious denomination in the United States by the mid nineteenth century. Many colonial governments had actually banned Catholicism, but the American Revolution brought more toleration. However, anti-Catholic sentiment renewed in the 1800s as immigrants from Ireland and Germany, many of whom were Catholic, arrived in ever-increasing numbers. The arrival of Italian immigrants in the late 1800s and early 1900s also increased Protestant-Catholic tension in America. Many Americans feared that Catholic immigrants would be more loyal to Pope than they would be to the Constitution. This led to the creation of the **Know Nothing** movement, which sought to limit immigration and precipitated violence against Catholics. Anti-Catholic sentiment remained an issue until the presidential election of 1960 when John F. Kennedy, a Catholic, won the Democratic nomination. Kennedy helped allay fears by promising to respect the separation of church and state. Since then, anti-Catholicism has largely disappeared.

The Free-Soil Movement

Many Northerners didn't view slavery as immoral; instead, they objected to the expansion of slavery into western territories because it suppressed the wages of white migrants, thus undermining the free-labor market. After President James K. Polk annexed Texas in 1845 and prepared to declare war on Mexico, Northern politicians rushed to pass a proposal known as the **Wilmot Proviso**, which would've outlawed slavery in all of the territory acquired in the upcoming conflict. Southerners shot down the Wilmot Proviso in the Senate, but Northern opposition to slavery's expansion triggered the formation of the **Free Soil Party** during the 1848 presidential election.

The Free Soil Party garnered significant support across most Northern states, especially in New England. By the late 1840s, manufacturing dominated the Northern economy, so there was little fear of economic

fallout if slavery declined. Significant amounts of the working poor also hoped to pursue economic opportunities in Western territories, so they had a vested interest in preventing slavery from undermining the free-labor market. However, the Free Soil Party's cautious approach to abolitionism led to its dissolution in the 1850s. Following the Compromise of 1850 and a series of bloody territorial conflicts, the **free-soil movement** merged with the newly formed Republican Party, which more strongly denounced slavery in the United States.

Anti-Slavery Efforts by African Americans and White Abolitionists

African Americans and abolitionists resisted slavery in a variety of ways. Frederick Douglass and William Lloyd Garrison led the charge in building anti-slavery coalitions and spreading awareness about slavery's deep-rooted immorality. Anti-slavery activists often leveraged the extensive influence and reach of the American publishing industry. For example, Harriet Beecher Stowe's *Uncle Tom's Cabin* was the bestselling novel in the nineteenth century, only trailing the Bible in terms of total publication. While these moral arguments carried the Republican Party into national prominence, many anti-slavery activists pursued more direct action.

Abolitionists tirelessly worked to expand the **Underground Railroad**—a series of secretive networks across the United States that helped slaves escape to the northern U.S. and Canada—in defiance of federal Fugitive Slave Acts. Estimates vary but it's likely as many as 100,000 slaves escaped to Canada during the nineteenth century. Other direct actions were more controversial. Following the enactment of the **Kansas-Nebraska Act** of 1854, pro- and anti-slavery settlers raced into Kansas, sparking a mini civil war known as **Bleeding Kansas** (1854–1861). One abolitionist leader, John Brown, left the fighting in Kansas to organize a slave revolt in Virginia. Brown attempted to seize a federal weapons depot at Harpers Ferry prior to the planned revolt, but the plot was foiled.

Slavery Supporters

Slavery's supporters raised racial, moral, and legal arguments to defend its continuation. Racial arguments justified the enslavement of Africans based on beliefs about white supremacy. Generally speaking, slave owners believed might made right and characterized the enslavement of Africans as an expression of the natural order. White supremacy was also closely tied to moral arguments claiming that slavery actually benefited Africans. Devout Christians were the most likely to adopt moral arguments because they genuinely believed the gift of eternal salvation outweighed the burden of enslavement. Furthermore, many plantation owners portrayed slavery as a social good since the institution boosted economic output and stabilized societal power structures.

While racial and moral arguments were commonly asserted to gain public support for slavery, legal arguments ensured that slavery would be protected from government interference. According to slave owners, the United States Constitution's references to slavery without expressing any reservations or limitations, except for a nominal compromise over the international slave trade, were conclusive proof of slavery's legality. In addition, slave owners relentlessly cited the Tenth Amendment to classify slavery as one of the rights reserved to the states. Although many Southerners sincerely believed in federalism, arguments about states' rights were almost always connected to slavery.

Failure of Compromise

The End of the Second Party System

During the 1850s, the **Second Party System** collapsed due to a host of intensely controversial issues, including anti-immigration nativism and controversies over slavery.

Nativism surged in the 1840s in response to rapidly rising rates of immigration, particularly in Northern cities. Nativists opposed all immigration, but they held a special disdain for Irish Catholics who were alleged to be part of a papal plot to overthrow the United States. When the Whigs and Democrats failed to limit immigration, nativists formed their own political party, the **Know Nothings**. Although the Know Nothings never achieved mainstream political success, they severely undermined the Whigs and Democrats in Northern cities during the mid-1850s.

Slavery drove a stake through the heart of the Second Party System. To appease Southern voters and remain a viable national political party, the Whigs refused to meaningfully oppose against slavery. As a result, when the Free Soil Party merged with the more vigorously anti-slavery Republican Party, the Whigs lost nearly all their Northern support. In response to the rise of the Republicans (primarily in the North), Southerners flocked to the Democrats. By the late 1850s, the Republicans and Democrats functioned as regionally dominant parties, with the issue of slavery deciding where citizens stood politically.

Election of 1860 and Secession

Lincoln's Election and Southern Secession

The sectional differences that emerged between the North and the South culminated in the presidential election of 1860. Abraham Lincoln led the new **Republican Party**, which opposed slavery on moral and economic grounds. This party was particularly strong and represented in the North. The question of how best to expand slavery into new territories split the Democratic Party into two different factions that each nominated a presidential candidate. A fourth candidate also ran on a platform of preserving the union by trying to ignore the slavery controversy.

Lincoln found little support outside of the North; in fact, he did not earn any Southern electoral votes. However, Lincoln managed to win the White House since the Democratic Party was divided. Southern states felt threatened by Lincoln's anti-slavery stance and feared he would abolish slavery throughout the country. South Carolina was the first Southern state to secede from the Union and ten more eventually followed. Lincoln declared that the Union could not be dissolved and swore to defend federal installations. The **Civil War** began when Confederate troops fired on **Fort Sumter** in Charleston in 1861.

Military Conflict in the Civil War

Societal Mobilization and Opposition to the Civil War

The Union and the Confederacy both quickly adopted a total war military strategy during the American **Civil War** (1861–1865). Total war involved mass mobilization of economic and societal resources for military purposes. The Union and the Confederacy both instituted military drafts after a year of fighting

discouraged volunteerism. Along with a draft, the Union granted immigrants citizenship if they joined the military. As in the world wars, women achieved significant socioeconomic gains due to the wartime reduction in the workforce.

Mounting military costs eventually forced the Union and the Confederacy to alter economic policies. Both sides issued paper money backed by government credit rather than precious metals. Governments also regularly explicitly ordered or tacitly permitted the seizure of food, manufactured goods, and railway systems to support the war effort.

The Union and the Confederacy each faced considerable domestic resistance to the war. In the early stages of the conflict, President Lincoln suspended some civil liberties in Baltimore to quell rioting that threatened the capital. Many Northern cities also experienced violent draft riots. For example, President Lincoln diverted forces from the **Battle of Gettysburg** (1863) to suppress draft riots in New York City. Confederate leaders similarly moved to suppress slave insurrections that would have undermined agricultural production.

The Union Eventually Succeeds

The **First Battle of Bull Run** (also known as the **First Battle of Manassas**) in 1861 was the first major infantry engagement of the Civil War. Both the Northern and Southern troops were inexperienced and, although they had equal numbers, the Confederates emerged victorious. Many had thought the war would be short, but it continued for another four years.

The Union navy imposed a blockade on the Confederacy and captured the port of New Orleans in 1862. The Union navy was much stronger than the Confederate fleet and prevented the Southern states from selling cotton to foreign countries or buying weapons.

In 1862, Union forces thwarted a Confederate invasion of Maryland at the **Battle of Antietam**. This engagement was the single bloodiest day of the war and more than 23,000 men on both sides were killed or wounded. Union troops forced the Confederates to retreat, and that gave Lincoln the political capital he needed to issue the **Emancipation Proclamation** in 1863. This declaration did not abolish slavery, but it did free slaves in the Southern states that were in rebellion against the Union. It also allowed African Americans to join the Union Army and Navy and about 200,000 did so. The 54th Massachusetts Infantry was a famous unit of African American soldiers who led an assault on Fort Wagner in South Carolina in 1863. Although the attack failed, the 54th Massachusetts demonstrated African American troops fighting bravely under fire.

The **Siege of Vicksburg** in 1863 was a major Union victory because the Union gained control of the Mississippi River and cut the Confederacy in half. This made it difficult the Confederacy to move troops around and communicate with their forces. General **Ulysses S. Grant** commanded the Northern forces in the siege and eventually became the Union army's top general.

The **Battle of Gettysburg** in 1863 marked the turning point of the Civil War. General **Robert E. Lee** led Confederate troops into Pennsylvania, but in three days of heavy fighting, the Union army forced them to retreat. The victory bolstered Northern morale and weakened Southern resolve. Never again would Confederate forces threaten Northern territory.

In 1864, Union general **William T. Sherman** captured Atlanta, Georgia, and then marched more than 200 miles to Savannah. Along the way, he destroyed anything that could support the Southern war effort,

such as railroads and cotton mills. At this point, the Southern economy was beginning to collapse. The North had more manpower than the South and could afford to sustain more casualties. The North also had more industrial capacity to produce weapons and supplies and more railroads to transport men and equipment.

Eventually, Robert E. Lee surrendered to Ulysses S. Grant at Appomattox, Virginia, on April 9, 1865. Five days later, **John Wilkes Booth** assassinated Lincoln in Washington, D.C. Vice President **Andrew Johnson**, a Democrat, succeeded him and soon came into conflict with Republicans in Congress about how to reintegrate Southern states into the nation. This process was known as **Reconstruction** and lasted from 1865 to 1877.

Government Policies During the Civil War

The Emancipation Proclamation's Role in the War

Most Union supporters and President Lincoln began the Civil War with the goal of preserving the Union and ending the Southern rebellion, but the means of achieving these goals changed after the first couple of years. While the **Emancipation Proclamation** did not completely abolish slavery, it did free slaves in the rebellious Southern states and allowed African Americans to join the Union Army and Navy. This was crucial in the Union's ultimate triumph in the war because it further crippled the South's economy and roughly 200,000 African Americans (many of whom were freed slaves from southern plantations) helped bolster the Union's forces and undermine the Confederacy.

The Gettysburg Address

Abraham Lincoln was inarguably one of the greatest politicians in American history in terms of how he nimbly balanced his support for reunification and arguments about the immorality of slavery.

Immediately upon the Southern states' secession, Lincoln chose to frame the conflict as a matter of national unity. Most historians believe Lincoln personally found slavery to be an abhorrent stain on the nation's character, but he publicly showed a willingness to negotiate with the Southern slave states to avoid a civil war. When peace failed, Lincoln moved quickly to secure the support of slave-owning border states—Delaware, Kentucky, Maryland, and Missouri—within the Union to avoid a military catastrophe. For example, if the Union lost Maryland, it would've needed to withdraw from Washington, D.C. However, in private communications, Lincoln regularly placed pressure on the border states to abolish slavery on moral grounds.

Lincoln was a master of using strategic proclamations and speeches to secure his goals. Following a brutal bloodbath at the Battle of Antietam, Lincoln issued the Emancipation Proclamation (1863) to free the Confederacy's slaves as a wartime measure. Later that same year, Lincoln delivered the famously succinct **Gettysburg Address** to reaffirm the nation's commitment to reunification and moral ideals.

Reconstruction

Ideas of Citizenship and Federal and State Government Relationships

The **Reconstruction Era** (1865–1877) transformed the relationship between the federal government, states, and citizens. Despite the moderating forces within President Andrew Johnson's administration,

the more radical branch of the Republican Party successfully forced the federal government to take some unprecedented action.

Radical Republicans won the debate over citizenship for former slaves and people of color. After ratifying the Thirteenth Amendment to abolish slavery, they spearheaded the passage of the Fourteenth and Fifteenth Amendments to guarantee due process under the law and universal male suffrage regardless of "race, color, or previous condition of servitude." Other minority groups, such as Chinese and Mexican immigrants, celebrated the Reconstruction amendments for the progress they made toward racial equality; however, the women's rights movement was much more divided. The Fourteenth Amendment added "male" to the U.S. Constitution for the first time, and many suffragettes believed the use of gendered terminology would impede the fight for women's rights. The Fifteenth Amendment proved even more controversial because it only applied to men.

Federal forces conducted a large-scale occupation of states' territories for the first time in American history. This occupation was not strictly a punitive measure; the goal was to enforce the Reconstruction Amendments in the former Confederate states. Consequently, African Americans gained new commercial opportunities and were elected to myriad public offices for the first time. However, white Southerners deeply resented this occupation and intervention, decrying it as yet another act of Northern aggression. Northern support for Reconstruction faded in the mid-1870s as white Southerners mounted more violent resistance, and President Rutherford B. Hayes officially withdrew federal forces in 1877. Immediately afterward, Southern states passed Jim Crow laws to legalize racial segregation and disenfranchisement, which obstructed the Reconstruction Amendments' enforcement for nearly a century.

The Thirteenth, Fourteenth, and Fifteenth Amendments

The **Thirteenth Amendment** abolished slavery and involuntary servitude, except as punishment for a crime. The issue of slavery was no longer in the states' hands. Although the Emancipation Proclamation freed slaves in the Confederacy, the status of former slaves remained uncertain as the war neared its conclusion. Many Northerners did not hold strong views on slavery, but most wanted to punish the South and resolve the primary cause of the bloody Civil War. The Northern states all immediately ratified the amendment, and in December 1865 enough reconstructed Southern states ratified the amendment for it to be adopted into law.

The **Fourteenth Amendment** (1868) granted citizenship to all persons born or naturalized in the United States; prohibited states from depriving any citizen of life, liberty, or property without due process of law; and prevented the states from violating equal protection based on race, color, or previous condition of servitude. Although revolutionary for the theoretical rights of all American citizens, newly freed or otherwise, the Fourteenth Amendment was not federally enforced until the **Civil Rights Act** of 1964.

The **Fifteenth Amendment** prohibits the government from denying a citizen the right to vote for reasons of race, color, or previous condition of servitude. Adopted in 1870, the last of the **Reconstruction Amendments**, the Fifteenth Amendment sought to protect newly freed slaves' right to vote. As discussed below, most states interpreted the amendment to only apply to male suffrage. In addition, Southern states passed a series of laws to systematically disenfranchise African Americans including poll taxes, literacy tests, and residency rules. The use of violence and intimidation for political purposes was also common. Meaningful change did not occur until the Civil Rights Movement, nearly one hundred

91

years later. In 1964, the **Twenty-Fourth Amendment** prohibited the states and federal government from charging a poll tax or fee to vote. Later, the **Voting Rights Act** of 1965 empowered the federal government to enforce the Fifteenth Amendment in the states for the first time.

The Women's Rights Movement

Debate over the Fourteenth and Fifteenth Amendments sharply divided the women's rights movement. Suffragettes had strongly supported abolitionism to generate intersectional solidarity among oppressed Americans, and many women's rights leaders felt abandoned by the Reconstruction Amendments' failure to address gender inequality.

Tensions within the women's rights movement reached a boiling point at the **American Equal Rights Association** (AERA) annual meeting in 1869, which was held during the run-up to the ratification of the Fifteenth Amendment. Two of the movement's preeminent leaders, Susan B. Anthony and Elizabeth Cady Stanton, stridently opposed the amendment, and Anthony went so far as to tell Frederick Douglass that white women were currently more oppressed than African Americans. In contrast, the majority of attendees and some important leaders, such as Lucy Stone and Julia Ward Howe, viewed the enfranchisement of African Americans as a positive step toward universal suffrage.

The AERA collapsed shortly after this meeting, and two competing organizations took its place. Anthony and Stanton formed the National Woman Suffrage Association, and Stone and Howe established the American Woman Suffrage Association. The organizations' relationship remained contentious until the formation of the National American Woman Suffrage Association in 1890.

Radical Republicans

Johnson opposed equal rights for African Americans and pardoned many Confederate leaders. However, many Congressional Republicans wanted to harshly punish Southerners for their attempts to secede from the Union. They were known as **Radical Republicans** because they also wanted to give former slaves equal rights.

Johnson vetoed bills that were designed to protect the rights of freed slaves, but Congress overrode his vetoes. This led to increasing conflict between Johnson and Congress, which eventually caused Radical Republicans to impeach him. Although Johnson was acquitted in 1868, he had very little power, and Radical Republicans took control of the Reconstruction process.

Republicans passed three important constitutional amendments as part of the Reconstruction process. The Thirteenth Amendment was ratified in 1865, and it abolished slavery throughout the country. The Fourteenth Amendment was ratified in 1868 and gave equal rights to all citizens. The Fifteenth Amendment was ratified in 1870 and specifically granted all men the right to vote regardless of race.

Failure of Reconstruction

Sharecropping

Policies enacted and implemented during the Reconstruction era failed to achieve long-term, meaningful land reform. While the Radical Republicans did greatly expand newly freed slaves' political rights and protections through the Reconstruction Amendments, economic measures missed the mark.

At the tail end of the American Civil War, Union General **Tecumseh Sherman** had implemented orders to seize plantations and provide every former slave with "forty acres and a mule." However, President Andrew Johnson reversed Sherman's orders. This reversal allowed wealthy plantation owners to retain the vast majority of their land despite the material support they had provided to the traitorous Confederacy.

Once Reconstruction drew to a close, Southern state legislatures immediately passed legislation to obstruct African Americans and other people of color from exercising political rights as granted under federal law. The federal government refused to intervene, and disenfranchisement only compounded the already minimal economic opportunities available to African Americans.

Given the lack of open land and economic opportunity, poor whites and Africans Americans were forced into **sharecropping**, meaning they farmed small plots of rented land in exchange for a small portion of the harvest while the rest went to the landowner. Some sharecroppers lived on what little they could raise in subsistence farming, and some went into debt to their landlords so they could buy food and other goods. Sharecropping was incredibly exploitative, a problem which only increased as time went on since agricultural outputs steadily declined due to rapid soil degradation.

The Basis of Civil Rights in the Twentieth Century

Reconstruction officially ended with the Compromise of 1877. After the intensely disputed election of 1876, the Democrats offered to let the Republicans have the White House if they agreed to end Reconstruction. After the Republicans agreed, federal troops were withdrawn and African Americans in the South were subjected to discrimination until the Civil Rights movement of the 1960s. Scholars often consider the Reconstruction era the beginning of **Jim Crow** and a transition into a new form of "institutionalized racism."

Practice Quiz

1. What was a consequence of the industrialization that followed the Civil War?
   a. Decreased immigration
   b. Increased urbanization
   c. Decreased socioeconomic inequality
   d. Increased rights for workers

2. Which of these is NOT a protection within the Bill of Rights?
   a. Right to due process
   b. Freedom of speech
   c. Right to privacy
   d. Right to a speedy and fair trial

3. The establishment clause deals with which of the following?
   a. The relationship between government and labor unions
   b. The relationship between government officials and lobbyists
   c. The relationship between government and the creation of new federal courts
   d. The relationship between government and religion

4. The Supreme Court has ruled that the federal government may limit a certain type of speech without violation of the First Amendment. What is an example of that type of speech?
   a. Students wearing black arm bands to protest a war
   b. A person writing a newspaper article using falsified quotes to attack a rival's character
   c. A student giving a speech outside of Congress protesting the passing of a bill that cuts school funding
   d. A citizen publishing a flier about the dangers of the government's new hunting regulations and hanging them up all over town

Question 5 is based on the following passage:

> Now, therefore I, Abraham Lincoln, President of the United States, by virtue of the power in me vested as Commander-in-Chief, of the Army and Navy of the United States in time of actual armed rebellion against the authority and government of the United States, and as a fit and necessary war measure for suppressing said rebellion...
>
> And by virtue of the power, and for the purpose aforesaid, I do order and declare that all persons held as slaves within said designated States, and parts of States, are, and henceforward shall be free; and that the Executive government of the United States, including the military and naval authorities thereof, will recognize and maintain the freedom of said persons.
>
> President Abraham Lincoln, Emancipation Proclamation, January 1, 1863

5. How does President Lincoln justify freeing the slaves in designated areas of the South?
   a. Emancipation is necessary since slavery is evil.
   b. Emancipation is necessary to boost the morale of the North.
   c. Emancipation is necessary to punish the South for seceding from the Union.
   d. Emancipation is necessary to strengthen the war effort of the North. **See answers on next page.**

Answer Explanations

1. B: Choice *B* is correct. Industrialization directly caused an increase in urbanization. Factories were located near cities to draw upon a large pool of potential employees. Between 1860 and 1890, the urbanization rate increased from about 20 percent to 35 percent. The other three choices are factually incorrect. Choice *A* is incorrect because immigration increased during industrialization, as immigrants flooded into America to search for work. Choice *C* is incorrect because socioeconomic problems plagued the period due to social ills caused by rapid urbanization. Choice *D* is incorrect because labor unrest was common as unions advocated for workers' rights and organized national strikes.

2. C: The Bill of Rights grants protections for almost all conceivable parts of life. The Framers were quite adamant that freedom was the ultimate right that the federal government could protect for its people, and so they worked hard to ensure that that was exactly what the federal government did. Right to privacy, however, is not considered one of these protections. While some have recently argued that it is implied, this protection is not explicitly given in the Bill of Rights. Choice *A* is incorrect because due process is one of those key pieces, guaranteeing every American gets equal protections under the law. Choice *B* is incorrect because freedom of speech grants this protection too, as one of the more well-known guarantees of the Constitution. Choice *D* is incorrect because the right to a fair and speedy trial is also one of those crucial protections.

3. D: The term "establishment clause" refers to the part of the First Amendment that applies to freedom of religion. It says: "Congress shall make no law respecting an establishment of religion." Choices *A*, *B*, and *C* do not describe the establishment clause.

4. B: Choice *B* is libel and is a type of speech that can be restricted and is even punishable by law. Choice *A* is incorrect because it is the subject of a famous legal case where students wore bands to protest a war and won their case against their school district. Choice *C* is incorrect because protest is legal, no matter the subject, as long as it is peaceful and approved. Choice *D* is incorrect because fliers are legal as long as they are not impeding a war effort.

5. D: Choice *D* is correct. President Lincoln issued the Emancipation Proclamation to free the slaves in the Confederacy, allowing the institution to continue in states and territories that didn't secede. The excerpt justifies the decision as a "fit and necessary war measure for suppressing said rebellion." Therefore, per the excerpt, emancipation was necessary to strengthen the war effort for the North. Choice *C* is the second-best answer, but the excerpt supports the contention that emancipation was part of an active war effort, rather than merely a punishment. Choices *A* and *B* are incorrect because nothing in the excerpt describes the evil of slavery or the effect of emancipation on morale in the North.

Period 6: 1865–1898

Westward Expansion: Economic Development

Mechanization Improvements

Technological innovations dramatically increased agricultural production, which resulted in steep reductions in food prices. Several American inventors, including the famed **Cyrus McCormick**, developed mechanized and steam-powered reaping, threshing, and winnowing equipment during the mid-nineteenth century. These inventions represented a seismic jump in terms of efficiency and agricultural production. During the latter half of the nineteenth century, northern factories began mass producing and marketing agricultural machines. Mechanization again increased at the end of the nineteenth century as tractors began to replace horses and mules in the operation of agricultural machines.

Mechanization caused an exponential increase in the size of harvests. Combine harvesters were especially efficient because they combined reaping, threshing, and winnowing operations for a number of essential food products including corn, oats, soybeans, and wheat. As the supply of food rapidly expanded in the United States, food prices dropped to historic lows. This resolved some of the societal issues related to industrialization and urbanization; namely, that the working poor struggled to afford food, resulting in inferior nutritional consumption as compared to subsistence farmers. Overall, the agricultural boom strengthened food security for working-class households, and improved nutritional outcomes were evident based on the corresponding increase in Americans' average height.

Farmers' Cooperative Organizations

During the latter half of the nineteenth century, farmers sought to overcome challenges such as exorbitant railroad fees and unfavorable governmental policies by entering cooperative organizations and organizing themselves politically.

Local collectives at the township and county level were commonplace, and these groups often entered into coalitions at the regional and national level. Most generally, cooperative organizations opposed the creeping power of the federal government and railroads. Farmers especially objected to the construction of transcontinental railroads and homestead acts due to the resulting reductions in land prices. Furthermore, cooperative organizations strengthened farmers' bargaining position vis-à-vis railroads and the powerful trusts spurring the consolidation of agricultural markets.

Cooperative agreements specialized in a variety of services including splitting marketing and production costs, negotiating collective prices for transportation and market access, sharing expensive agricultural tools, and building political coalitions. One of the most important national cooperative organizations was the **Farmers Alliance**, an umbrella political advocacy group consisting of several high-profile cooperative organizations including the National Farmers' Alliance and Industrial Union (Southern white farmers), Colored Farmers' National Alliance and Cooperative Union (Southern black farmers), and the National Farmers' Alliance (Midwestern farmers). The Farmers Alliance would later fuel the rise of the **Populist Party** (1892–1909).

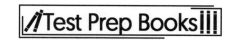

New Markets in North America

After the end of the Civil War, America experienced a period of intense industrialization, immigration, and urbanization, and all three trends were interrelated. The process of industrialization had begun before the Civil War but expanded into more sectors of the economy in the later part of the century. This era is often called the **Second Industrial Revolution** and included growth in the chemical, petroleum, iron, steel, and telecommunications industries, which were fueled by government subsidies. For example, the Bessemer process made it much easier to produce high quality steel by removing impurities during the smelting process.

Causes of Economic Growth

Three large-scale trends contributed to an economic boom and development of new commercial centers during the late nineteenth century. First, the completion of the **First Transcontinental Railroad** (1869) and the further development of interconnected regional railway networks significantly reduced the costs of traveling west. Second, mineral resources triggered mass migrations to boomtowns. Gold generally attracted the largest crowds (in "gold rushes"), and industrial demands boosted the commercial value of other minerals including copper, lead, silver, and zinc. Third, government policies such as homestead acts, commercial subsidies, and the unwavering support of the United States military in conflicts with American Indians over resources facilitated and further incentivized westward expansion.

The wholesale acquisition of Western resources fueled an economic boom like few others in history. Midwestern cities experienced exponential population growth, rivaling and surpassing Northeastern metropolitan areas. By 1900, Chicago was the second most populous city in the United States, and more than half of America's top 25 largest cities were located in the Midwest and West. More localized centers of commerce also developed all throughout the continental United States. Sudden influxes of migrants turned rural areas into boomtowns, and skyrocketing economic growth incentivized the construction of large-scale housing, roadways, and local industries.

Westward Expansion: Social and Cultural Development

Migrating West for Opportunities

Floods of migrants traveled West to pursue greater independence, self-sufficiency, and economic opportunities after the American Civil War. Many migrants sought religious freedom, such as the Mormons who settled in Utah. Likewise, many Americans simply wanted to be landowners and establish livelihoods where they weren't entirely dependent on the whims of employers or markets to survive.

Many migrants sought fabulous riches working for the railroads and mines. The construction of railroads increased land values and provided a steady stream of employment opportunities. Migrant miners hoped to literally strike gold, but most eventually found work in the local economy as it developed in the surrounding area. Some boomtowns quickly went bust while others continued to thrive even after the initial rush. For example, successive gold rushes led to San Francisco becoming one of the top ten most populous American cities by the late 1890s.

Rural areas also experienced substantial population growth during the late nineteenth century. Family farms profited from their proximity to boomtowns and the railway networks that provided access to a

national marketplace. Furthermore, ranching became a major industry as settlers seized control over sufficiently large areas of land that livestock could freely roam.

Competition for Land and Resources in the West

As waves of white settlers migrated westward in pursuit of economic prosperity, the region's long-established societies faced incredible cultural, economic, military, and political pressure. Mexican Americans were largely denied the right to consolidate control over valuable natural resources. Furthermore, when Mexican Americans attempted to assimilate, they suffered systematic discrimination. In effect, Western states' **Anti-Vagrancy laws** functioned in the same way Jim Crow laws did in the New South.

American Indians similarly struggled to survive the onslaught of settlers, who were backed by a federal government that did everything in its power to deny American Indians critical resources. For example, the United States military routinely ordered the slaughter of bison herds in order to drive American Indians away from valuable land. Unsurprisingly, military conflicts regularly erupted when white settlers seized indigenous lands.

The **Great Sioux War** of 1876–1877 was one of the last major armed conflicts in the West. The discovery of gold in the Black Hills of South Dakota caused prospectors to flood into the area although the U.S. government had recognized the territory as belonging to the Sioux. **Lieutenant Colonel George Armstrong Custer** brought in troops to try and take possession of the Black Hills. This led to disaster when Custer and more than 250 soldiers died at the **Battle of Little Bighorn** in 1876 fighting against **Crazy Horse**, who initially led the Lakota Sioux and Cheyenne forces. Bands of Sioux and Cheyenne fought several battles against the U.S. troops, but one by one the politically fractured groups surrendered. On February 28, 1877, the **Agreement of 1877** took effect, removing all land from Sioux ownership and establishing permanent reservations. Crazy Horse died in September 1877 while trying to escape U.S. custody.

Chief Joseph was a leader of the Nez Perce tribe who refused to live on a reservation and tried to flee to Canada. The amazing skill and bravery of the Nez Perce during their fighting retreat, which became known as the Nez Perce War (1877), earned the admiration of both military and civilians in the U.S. However, the U.S. captured Chief Joseph and his tribe and forced them onto a reservation.

The U.S. government continued its efforts to control Native American tribes. The **Dawes Act** of 1887 encouraged Native Americans to settle on reservations and become farmers in exchange for U.S. citizenship. Reformers also required Native Americans to send their children to boarding schools where they had to speak English and dress like Caucasians instead of maintaining their traditional culture. The schools were often crowded, and students were also subjected to physical and sexual abuse. In 1890, after broken treaties, reductions in government rations, drought, and a brutal winter pushed them to the brink of starvation, the **Lakota** Indians turned in desperation to the **Ghost Dance** ceremony, part of a movement that promised an end to white westward expansion. U.S. government officials felt threatened and sent soldiers to try and disarm the Lakota. This led to the **Massacre at Wounded Knee** in 1890 where at least 150 Lakota, including many women and children, were slaughtered. It was the last major conflict between Native Americans and U.S. forces.

Violated Treaties with American Indians

The United States repeatedly violated treaties with American Indians throughout the nineteenth century.

Prior to 1871, interactions between the federal government and American Indian tribes consistently followed the same pattern. First, white settlers would infringe on American Indians' historical territory. Second, a military conflict would ensue in which the federal government ultimately intervened on behalf of the settlers. Third, the federal government would sign a treaty with a specific American Indian tribe to acquire ownership of conquered territory and/or establish terms for peaceful relations. Fourth, white settlers would violate the terms of the agreement, triggering the beginning of another cycle.

The **Indian Appropriations Act** of 1871 went a step further than previous policies. According to this law, the United States unilaterally declared that tribes didn't qualify as foreign nations, meaning the federal government would no longer sign treaties of any kind with American Indian tribes. While the Indian Appropriation Act did have a provision to preserve preexisting treaties, meaningful enforcement was nonexistent. The United States then proceeded to pass a variety of laws to more fully deny tribal sovereignty. Most infamously, the **Dawes Act** (1887) seized approximately 93 million acres of American Indian land and then parceled it out to white settlers.

Assimilation v. Preservation of American Indians' Identity

The assimilation of American Indians was a longstanding policy ambition for the United States, dating back to the Washington administration. Federal policymakers believed American Indian culture would find its place in the American melting pot in the same way immigrants' cultures had. During the late nineteenth century, the federal government took a variety of aggressive actions to Americanize and assimilate American Indians. Most infamously, the Department of the Interior enforced the **Code of Indian Offenses** (1883) to prohibit any indigenous cultural practice that the federal government deemed an obstacle to assimilation.

Despite federal attempts at forced Americanization, indigenous populations resisted and actively sought to preserve their way of life. Many American Indians took up arms to defend their homeland from hordes of white settlers, and, even when forced onto reservations, American Indians sought to become economically self-sufficient. Oftentimes, American Indians attempted to create a self-sufficient economy on the reservation to minimize their dependence on and interactions with the United States.

American Indian leaders also pressed legal challenges against the federal government, and when the Supreme Court rejected their claims, many tribes bypassed federal prohibitions on indigenous cultural practices with many historians drawing comparisons to how slaves resisted white supremacy and preserved traditions in private wherever possible.

The "New South"

The "New South" Economy

Following the Reconstruction era, the Southern economy underwent a modest industrialization period. The abolition of slavery threatened the Southern plantation-based economic system, and some Southern leaders believed the region needed to model itself after the North to sustain economic

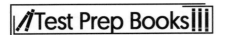
growth. As a result, some Southern politicians envisioned a **New South** based on urbanization and industrialization. The New South had some notable successes. For example, modernization programs in Atlanta featured investments in higher education and a railway transportation system, and, by 1880, Atlanta overtook Savannah as Georgia's largest city by population. However, much remained the same in the New South.

Almost immediately after President Rutherford B. Hayes withdrew the remaining federal forces from the South in 1877, Southern states rushed to enact **Jim Crow laws**. These laws functioned as a racial caste system, denying African Americans' rights and lending support to white supremacy.

Faced with an oppressive political system and minimal economic opportunities, African Americans were forced into sharecropping and tenant farming. This exploitative system undercut the New South's progressive vision since sharecropping simply replaced slavery as the dominant labor system. While African Americans enjoyed more personal freedom as sharecroppers than they had as slaves, sharecropping sustained the hierarchical dominance of wealthy white landowners.

Plessy v. Ferguson

Although the Declaration of Independence declared "all men are created equal," blacks, women, and other minorities struggled for more than a century to make this dream a reality. Slavery was not abolished until the Thirteenth Amendment to the U.S. Constitution was ratified in 1865. The Fourteenth Amendment, ratified in 1868, granted African Americans citizenship, and the Fifteenth Amendment, ratified in 1870, explicitly granted them the right to vote. However, Jim Crow laws in the South prevented blacks from exercising their rights and, when that failed, Southern whites often relied on violence and intimidation to oppress African Americans. For example, many Southern states required voters to pass literacy tests and used them to prevent blacks from casting a ballot. Whites were either exempt from the test or were held to much lower standards. Blacks who protested their oppression could be assaulted and even killed with impunity. The 1896 Supreme Court decision **Plessy v. Ferguson** upheld segregation, ruling that segregation laws did not violate the U.S. Constitution as long as equal facilities were available for each race. This led to the "separate but equal" doctrine; however, in reality, black facilities were almost always inferior to those provided for whites.

Technological Innovation

Increasing the Production of Goods

Five factors contributed to the rapid acceleration of industrialization after the American Civil War.

First, technological innovation continued to progress throughout the latter half of the nineteenth century. Along with the further advancement of interchangeable parts and complex assembly lines, important innovations occurred in steam power, glass making, chemical manufacturing, and transportation networks. Additionally, between 1865 and 1898, the Bessemer process fueled a 500% increase in American steel production.

Second, natural resources provided a major boost to industrialization. The discovery of precious metals functioned as an easily accessible source of capital for industrialists, and coal mining was invaluable due to industrialization's energy demands.

Third, new corporatized management structures increased efficiency in production, and the development of more advanced banking and credit systems helped business owners consolidate capital and invest in expansion.

Fourth, companies engaged in mass marketing for the first time in history due to the country's improved literacy rates, robust publishing industry, and strong class of consumers.

Fifth, the United States enjoyed an enormous labor force that rapidly outpaced its European rivals. In the aftermath of the American Civil War, African Americans living in the North secured employment at factories at high rates, and successive waves of immigration carried a steady supply of cheap labor to American businesses.

The Rise of Industrial Capitalism

Rapid Economic Development and Business Consolidation

During the **Second Industrial Revolution** (1870–1914), the American economy underwent a radical transformation due to the rise of large-scale industrial systems, technological advancements, and modern business organizations.

Innovations in assembly lines, the mass production of interchangeable parts, and electrification spurred rapid growth in American industrial production. As a result, the supply of consumer goods exponentially increased across nearly all economic sectors, which led to steep price reductions for consumer goods. Consumerism also increased due to the creation of new industrial employment opportunities, especially in terms of middle-class management positions, which boosted households' discretionary spending. In addition, businesses applied management principles known as **Taylorism** to reorganize departments, enhance supervision, and provide more detailed instructions to employees. Increased efficiency and profits led to more business consolidation, including the establishment of corporate trusts with widespread investments. For example, John D. Rockefeller's Standard Oil Company established a monopoly over the oil industry through the vertical integration of smaller companies it acquired.

Myriad technological breakthroughs drove this economic expansion, particularly in terms of advancements in steel, chemicals, fertilizers, electrical power, and mechanical engines. Several additional breakthroughs revolutionized international commercial networks. Intercontinental railways expedited the shipment of goods across North America, and modernized ships cut down travel times abroad. In addition, the invention of the telegraph facilitated communication with international business partners, which increased business investments and the dissemination of technical knowledge.

Democrats and Republicans both supported pro-growth economic policies such as low taxes, limited regulations, and minimal oversight mechanisms. For much of this era, trade policy was the most divisive economic issue. Republicans favored maintaining high tariffs to protect domestic industries, and Democrats advocated for free trade to help businesses access foreign markets.

Corporate Consolidation

Business leaders maximized profits through corporate consolidation, particularly in terms of reorganizing commercial enterprises into large trusts and holding companies. Large trusts and holding companies led to vertical integration, meaning a large corporate entity controlled an entire supply chain

and produced everything from individual parts to the finished product. For example, John D. Rockefeller's Standard Oil trust implemented **vertical integration** to streamline the construction of refineries and better coordinate logistics.

Vertical integration allowed large corporate enterprises to achieve economies of scale, meaning that economic costs declined as production increased. So vertical integration generally benefited consumers by reducing the price of goods and services. However, vertical integration also had critical drawbacks. Large corporate enterprises were able to wield their disproportionate economic power to undercut competitors and establish monopolies. Less competition resulted in a greater concentration of wealth amongst business elites who owned monopolies that systematically destroyed smaller enterprises. Likewise, the displacement of competition reduced employment opportunities in some sectors, and monopolies naturally held a coercive power to limit wages and benefits for employees. Lastly, since wealth so easily translated into political power, the rise of monopolies created critical issues related to political corruption.

Efforts to Control Markets in Asia and Latin America

The United States sought to expand American diplomatic influence and commercial networks across the world, especially in Latin America and Asia.

The United States historically viewed itself as the hegemonic power within the Western Hemisphere. During the early 1880s, President Benjamin Harrison's Secretary of State James G. Blaine pursued a strategy known as the **Big Brother policy** to extend the Monroe Doctrine by gathering Latin American nations under U.S. leadership and opening their markets to the U.S. For example, the United States intervened in the Venezuelan crisis of 1895 to force the United Kingdom and Venezuela to settle their territorial dispute through arbitration.

The United States also leveraged its military prowess for commercial gain. Following the mysterious sinking of the **USS Maine**, the United States entered into the Cuban War of Independence against Spain and sparked the **Spanish-American War** (1898) to protect American plantations in Cuba and increase its presence in the Pacific Rim. The United States decisively defeated Spain and gained control over Cuba, Puerto Rico, Guam, and the Philippines. Based on its improved geopolitical position in the Pacific Rim, the United States pushed for an **Open Door Policy** in China to undermine its European and Japanese competitors. While the Open Door Policy was ultimately unsuccessful, it cemented the United States as a global power.

Labor in the Gilded Age

Improvements in Americans' Standards of Living

Americans' standard of living changed dramatically over the latter half of the nineteenth century. Prior to the Industrial Revolution, the overwhelming majority of Americans were employed in the agricultural sector. As industrial production expanded throughout the nineteenth century, Americans became increasingly more likely to live in cities and work in factories. These changes had a mixed effect on Americans' standard of living.

On the one hand, industrialization triggered a steep decline in the price of goods, a greater diversification of goods and services, and the growth of a middle class. Consequently, a consumer

102

culture swept across the United States as retail outlets attained the status of cultural centers. Cities also attracted diverse migrants from outlying rural areas as well as foreign countries, resulting in dynamic and syncretic cultural exchanges. Furthermore, literacy rates, life expectancy, and childhood survival rates generally increased, especially at the end of the nineteenth century.

Conversely, capital consolidation wildly outstripped real wage growth, which is why this period is known as the **Gilded Age** (1870–1900). As business elites achieved unprecedented levels of wealth, the working poor struggled to make ends meet. Conditions were the worst in working class neighborhoods due to the prevalence of overcrowding, dilapidated buildings, and untreated sewage.

Labor and Management Battles

The writer Mark Twain called the late nineteenth century the Gilded Age because the era was one of extreme social inequality where the top "gilded" levels of society covered a rotten underbelly. Some corporations expanded and began to control entire industries. For example, by 1890, the Standard Oil Company produced 88 percent of all the refined oil in the nation. This made a few individuals, such as Standard Oil owner **John D. Rockefeller**, extremely wealthy. On the other hand, many workers earned low wages and began to form labor unions, such as the American Federation of Labor in 1886, to demand better working conditions and higher pay.

Strikes were one of the most common ways workers could express their dissatisfaction, and the **Pullman Strike** of 1894 was one of the largest such incidents in the nineteenth century. Workers went on strike after the Pullman Company, which manufactured railroad cars, cut wages by about 25 percent. More than 125,000 workers around the country walked off the job and attacked workers hired to replace them. Federal troops were sent in to end the strike, and more than eighty workers were killed or wounded during confrontations. The strike was unsuccessful, but Congress passed a law making Labor Day a federal holiday in order to placate union members.

Increases in Child Labor

Business magnates sought to enlist rural migrants, immigrants, children, and women into their workforces between 1865 and 1898. This trend had begun in northern cities in the run-up to the American Civil War, but the pace quickened afterward due to a massive spike in the demand for industrial labor.

Women and children joined the workforce in record numbers during this period. Both groups primarily worked for textile manufacturers, and they were often the least compensated. Some industries especially valued orphaned children because they were viewed as expendable assets capable of working in tight spaces such as coal shafts.

Immigration and Migration in the Gilded Age

Diversification of the Industrial Workforce

As the industrial workforce expanded, business owners had to diversify the employee pool. They enlisted rural migrants, immigrants, children, and women in increasing numbers in the second half of the nineteenth century.

Rural migrants generally moved to urban cities for economic opportunities, and since this group had previously worked in the agricultural sector, they were mostly placed in entry-level jobs on factory assembly lines. Likewise, immigrants frequently remained in port cities, working in factories to secure basic needs and potentially save enough to travel west. Consequently, factories became the most diverse workplaces in America. Along with immigration from Britain, Ireland, and Germany, immigration from Central and Eastern Europe increased markedly after 1880. In the West, railroads and factories hired Chinese immigrants, but a racist backlash led to the passage of the Chinese Exclusion Act (1882), which prohibited Chinese laborers from immigrating into the United States.

Immigrants Came Seeking Better Lives

Immigration also played an important part in the economic and social changes that occurred during the late nineteenth century. Immigration patterns changed during this time and immigrants from Southern and Eastern Europe, such as Italy and Poland, began to surpass the number of arrivals from Northern and Western Europe. An increasing number of immigrants also came from Asia. The immigrants sought economic opportunity in the United States because wages for unskilled workers were higher than in their home countries. Immigrants and internal migrants also moved to escape religious persecution and either poverty or the inability to readily improve their socioeconomic status. Some Americans resented the influx of immigrants because they spoke different languages and many practiced Catholicism. As a result, in 1924 Congress passed the **Immigration Act of 1924**, which included the Asian Exclusion Act and the National Origins Act, that prohibited immigration from Asian and significantly restricted immigration from Southern and Eastern Europe.

Urban Neighborhoods

Increased urbanization was the last factor that contributed to the rapid changes of the Gilded Age. Factories were located near cities in order to draw upon a large pool of potential employees. Immigrants flooded into cities in search of work, and new arrivals often settled in the same neighborhoods where their compatriots lived. Between 1860 and 1890 the urbanization rate in the United States increased from about 20 percent to 35 percent. City dwellers with similar races, ethnicities, or socioeconomic classes often formed their own closely knit urban neighborhoods. However, cities struggled to keep up with growing populations, and services such as sanitation and water often lagged behind demand. Immigrants often lived in crowded conditions that facilitated the spread of diseases.

Responses to Immigration in the Gilded Age

Assimilation and Americanization

Americans continually and fiercely debated whether the government should encourage assimilation and Americanization as immigration rates skyrocketed over the latter half of the nineteenth century.

The United States Census Bureau estimated that at least 20% of Americans were first- or second-generation immigrants. In addition to the sheer rise in total arrivals, immigrants' country of origin shifted dramatically in the 1880s. Prior to this, approximately 90% of immigrants to the U.S. came from Northwestern Europe. In contrast, the vast majority of immigrants arriving at the end of the century were Southern and Eastern Europeans. Unlike earlier immigration waves, Southern and Eastern Europeans were less likely to speak English.

Societal elites feared the immigrants would struggle to be integrated, while the working classes generally feared immigrants would potentially drive down labor costs. As a result, public and voluntary organizations developed **assimilation** programs, such as English lessons and basic social services. Settlement houses were especially active in assimilating groups, particularly when located within ethnic urban neighborhoods. **Americanization** was also common, and it refers to a more forceful, if not mandated, mode of assimilation. Accordingly, immigrants were often forced to navigate how much American culture they would adopt, possibly at the expense of generational family traditions and values.

Social Darwinism

A new phase of American territorial expansion occurred as a result of the Spanish-American War in 1898. New ideas arose in the late nineteenth century that helped justify this further expansion. Some intellectuals applied Charles Darwin's idea of natural selection, often summarized as "survival of the fittest," to the human race and called this new concept **Social Darwinism**. They used this idea to justify stronger groups of people colonizing and exploiting weaker groups. In addition, imperialists also used the idea of the **White Man's Burden** to justify further expansion. They claimed that Caucasians were obligated to civilize and govern groups thought to be less advanced.

These ideas were used to justify America's new status as a colonial power as a result of the **Spanish-American War**. Although Spain had once been a powerful empire, it had been in decline. The United States went to war against Spain in 1898 when the American battleship **USS Maine** exploded in Havana Harbor and killed more than 250 sailors. The U.S. Navy defeated the Spanish fleet in several engagements and then the Army followed up with a victory at San Juan Hill, which included the famous charge by Teddy Roosevelt and the Rough Riders.

The war lasted less than four months and made the United States a world power. The U.S. also acquired several Spanish colonies including Puerto Rico, Guam, and the Philippines. Guam became an important refueling station for American naval forces in the Pacific and remains a U.S. territory today, along with Puerto Rico. While the **Treaty of Paris** ended the war with Spain in 1898, the First Philippine Republic objected to the terms of the treaty. The Philippine-American War, which the Filipino people considered to be a continuation of their war for independence against Spain, lasted for three years, with individual groups in the Philippines continuing to fight until 1913. While the U.S. eventually won the war, hundreds of thousands of Filipino civilians died, largely as a result of famine and disease. There were also reports of atrocities committed on both sides. The Philippines would remain an American territory until 1946.

Jane Addams and Gender Equality Efforts

Women increasingly pursued educational and professional opportunities between 1865 and 1898. Industrialization generated a greater amount and broader range of employment opportunities, and women often entered the workforce to supplement the household income. Several universities were also founded in this period to educate women. For example, in 1871, Sophia Smith founded Smith College to provide women with the same educational opportunities as men.

As women seized upon educational and professional opportunities, they sought more active roles in voluntary organizations and progressive reform movements. The **Women's Christian Temperance Union**, which combatted the disruptive effect of alcoholism on American households, was the largest women-led voluntary organization in the United States. Aside from protecting families, women were

incredibly active in combatting urban poverty, especially in connection with the settlement movement. Settlement houses offered free housing and social services to low-income and immigrant communities.

Voluntary organizations provided women with leadership experience that was vital to the women's suffrage movement. Jane Addams and Ellen Gates Starr co-founded Hull House, a legendary settlement house in Chicago, and they became leading activists for gender equality. Likewise, Elizabeth Cady Stanton and Susan B. Anthony were abolitionists and social activists who founded the National American Woman Suffrage Association.

Jane Addams is known as one of the most prominent reformers of the Progressive Era. She was a pioneer in Social Work and advocated for the health of mothers, the needs of children, world peace, and public health. She was also an activist, author, and leader in the women's suffrage movement. In 1931, she became the first American woman to be awarded the Nobel Peace Prize.

John Stuart Mills (1806–1873), an English philosopher and political economist, was considered the "most influential English-speaking philosopher of the nineteenth century" and was best known for being the first member of Parliament to advocate women's suffrage. His book *On Liberty* promoted utilitarianism, which advocates that people should always make decisions based on what would achieve the greatest utility, or well-being. In his work, Mills sought to limit the power exercised upon the individual by any ruling body and stated that moral actions are those that promote utility and increase individuals' and society's well-being. He called for limited constraints upon individual behavior that only restrict those actions that cause harm to others.

Development of the Middle Class

The Growth of the Middle Class

The American middle class developed in the late nineteenth century due to the diversification of jobs in the workforce. As corporations attempted to implement vertical integration and stimulate growth, there was more demand for managers, logistical specialists, clerical workers, and others in white-collar jobs. These jobs generally paid significantly more than working-class factory jobs, and higher wages led to the development of a distinctive middle class. The middle class enjoyed unprecedented amounts of leisure time, which fueled the development of entertainment industries.

Increased disposable income also strengthened American consumerism. Sears distributed millions of mail-order catalogs in the 1890s, and the resulting competition caused a steep decline in the price of consumer goods as local establishments sought to keep pace with national distributors. Lastly, mail-order businesses and large corporations began offering credit lines directly to consumers for the first time in history, which further enhanced Americans' buying power.

Although they were generally paid considerably less than male employees, women especially benefited from greater employment opportunities. At long last, unmarried women could achieve financial independence. In addition, dual sources of income lifted many working-class households into the middle class. Stronger employment prospects also led to the establishment of private women's colleges and more offerings for women at public institutions.

The Gospel of Wealth

Some elite business leaders practiced philanthropy to improve the living conditions for the working poor. The philanthropic movement gained some traction after business titan **Andrew Carnegie** published an article titled "**The Gospel of Wealth**" in 1889.

In "The Gospel of Wealth," Carnegie asserted that the wealthy had a moral obligation to spend their money philanthropically in order to benefit the greater good and improve society. Therefore, Carnegie implored his fellow captains of industry to spend their riches on improving the lives of the working poor. The "Gospel of Wealth" had a profound impact on elites' philanthropic contributions with the bulk of money being spent on public education, higher education, cultural centers, and the revitalization of urban centers.

This new view of philanthropy was particularly important near the turn of the century. During the **Gilded Age** (1870–1900), some private fortunes grew to incredible levels. For example, after adjusting for inflation, John D. Rockefeller and Andrew Carnegie remain some of the richest men in modern history. Even with their magnanimous philanthropy, Gilded Age business leaders' consolidation of capital still generated tremendous family wealth, easily lasting for many generations to come. While Andrew Carnegie and other business leaders opposed a federal income tax, Carnegie himself advocated for significant inheritance taxes on large estates.

Reform in the Gilded Age

Critics Championed Alternative Visions for Society

A diverse array of critics challenged traditional economic and political power structures during the Gilded Age.

Artists played an essential role in popularizing progressive causes and spreading awareness about poverty. For example, cartoonist Thomas Nast frequently parodied corrupt public officials, racist organizations, and business elites in his popular political cartoons.

A late nineteenth century religious movement known as the **Social Gospel** believed the Second Coming of Christ would only happen when humanity purified itself of its social ills. Social Gospel leaders participated in a variety of progressive causes including public education, public housing, anti-corruption movements, and poverty reduction.

Socialists were another indispensable part of the progressive movement. In contrast to the established economic policy of the United States, socialists advocated for more labor protections, social programs to fight poverty, and limitations on capital consolidation. **Eugene V. Debs** was a prominent socialist leader who played an instrumental role in organizing strikes against railroads. Some socialists also formed utopian groups to establish independent communities, such as the Icarians' egalitarian communes. Like socialists, **agrarian reformers** pursued collective action to reduce the power of railroads and consolidated financial interests. During the 1890s, William Jennings Bryant led the left-wing, agrarian **Populist Party** to national prominence advocating for the gold standard and restrictions on financial speculation.

Controversies over the Role of Government in the Gilded Age

Arguments for Laissez-Faire Policies

The concept of **laissez-faire** developed during the Gilded Age and was particularly influential in economic policies. Generally speaking, supporters of laissez-faire economics oppose government intervention in the private sector based on a belief that the free market will most efficiently and effectively resolve economic crises. Overall, the laissez-faire economic approach asserts that free markets will generate the most economic growth over time.

During the late nineteenth century, some members of the Democratic Party, known as the **Bourbon Democrats**, explicitly adopted laissez-faire economics. The Bourbon Democrats believed limited government and free markets were the answer to the country's recurring economic crises, such as the Recession of 1882–1885 and Panic of 1893. Aside from opposing government regulation, the Bourbon Democrats supported the gold standard, anti-corruption legislation, reduced government spending, and lower tariffs. However, laissez-faire economics worked better in theory than in practice. For example, without the government actively engaging in trust busting, wealthy corporations inevitably consolidated power as they gained advantages related to economies of scale. Therefore, greater consolidation of wealth crushed competition, undermining the potential benefits of a free market.

Politics in the Gilded Age

Populism

Populism in the Gilded Age advocated for various social, political, and economic measures that would support the interests of the people rather than the dominant elites. It also advocated for more governmental control in regulating the economy, particularly in favor of small businesses and farmers against large corporate and financial interests. The term "populism" was popularized in the 1890s by farmers and labor unions in reaction to the Gilded Age and economic instability; the movement eventually grew into the Populist Party (1892–1909).

Political Parties Remained Divided on Issues

Despite the relative peace that followed the American Civil War, partisan divisions remained alive and well in the American political party system.

In the aftermath of the American Civil War, the South seethed with resentment over the federal military occupation, political restrictions, and legal interventions of Reconstruction. Despite their lack of popular support, Republicans maintained control of the South until the presidential election of 1876. Republican Rutherford B. Hayes narrowly won the election, but only after agreeing to the **Compromise of 1877**, which returned the right to self-rule back to the Southern states. The federal government's withdrawal effectively killed the Republican Party in the South, triggering the return of sectionalism and partisanship.

Following the Compromise of 1877, Democrats dominated the South and Republicans remained the most popular party in the North. Democrats primarily called for limited government, opposed tariffs, and supported racial segregation. During the 1890s, William Jennings Bryant's Populists took over the Democratic Party by condemning moneyed interests and political corruption. In contrast, the

108

Republicans pursued a pro-business political agenda, including tariffs to protect domestic industry. Some Republican reformers adopted progressive and anti-corruption platforms, but the party struggled to enact meaningful reforms due to its long-standing relationships with economic elites.

Political Machines

During the latter half of the nineteenth century, **political machines** rose to power and came to dominate American urban political institutions, especially in the North. Elite bosses led political machines, or political groups, and they exercised authority over socioeconomic systems through complex political patronage networks. Bosses provided "spoils" to loyal officials working with the political machine, such as the unlawful sharing of government revenue. For example, Tammany Hall's Boss Tweed paid twice as much to construct the New York County Courthouse as the United States paid for the Alaska Purchase.

However, despite overt corruption, political machines did serve an essential function in many Northern cities. The federal government didn't have the resources or power to adequately provide social services to the poor, and most local governments struggled to implement necessary reforms. Political machines somewhat successfully filled this void, though this admittedly came at a heavy cost. In addition, political machines seeking loyal voters often fought to assimilate immigrant groups and deliver essential services to them. For example, Irish Americans first obtained a meaningful voice in American politics through their rise in political machines.

Practice Quiz

Question 1 is based on the following passage:

> Those who are opposed to this proposition tell us that the issue of paper money is a function of the bank and that the government ought to go out of the banking business. I stand with Jefferson rather than with them, and tell them, as he did, that the issue of money is a function of the government and that the banks should go out of the governing business.
>
> If they dare to come out in the open field and defend the gold standard as a good thing, we shall fight them to the uttermost, having behind us the producing masses of the nation and the world. Having behind us the commercial interests and the laboring interests and all the toiling masses, we shall answer their demands for a gold standard by saying to them, you shall not press down upon the brow of labor this crown of thorns. You shall not crucify mankind upon a cross of gold.
>
> William Jennings Bryan, "Cross of Gold" speech, 1896

1. What is the main idea presented in the excerpt?
   a. Banks prefer the gold standard.
   b. Most Americans dislike the gold standard.
   c. Violence is justified when the government oppresses the masses.
   d. The government should set the monetary policy based on the will of the people.

2. Which of the following types of government intervention lowers prices, reassures the supply, and creates opportunity to compete with foreign vendors?
   a. Income redistribution
   b. Price controls
   c. Taxes
   d. Subsidies

3. What type of map would be the most useful for calculating data and differentiating between the characteristics of two places?
   a. Topographic maps
   b. Dot-density maps
   c. Isoline maps
   d. Flow-line maps

Question 4 is based on the following map:

Map of the United States by population density

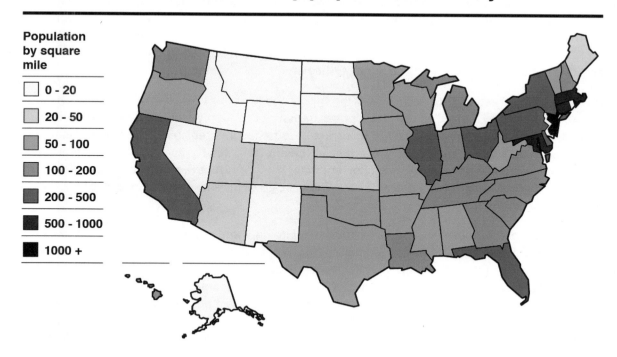

Population by square mile

☐ 0 - 20

☐ 20 - 50

☐ 50 - 100

☐ 100 - 200

☐ 200 - 500

■ 500 - 1000

■ 1000 +

4. According to the map, what area of the United States has the highest population density?
   a. Northwest
   b. Northeast
   c. Southwest
   d. Southeast

5. What accounts for different parts of the Earth experiencing different seasons at the same time?
   a. Differences in the rate of Earth's rotation
   b. Ocean currents
   c. Tilt of the Earth's rotational axis
   d. Elevation

See answers on next page.

Answer Explanations

1. D: Choice *D* is correct. William Jennings Bryan's "Cross of Gold" is one of the most famous speeches in American history, launching his candidacy in the 1896 presidential election. The speech advocates for abolishing the gold standard and adopting a bimetallic system to provide more government control over monetary policy. The excerpt condemns the influence of banks in monetary policy, and states that the masses should act to remove the gold standard. Choices *A*, *B*, and C are incorrect because, although they do accurately state assertions from the excerpt, they aren't the main idea.

2. D: Choice *D* is correct. By artificially increasing supply and lowering costs of production in various sectors of the economy, subsidies can lower prices, reassure the supply, and create opportunity to compete with foreign vendors. Choice *A* is incorrect because income redistribution moves wealth from some people in a society to others; it does not have the effects asked for in the question. Choice *B* is incorrect because, while price controls can lower prices, they do not have the other effects asked for in the question. Choice *C* is incorrect because taxes increase government revenue but do not have the effects asked for in the question.

3. C: Choice *C* is correct. Isoline maps are used to calculate data and differentiate between the characteristics of two places. In an isoline map, symbols represent values, and lines can be drawn between two points to determine differences. The other answer choices are maps with different purposes. Choice *A* is incorrect because topographic maps display contour lines, which represent the relative elevation of a particular place. Choices *B* and *C* are incorrect because dot-density maps and flow-line maps are types of thematic maps. Dot-density maps illustrate the volume and density of a characteristic of an area. Flow-line maps use lines to illustrate the movement of goods, people, or even animals between two places.

4. B: Choice *B* is correct. The map is a density map illustrating population density by state in the United States. Accordingly, the darker areas have higher population density. The darkest area of the map is the Northeast, so Choice *B* is correct. Choices *A*, *C*, and *D* show less population density than the Northeast.

5. C: Choice *C* is correct. The tilt of the Earth's rotation causes the seasons due to the difference in direct exposure to the Sun. For example, the Northern Hemisphere is tilted toward the Sun from June 22 to September 23, which creates the summer in that part of the world. Conversely, the Southern Hemisphere is tilted away from the Sun and experiences winter during those months. Choice *A* is factually incorrect—the rate of Earth's rotation is constant. Choices *B* and *D* are factors in determining climate, but differences in climate don't cause the seasons.

Imperialism: Debates

Imperialists' Arguments

Imperialism gained traction in the United States at the tail end of the nineteenth century. Prior to this period, Americans generally opposed imperialism due to America's history with European colonization. However, American foreign policy preferences became more fluid as the country increasingly entered the world stage and competed with European powers.

American imperialists had several interrelated justifications, ranging from cultural to economic. Most imperialists argued that it was a necessity for the United States to acquire foreign territory and resources to sustain economic growth. Hardcore imperialists went even further and applied principles of evolution to geopolitics, arguing that strong states would by necessity dominate and annihilate weaker states. This motivation only increased as Americans settled the western frontier and, for the first time in its history, faced a dwindling supply of undeveloped land.

Some imperialists combined pragmatic economic arguments with the narrative that the United States was destined for greatness, essentially refashioning Manifest Destiny on a global scale. Similarly, feelings of cultural superiority led to arguments that the United States had a moral obligation to spread democracy and commercial enterprise all over the world. This moral argument sometimes had a racial element as well, resembling that of the Spanish friars who defended the conquest and enslavement of indigenous populations in the 1500s and 1600s.

Anti-Imperialists' Arguments

Anti-imperialists denounced the growing popularity of ambitious and aggressive foreign policymaking as exploitative warmongering. In most cases, anti-imperialists criticized European powers for their oppressive colonial and imperial practices. Anti-imperialists commonly cited Enlightenment philosophers, America's Founding Fathers, and the Declaration of Independence (1776) to argue for the existence of an inalienable right to self-determination. Some radical anti-imperialists actually supported military interventions, but only to support local guerilla forces until they gained freedom from European powers. That being said, most anti-imperialists were isolationists who adopted arguments from George Washington's Farewell Address (1796). They viewed European imperialism as inherently destabilizing despite its economic benefits.

In addition, some anti-imperialists were nativists, and they adopted racial theories to protest territorial expansionism. Nativists viewed imperialism as a threat because local populations might one day be granted citizenship, similar to what occurred after the Mexican-American War (1846–1848). For example, in the run-up to the Spanish-American War (1898), nativists railed against an intervention because they believed Cuba and Puerto Rico might eventually become American states, potentially resulting in a million people of color becoming American citizens. Because nativists mostly hoped to preserve America's connection to Northwestern Europe, they championed anti-imperialism and isolationism.

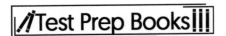

The Spanish–American War

American Victory in the Spanish-American War Effects

The United States' decisive victory in the **Spanish-American War** (April–August 1898) was a paradigm-shifting movement in American foreign policymaking, marking the beginning of the United States as an imperial force with a global reach. Spain was a crumbling empire prior to the conflict, and the United States landed the knockout blow, annexing Cuba, Puerto Rico, Guam, and the Philippines. This massive territorial acquisition reinforced American dominance over Latin America and served as a launching pad for American imperialists to challenge European control over the Southeast Pacific and Chinese mainland. However, great power presented its own challenges.

To gain Cuban support against Spain and guarantee Cuban independence, Congress passed the **Teller Amendment** which amended the United States' declaration of war against Spain to include the promise that the United States would not annex Cuba but merely support its independence. However, the United States immediately reneged on that promise after the fighting ended. American efforts to colonize the Philippines were similarly imperial in nature. The **Treaty of Paris** ended the war with Spain in 1898, but the Filipinos were in the midst of revolting against Spanish rule, and the nationalist movement felt no differently about the American imperialists. This inaugurated the **Philippine-American War** (1899–1902), which the Filipino people considered to be a continuation of their war for independence against Spain, while the U.S. considered it to be a rebellion. The war officially lasted for three years, but individual groups in the Philippines continuing to fight until 1913. Approximately 18,000 Filipinos died in the fighting, and somewhere between 250,000 and 1 million civilians died of war-related famine and cholera outbreaks. There were also reports of atrocities and war crimes committed on both sides.

The Progressives

Goals of Progressives

The social inequalities and economic abuses of the Gilded Age did not go unnoticed, and in the 1890s, many reformers began to demand change. This period was called the **Progressive Era** and included activists in both the Democratic and Republican parties. The Progressives wanted to use scientific methods and government regulation to improve society. For example, they advocated the use of direct democracy procedures such as the ballot initiative (citizens changing a law directly rather than through their legislatures), the referendum (a direct vote on a law passed by Congress), and recall (voters removing public officials from office) to make government more responsive to its citizens.

Progressives also argued that it was necessary to breakup large monopolies (known as **trust busting**) in order to promote equal economic competition. In 1911, Rockefeller's Standard Oil was split up into thirty-four different companies in order to promote competition, and the Federal Trade Commission was established in 1914 in order to prevent other monopolies from forming. Many Progressives also supported several constitutional amendments that were ratified in early twentieth century, including the Seventeenth Amendment, which established the direct election of U.S. Senators in 1913 (previously state legislatures had elected senators). They also favored the prohibition of alcohol that went into effect with the Eighteenth Amendment in 1919. Progressives also advocated for women's rights and backed the Nineteenth Amendment, which gave women the right to vote in 1920.

Disagreements Among Progressives

Progressives disagreed on a host of issues. Many Progressives emphasized democratizing the political system, promoting labor reform and social welfare, creating economic reform, and curing societal issues, especially in regard to working-class households in urban areas. These types of Progressives tended to be political activists, social workers, suffragettes, socialists, labor organizers, and/or agrarian populists.

Other Progressives pursued democratic reform and economic fairness through technocracy. Under a **technocratic government**, elite experts enjoy extraordinary power and control over the government to maximize efficiency. Although Progressive support for experts was considerable, technocrats didn't always make strong politicians, drawing heavy criticism for their relationships with powerful business leaders and politicians. In general, Progressive technocrats were most influential in urban areas, particularly when posing as an alternative to overtly corrupt party bosses.

Some Progressives hoped to maintain the privileges and benefits they enjoyed under the status quo of the traditional establishment. This type of contradictory Progressivism was commonplace throughout the country. Many Progressives sought to restrict immigration, believing the influx of cheap labor would further impoverish the urban working class. Likewise, Southern Progressives generally didn't challenge racial segregation or the denial of African Americans' political rights, although they often supported more democratization in areas where their interests were more aligned.

Progressive Amendments

The Progressive movement pushed for economic, political, and social reform to address issues related to industrialization and urbanization, expand democracy, and create moral reform.

Progressives' economic agenda mostly consisted of labor reform, social programs, and wealth redistribution through introducing taxation at the federal level. Additionally, Progressives pushed for more regulation to prevent financial speculators from causing market turmoil and contributing to recessions.

In terms of political policies, Progressives advocated primarily for an increase in direct democracy and anticorruption legislation. A crowning political achievement for the Progressive movement was the **Seventeenth Amendment**, which required U.S. senators to be directly elected. Prior to this constitutional amendment, state legislatures elected U.S. senators. Anticorruption legislation at the local level sought to break the hold of party bosses and business elites over the political system.

Pressing social issues included gender inequality, racial discrimination, and rampant alcoholism. Progressives were incredibly divided on social issues, and progress was slow. Little was accomplished in regard to repealing Jim Crow laws in the South or outlawing racial discrimination in the North. However, Progressives did manage to successively ratify the **Eighteenth Amendment** (1920) to criminalize the sale of alcohol as well as the **Nineteenth Amendment** (1920), which legalized women's suffrage.

Preservationists and Conservationists

Preservationists and **conservationists** during the Progressive Era advocated for the government to establish national parks and address the overuse and potential depletion of natural resources.

Preservation aims are specifically geared toward protecting nature and natural resources from being used, whereas conservation focuses on using natural resources properly and in a sustainable way.

President **Theodore Roosevelt**, who led the nation between 1901 and 1909, is famous for a series of modernization and conservation projects. Additionally, Roosevelt is famous for adding the **Roosevelt Corollary** (1904) to the Monroe Doctrine. The Corollary stated that the U.S. would take on the role of an "international police power" to resolve disputes between European and Latin American countries, rather than allowing Europeans to intervene themselves. The Roosevelt Corollary, backed by an impressive U.S. Navy, allowed the United States to have unchecked power in Latin America for decades after the Roosevelt administration.

One result of the U.S. interest in Latin America was Roosevelt enthusiastically offering the Panamanian governor $10 million per year to build and operate the Panama Canal. Operating under U.S. leadership between 1914 and 1999, the Panama Canal remained a last symbol of Roosevelt's diplomatic legacy in Latin America. The canal is a beacon of the United States' strong-armed diplomatic influence in Latin America during the years of the Roosevelt Corollary. During Roosevelt's presidency, the United States occupied many Latin American countries for self-serving reasons. Nevertheless, not all of Roosevelt's policies were as self-serving—the rough-and-tumble president is also responsible for establishing the National Park System in the United States and setting aside hundreds of thousands of acres of land for conservation.

World War I: Military and Diplomacy

The United States Enters WWI

World War I began in 1914 with the assassination of **Franz Ferdinand**, the heir apparent of the Austro-Hungarian Empire. A network of secret alliances meant that most European nations were quickly drawn into the conflict, although President **Woodrow Wilson** initially tried to keep the United States neutral. This decision was consistent with the United States' foreign policy tradition of staying out of European affairs. The majority of Americans agreed with this decision.

The war involved two major European alliances: the **Triple Entente** of the United Kingdom, France, and Russia and the **Central Powers** which included Germany and Austria-Hungary. The British implemented a naval blockade that was very successful, and the Germans retaliated by launching submarine attacks. German submarines attacked any ship carrying supplies to the Triple Entente, including the passenger ship **RMS Lusitania** in 1915. About 1,200 people died, including more than 100 Americans. The Germans temporarily halted their unrestricted submarine campaign but eventually resumed the attacks in 1917.

In addition, in 1917, Germany asked Mexico to attack the United States in a communiqué known as the **Zimmerman telegram**. These events led the United States to join the Triple Entente in April 1917, although significant numbers of American troops did not arrive in Europe until 1918. American reinforcement helped the British and French, who had been fighting continuously since 1914, launch a final offensive that defeated Germany in 1918. American forces suffered about 320,000 casualties. World War I also led to significant changes on the home front as women took on new responsibilities and thousands of African Americans migrated north in search of work. World War I also led to a communist revolution that transformed Russia into the U.S.S.R. in 1922.

116

The American Expeditionary Force

During the summer of 1917, the **American Expeditionary Force** (AEF) made their debut in Europe and changed the course of World War I. Although the United States had already been bankrolling and providing material assistance to the Allied powers for years, the establishment of the AEF laid bare the United States' commitment to defeating the Central powers. Backed with an enormous number of fresh troops and nearly unlimited supplies, the Allied powers surged to victory approximately sixteen months after the AEF first landed in France.

The AEF primarily fought under the command of U.S. General **John J. Pershing**. His forces were slowly acclimated to the battlefield, functioning as supplemental support for battle-hardened British and French divisions. However, by the fall of 1918, the AEF had garnered enough combat experience to begin operating independently. Pershing commanded the largest offensive force in the American military at the Battle of Saint-Mihiel (September 1918), heavily contributing to the Allied victory. Less than a month later, Pershing led more than one million AEF and French forces to victory during the Meuse-Argonne offensive. Given the AEF's late arrival, American forces were spared from some of the carnage, although the 1918 influenza pandemic ravaged the AEF.

Refusal to Ratify the Treaty of Versailles

The United States' refusal to ratify the **Treaty of Versailles** (1920) was one of the most peculiar events in American history. President **Woodrow Wilson** held disproportionate influence over the negotiations, and he secured the inclusion of his most prized policies, including the League of Nations, in the final draft. However, the U.S. Senate refused to ratify the treaty due to concerns including the League of Nations affecting U.S. sovereignty, effectively submarining Wilson's plans. Few states have ever enjoyed the luxury of crafting a new world order for their benefit, and even fewer have proceeded to reject the ultimate agreement.

President Wilson had been a vocal supporter of self-determination to prevent imperial ambitions from triggering another devastating global conflict. In his **Fourteen Points** speech, Wilson laid out policies to restrict colonization, support independence movements, implement global disarmament, and promote free trade. Furthermore, President Wilson advocated for the establishment of an international organization tasked with promoting peaceful international relations, which led to the founding of the **League of Nations** (1920).

The U.S. Senate was intensely skeptical of ceding any degree of sovereignty to an international organization. Given Americans' lukewarm and hostile support for World War I, American nationalists and isolationists had a relatively easy time rallying opposition to further enmeshing the United States in foreign affairs.

World War I: Home Front

Freedom of Speech Restrictions

Restrictions on Americans' **First Amendment** rights (the freedom of speech) increased during World War I. The conflict was deeply unpopular among the working classes; therefore, the federal government sought to suppress and strangle the antiwar movement in its infancy.

Congress passed the **Espionage Act** of 1917 and an amendment strengthening its provisions, the **Sedition Act** of 1918, to prevent speech that was viewed as undermining the war effort. The Supreme Court later affirmed the constitutionality of this extremely broad legislation, effectively allowing the federal government to suppress any negative or unfavorable speech proven to be even tangentially related to World War I. The federal government and business leaders used the acts to wage war against radicals and the organized labor movement, particularly after the beginning of the **Russian Revolution** (1917–1923). The Sedition Act of 1918 was repealed in 1920.

Despite the lack of meaningful evidence, in response to strikes and labor unrest, as well as anarchist bombings, American leaders argued that American labor unions were part of a Bolshevik plot to overthrow the federal government, triggering the **First Red Scare** (1917–1920). During the Red Scare, the federal government forcibly broke labor unions and arrested America's most famous socialist leader and labor organizer, **Eugene V. Debs**, over a speech expressing his opposition to draft and support for protests. After the Supreme Court upheld his conviction, Debs entered the presidential election of 1920 from prison, finishing in a distant third place.

Immigration Restrictions

The peak of European immigration occurred in 1907, just a few years before World War I. Nativist campaigns targeted at certain ethnic groups during and after World War I resulted in quotas being passed that placed restrictions on immigration for certain countries and regions or increased barriers to immigration.

However, these restrictions did not just crop up during the war; the late 1800s and early 1900s witnessed increased restrictions in immigration. Passed by President Chester A. Arthur, the **Chinese Exclusion Act** of 1882 inaugurated a decade-long moratorium on Chinese labor immigration.

Nationalist sentiment certainly played a part in limiting immigration. For some this was due to racism, while others were simply looking to build a strong, successful nation. As a result, the **Immigration Act of 1917** was enacted. It barred people who were insane, alcoholics, paupers, those with contagious diseases, felons, polygamists, prostitutes, and those who attempted to procure or import prostitutes. Additionally, it barred immigrants from Asia, with the exception of those allowed by existing treaties, those with specific professions, and those living in American-held territories. It also established literacy requirements for immigrants, requiring that they be able to read in English or some other language or dialect. It did also include an exception for anyone seeking asylum in the U.S. to avoid religious persecution. Likewise, the **Johnson-Reed Immigration Act of 1924** placed semi-permanent limitations on the number of immigrants who could enter the United States per year. The act established quotas based on national origin, limiting immigration from the Asia-Pacific Triangle. The act also placed quotas on European, African, and Middle Eastern immigration. Instead, it heavily favored immigrants from Northern and Western Europe, particularly Great Britain, Germany, and Ireland.

Economically-Motivated Migration to Urban Centers

Americans migrated from rural communities to urban centers during **World War I** (1914–1918), the **Great Depression** (1929–1941), and **World War II** (1939–1945) to pursue greater economic stability.

The American economy underwent a radical transformation during World War I. This conflict marked the first time the United States adopted a total war strategy, meaning every economic resource was

directed toward the war effort. Cities were the centers of mass production, and the resulting increase in economic activity generated tremendous employment opportunities. Given the shortage of labor caused by men joining the armed services, women entered the workforce in large numbers for the first time. Likewise, African American sharecroppers migrated to cities and secured higher pay working on assembly lines.

The Great Depression decimated rural communities. Debt is an inherent part of farming, and millions of farmers defaulted during the Great Depression due to unstable food prices, insufficient labor, environmental issues, and/or the stress placed on supply chains. Non-agricultural rural employment also largely depended on agricultural production and/or farmers' discretionary spending. Lacking alternatives, millions of displaced families migrated to urban areas and sought entry-level work in manufacturing and construction.

Like in World War I, the United States adopted a total war strategy during World War II, and the urban manufacturing boom attracted rural migrants and opened new opportunities for historically oppressed groups. Many farmers and African Americans also migrated to rapidly industrializing West coast cities. Industrialization increased at such a frantic pace that urban areas experienced intense housing shortages due to the expansion of the urban workforce. As a result, many cities achieved all-time low levels of unemployment, which officially brought an end to the Great Depression.

The Great Migration

During the **Great Migration** (1916–1970), approximately six million African Americans left the South to pursue more lucrative economic opportunities and political rights in the Northeast, Midwest, and West.

Labor shortages during World War I triggered the Great Migration as companies opened new jobs to meet industrial demands. More than 350,000 African Americans served in the **American Expeditionary Force** (AEF), and after fighting for their country, many joined the Great Migration to continue working as respected professionals. Several African American organizations, including the National Association for the Advancement of Colored People (NAACP) and the New Negro political movement, helped settle African Americans during the Great Migration.

Despite African Americans' improved economic mobility and political representation, the North was far from an idyllic paradise for people of color. Jobs on offer to African Americans were generally the most dangerous with the least compensation, and numerous private businesses openly refused to hire people of color. While organizing labor unions in the 1930s and 1940s did help mitigate some of the wage and employment discrimination, African Americans continued to face employment discrimination throughout the period of the Great Migration. Housing was another major obstacle for African American migrants due to redlining, or the practice of barring African American families from certain communities. As a result, African Americans were routinely forced to settle in the most dilapidated housing units in neighborhoods with the least access to public services.

1920s: Innovations in Communication and Technology

Technological and Manufacturing Improvements

The American economy underwent dramatic changes between 1890 and 1945 due to a variety of modernizing factors. The creation of a complex credit system and increased white-collar employment

increased Americans' disposable income, influenced the development of a consumer culture, and broadly raised the standard of living.

Americans' personal mobility increased through improvements in public transportation and mass production of automobiles. **Henry Ford** drove down the price of automobiles by using standardized parts and assembly lines. By 1918, Ford's innovative manufacturing techniques resulted in his Model T outnumbering the combined total of all other American cars. This success led to **Fordism**—the implementation of a system of mass production—gaining widespread acceptance in the manufacturing of consumer products.

New technological innovations and manufacturing procedures revolutionized the American economy by providing larger amounts of higher-quality products at lower prices. Some of the most important innovations, such as the combustion engine and petrochemicals, came from the discovery of new uses for petroleum. Other important innovations occurred in the construction of electric grids and skyscrapers, especially after the invention of reinforced concrete. Technology also strengthened communication systems and modernized entertainment. During the early twentieth century, telephones and radios became staples in American households. People were better able to stay connected and communicate with others. Additionally, movies gained steam in the 1930s when filmmakers incorporated sound.

Mass Media

A more unified national culture, as well as the awareness of diversity and different regional cultures, rapidly spread as new forms of mass media, such as the radio and cinema, were developed and became more commonplace. **Mass media** refers to the various methods by which the majority of the general public receives news and information. Today mass media includes television, newspapers, radio, magazines, online news outlets, and social media networks. The general public relies on mass media for political knowledge and cultural socialization, as well as the majority of their knowledge of current events, social issues, and political news. The points below outline the general evolution of mass media in the United States:

- Until the end of the nineteenth century, print media such as newspapers and magazines was the only form of mass communication.

- In the 1890s, after the invention of the radio, broadcast media become a popular form of communication, particularly among illiterate people. By 1944, 32.5 million American households owned radios.

- In 1933, President Franklin D. Roosevelt delivered his first Fireside Chat over the radio, recognizing the incredible opportunity it presented for the leader of the nation to speak with the people directly.

- In the 1940s, television superseded both print and broadcast media as the most popular form of mass media.

- In 1947, President Harry Truman gave the first political speech on television.

- In 1952, Dwight Eisenhower was the first political candidate to air campaign ads on television.

- Today, the internet is the most widespread mass media technology, and citizens have instant access to news and information, as well as interactive platforms on which they can communicate directly with political leaders or share their views through social media, blogs, and independent news sites.

The growth of mass media had a powerful effect on spreading culture and ideas and shaping public opinion and politics.

1920s: Cultural and Political Controversies

Urban Growth

Population growth and modernization, sparked by the technological transformations of the Industrial Revolution, catalyzed the growth of urban centers. By 1920, urban centers were home to the majority of the population in the United States due to better economic opportunities than rural communities, particularly for women and immigrants. Nearly 75% of the population in New York City, for example, was composed of new immigrants and first-generation Americans in 1910.

Migration Affected Art

Migration between 1890 and 1945 led to the development and/or evolution of stronger regional and ethnic identities. At the tail end of the nineteenth century, most American art and literature movements shared a deep commitment to realism; however, this largely gave way to more experimentation, which allowed artists to express more of their individual and collective lived experiences.

During the early twentieth century, American art movements developed with incredible regional and cultural diversity. The mass arrival of European immigrants in Northeastern urban areas energized the Ashcan, modernist, cubist, and abstract expressionist movements. Additionally, New York City birthed the **Harlem Renaissance** (1918–1937) as African Americans left the South to pursue economic opportunities in the North during the **Great Migration** (1916–1970). The Harlem Renaissance reflected the experience of African Americans in a diverse array of artistic endeavors, including experimental jazz music and revolutionary literature. Other major early twentieth century artistic movement developed as settlers moved into the American Southwest, resulting in artistic works based on iconographic desert landscapes and wildlife.

Literature movements similarly reflected socioeconomic changes, ethnic experiences, and regional identities. The literature of **William Faulkner** (1897–1962) and **John Steinbeck** (1902–1968) reflected and shaped Southern and Western regional identities, respectively, during the Great Depression.

Cultural and Political Controversies

Cultural and political controversies roiled the United States during the decade known as the **Roaring Twenties**, which matched this contradictory period's defining characteristics of economic prosperity and generational poverty. Progressives wielded scientific innovations and social reform to lift the United States into modernity. By the 1920s, most Americans enjoyed access to running water, electricity, radios, telephones, sanitation systems, automobiles, and cheap consumer and household products.

121

Many groups acted to protect traditional American society. Nativists secured the passage of the **Immigration Act of 1924** to restrict immigration for the alleged purpose of protecting American culture and jobs. Likewise, Southern states sought to reinforce Jim Crow laws to prevent the growing calls for racial equality after African Americans returned from fighting in World War I. Similar discrimination was also prevalent throughout the North, even in the most liberal states and communities. Conservative evangelicals successfully censored and criminalized certain scientific theories in many public school systems; however, the national conversation shifted toward secularism after **Clarence Darrow** defended a biology teacher's right to teach evolution in the infamous **Scopes Monkey Trial** (1925). Religious and women's rights groups were also at the forefront of passing **Prohibition**, which remains one of the most controversial and counterproductive policies in American history. Gender roles and women's rights issues were also debated.

The Great Depression

Economic Transitions

Millions of Americans began migrating from rural to urban areas during the run-up to World War I, and this migration continued during the Great Depression. Three factors heavily contributed to the continuation of this transition.

Between 1934 and 1940, a string of droughts, combined with decades of inexperienced farming by settlers, created a series of dust storms that wracked the Great Plains in an event commonly referred to as the **Dust Bowl**. Insufficient knowledge of ecology and the proliferation of mechanized farming equipment, combined with drought, triggered this man-made catastrophe. During the late 1920s and early 1930s, farmers plowed deep into virgin topsoil, displacing the native grass that provided structure and moisture to the land. Consequently, droughts turned the topsoil into dust, and high winds blew it all away. Without access to arable land, farmers defaulted on their farms and abandoned rural communities en masse.

Although the Great Depression caused a massive downturn in urban areas, the sheer size of urban industries offered more economic opportunities than rural communities. In addition, New Deal programs more effectively provided social assistance and stimulated more economic growth in urban areas. For example, cities directly received money for social assistance through the **Federal Emergency Relief Administration** (FERA), and the **Public Works Administration** (PWA) provided funds to revive the construction industry. Large corporations also received substantial government funding to retain and hire more workers, and most of those corporations operated in American cities. As a result, unemployed people from rural communities migrated to find work on assembly lines, which didn't typically require prior industrial experience.

Calls for a Stronger Financial Regulatory System

Although the United States produced dynamic levels of economic growth, the country's financial system was a near-perpetual disaster during the early twentieth century. Between 1890 and 1945, America's systematic lack of regulation and government oversight led to at least six distinct major recessions before culminating in the **Great Depression** (1929–1933).

The American banking system had been unstable since its founding in the early nineteenth century, and by the early twentieth century the system lacked a central authority capable of injecting liquidity and

enforcing a rules-based order. On **Black Tuesday**, October 29, 1929, unsustainable levels of American consumer debt combined with reckless financial speculation caused the stock market to plummet. Although this was relatively common for the era, Black Tuesday occurred in the context of a global economic downturn, which soon turned into a global depression. The stock market collapse triggered cascading credit defaults, panic-based bank runs, and the collapse of consumer spending, as well as the call for a stronger national financial regulatory system to prevent similar events from occurring.

President Franklin D. Roosevelt made regulating the American financial system a major plank in his presidential platform and in a series of policies, programs, and reforms that he called the **New Deal** (1933–1939). Among other initiatives, New Deal policies strengthened the Federal Reserve central banking system, established the Federal Deposit Insurance Corporation (FDIC), and introduced regulations to increase transparency and thwart financial speculation.

A Limited Welfare State

The Great Depression upended liberalism in the United States. American liberalism had traditionally focused on maximizing individual liberties over addressing economic issues, but the sudden influx of displaced, unemployed, and homeless Americans led to liberals establishing and defending a limited welfare state. President Franklin D. Roosevelt explicitly campaigned against liberal beliefs regarding limited government, and the incredible popularity of his economic reforms tied American liberalism to poverty mitigation.

The **New Deal** represented the first large-scale effort to mitigate poverty through government spending. President Roosevelt created federal agencies and spearheaded legislation to reduce social upheaval by helping Americans meet their basic needs. The primary focus was on reducing unemployment. For example, the Civil Works Administration (1933–1934) and Works Progress Administration (1935–1943) combined to fund the creation of more than 10 million jobs. Other New Deal programs focused on housing and food subsidies, such as the Food Stamp Program (1939–1943) and Housing Act of 1937. One of the most effective and influential New Deal policies was the Social Security Act of 1935, which provided universal retirement pensions, unemployment insurance, and social assistance for poor children and disabled people. To fund these new agencies and policies, President Roosevelt introduced new taxes on wealthy Americans and corporations. The combination of limited social assistance and taxation on the wealthy has since remained the hallmark feature of American liberalism.

Despite conservative and business owners' hostility toward the new liberal conception of "big government," the New Deal was firmly committed to free market capitalism. For example, the United States handed over a significant amount of the funding for unemployment programs to private employers who promised to hire workers for specific projects. This reflects elite liberal policymakers' unbroken faith in the efficiency of free markets as well as their desire to undercut Socialist and Communist movements.

The New Deal

Franklin Roosevelt's New Deal

In 1932, in response to the looming global Great Depression of the 1930s, U.S. voters elected President Franklin D. Roosevelt (FDR) to office because his presidential campaign promised to pull the United States out of economic despair. Unlike his predecessor—President Herbert Hoover—FDR eventually

123

accepted the fact that the federal government would have to play a role in reviving the tattered U.S. economy. On March 4, 1933, FDR pledged a **New Deal** to the American people, one that would regain the trust of down-and-out American workers. This promise of a New Deal was followed by a deluge of socialist-democratic legislation. The New Deal attempted to revive the American economy and end the Great Depression through public works projects carried out by organizations such as the U.S. Civilian Conservation Corps. These public works projects and government-backed organizations provided jobs to unemployed men and women across the country and helped stimulate economic recovery for the U.S.

Reception of the New Deal

By the end of the 1930s, the FDR administration had spent nearly $10 billion on the construction of hundreds of thousands of public buildings, roads, bridges, and airports. The New Deal also created new government agencies to help struggling businesses and farms and dispersed billions of dollars to welfare and relief programs for the poor. The New Deal, however, was just the beginning of socialist-democratic policies being infused into the economic fiber of the United States. Populist and radical movements pushed FDR toward expanding the New Deal and working to further the efforts to change the national economy. At the same time, conservative opponents in Congress and the Supreme Court fought to limit the scope of the New Deal.

Although the New Deal economy only improved slowly prior to the advent of World War II, the changes brought about by FDR's administration transformed the entire essence of the U.S. government's beliefs regarding the role of government in business and the economy. Some describe FDR's policies as the beginning of a **New Deal Order** that continued well into the Obama administration of the early 2000s. Others call his policies the beginning of the U.S. welfare state. Regardless of the terminology used to describe the New Deal programs, one cannot deny that the New Deal revolutionized the relationship between the federal government and the economy. The New Deal extended the reach of federal government, paving the way to expanded executive powers.

The New Deal's Legacy

The New Deal (1933–1939) is largely responsible for shaping the modern American regulatory system. Along with constructing the regulatory system that survived for decades after the end of the Roosevelt administration, the New Deal established numerous critical federal agencies, commonly referred to as the **alphabet agencies** due to the popularity of their acronyms. Examples of present-day alphabet agencies with roots in the New Deal include the Social Security Administration (SSA), National Labor Review Board (NLRB), and Securities and Exchange Commission (SEC).

President Roosevelt's political coalition also lasted for decades, ensuring the Democratic Party's intractable national relevance. The New Deal coalition is commonly described as a "big tent" political coalition because it consisted of working-class whites, African Americans, immigrants, environmentalists, socialists, technocrats, and elite liberals. Never before in American history had the working classes been politically united.

Historians and economists continue to debate the New Deal's impact on the Great Depression. Although the New Deal was not solely responsible for ending the Great Depression, it certainly helped restore the faith of the American people in their government. Additionally, the New Deal's expansion of the federal government's economic role was invaluable in World War II, facilitating and centralizing processes for

wartime production. There are many debates still today about the long-term effect of the New Deal and whether or not it was ultimately good for the American people and system of government.

Interwar Foreign Policy

Unilateral Foreign Policy

Due to concerns about various provisions of the **Treaty of Versailles** (1919), which ended World War I, and a desire to avoid becoming enmeshed in future European conflicts, Congress refused to ratify the Treaty of Versailles or join the League of Nations. However, the United States did anything but retreat from the international world order.

The United States held the diplomatic influence and military power to unilaterally intervene in a variety of conflicts in pursuit of its national interests. During the 1920s and 1930s, the United States organized several disarmament treaties, such as the London Naval Treaty (1930). The United States also worked to protect its financial investment in a recovered Europe, particularly by acting as the mediator in disputes over German debts owed to France under the Treaty of Versailles. For example, the United States played a key role in negotiating the Dawes Plan (1924) to create a more feasible debt-servicing plan.

Aside from diplomacy and investments, the United States also frequently leaned on its immense military power. The most brutal interventions occurred during the **Banana Wars** (1898–1934). Between 1915 and 1934, the United States successfully occupied and/or coerced more than a half dozen Latin American countries to protect American economic and geopolitical interests. Likewise, immediately after the end of World War I, the United States sent AEF divisions to support capitalist factions fighting Communists in the Russian Revolution (1917–1923).

Fascism and the Attack on Pearl Harbor

In the period between the world wars, **fascism** became popular in many European countries that were ravaged by the Great Depression. Fascism is a political ideology that advocates for a dictatorship in order to provide stability and unity. Adolf Hitler emerged as a prominent fascist leader in Germany and eventually brought the Nazi party to power in 1933. Germany aligned with Italy and Japan in 1940 to form the **Axis Alliance**. Their goal was to establish a German empire in Europe and place Japan in control over Asia. The League of Nations could not diffuse the conflict. World War II broke out when Germany invaded Poland in 1939 and France and Great Britain declared war on Germany. Germany and the Soviet Union had a nonaggression pact and the Soviet Union invaded Poland shortly after Germany; however, when Germany invaded the Soviet Union in June 1941, the Soviets immediately allied with Britain.

Hitler quickly conquered most of Europe with a strategy known as "blitzkrieg," or lightning war. By June of 1940 Great Britain was the only Western European nation still independent from Germany. Germany relentlessly attacked Britain, including bombing raids known as the Blitz from September 1940 to May 1941, in preparation for an invasion, and attacked the U.S.S.R. in 1941. The United States sent military equipment and weapons to Britain and the U.S.S.R. but did not formally join the war until the Japanese attacked **Pearl Harbor** on December 7, 1941.

World War II: Mobilization

Economic Factors Helped End the Great Depression and World War II

Like nearly all other combatants, the United States adopted a total war strategy during World War II. Total war strategies involve mass mobilization of all resources and the entire workforce in support of the war effort. For example, the United States rationed consumer goods and seized control over private industries to better reallocate resources for the war effort. In effect, the free market gave way to a command-based economic system, meaning the government unilaterally directed everything from production to consumption. Wartime demand for industrial production triggered an unprecedented economic boom, and as a result, the number of unemployed Americans decreased from 7.7 million to 1.5 million between 1940 and 1942, effectively ending the Great Depression.

American industrial production was crucial for the Allied victory. When presented with projections on the United States' industrial capacity, Nazi leaders mocked it as propaganda. By the time American troops arrived in Europe, the United States had wildly exceeded the most optimistic projections. In addition to outfitting 16 million American soldiers with the latest weapons and equipment, the United States' **Lend-Lease Program** allowed Great Britain and the Soviet Union to withstand Nazi invasions and eventually launch crucial offensive campaigns. Overall, the United States provided the present-day equivalent of $560 billion worth of food, oil, steel, warships, warplanes, and weaponry to the Allied powers.

Wartime Opportunities for Women and Minorities

As during World War I, women played an important role on the home front by working in factories to build guns, tanks, planes, and ships. African Americans, Native Americans, and Japanese Americans also contributed by fighting on the front lines.

With 16 million Americans serving overseas and demands on industrial production reaching historic levels, factories loosened the restrictions on the employment of women and people of color during World War II. Many of these jobs disappeared after the soldiers returned from overseas; however, it had a lasting impact. Posters like those featuring "Rosie the Riveter" broke traditional gender norms, laying the foundation for more women to find work outside of the household. Similarly, African Americans who served in the U.S. Armed Forces or worked in factories learned valuable professional skills, which lifted many families into the middle class for the first time in generational history.

Despite this significant economic improvement, the United States maintained existing discriminatory policies and even introduced new ones as wartime measures. Even after 1.2 million African Americans fought for their country, the federal government still refused to intervene in the South to remove Jim Crow laws.

Additionally, Japanese Americans suffered great hardships. Without any supporting evidence, President Roosevelt issued an executive order to round up approximately 110,000 Japanese Americans and forcibly placed them in internment camps. Federal legislation intended to reimburse Japanese Americans was wildly insufficient, and many families permanently lost their homes and businesses to internment.

Immigration from the Western Hemisphere

Migration from the Western Hemisphere rapidly increased in the early twentieth century, particularly in comparison to immigrants coming from the Eastern Hemisphere. The **Immigration Act of 1924** outright banned all immigration from Asia, established the U.S. Border Control, and created a legal mechanism for deportation. Additionally, the Immigration Act of 1924 implemented restrictive quotas for Eastern and Southeastern Europeans. These immigration restrictions underscored the growing tide of nativism in the United States.

Along with restricting the arrival of new immigrants, nativists enacted and revamped anti-immigration legislation. For example, many Western states began enforcing anti-vagrancy legislation that was first passed to deny political and property rights to Mexicans. However, nativist groups failed to prevent Congress from carving out exceptions explicitly for Mexicans in the Immigration Act of 1917. Likewise, the Immigration Act of 1924 did not institute the same quota system for the Western Hemisphere, resulting in more immigration from the Caribbean and South America.

Congressional leniency toward Hispanic immigrants was the direct product of America's dependence on cheap labor. Once the Great Depression forced desperate white Americans to accept low-paying and dangerous work, the federal government immediately forcibly repatriated between 400,000 and two million people of Mexican descent, including American citizens.

World War II: Military

Fighting Against Fascism

The American foreign policy establishment characterized World War II as a global fight for the future of democracy. This wasn't anything new. Ever since the Revolutionary War (1775–1783), American politicians, journalists, and citizens had portrayed nearly every military conflict as an absolutely necessary measure for defending American freedom. World War II was different because the existential threat to democracy and freedom became increasingly self-evident as time progressed.

Nazi Germany and Japan were fascist powers willing to pursue global domination by any means necessary. Nearly every war involves some war crimes; however, the Axis powers differed in the strategic orchestration of mass killings. Nazi concentration and death camps systematically murdered an estimated two-thirds of European Jews during the Holocaust. On top of this, Nazi Germany oversaw the killing of approximately five million Slavs, Romani, and Soviet prisoners of war.

Although Americans didn't learn the full scope of the Holocaust until years after it commenced, Japanese war crimes in China and Korea were common knowledge. Overall, Japanese imperial forces killed between three million and fourteen million civilians in large-scale massacres and forced labor camps. As such, it wasn't hyperbolic or hysterical to describe the Axis powers as a genuine existential threat to democracy and freedom, a feeling that resonated with most Americans at the time.

The United States' Military Victory

The U.S. entered the war when Japan bombed Pearl Harbor in Hawaii on December 7, 1941. Battles raged in Europe and the Pacific, and the Allied forces won an important victory in June 1942 at the **Battle of Midway**. At this battle, the U.S. stopped the Japanese from advancing and prevented the

invasion of Australia. In 1943, Axis troops in North Africa surrendered to the Allies, who then began to invade Italy, and finally invaded France on June 6, 1944 (known as **D-Day**), which resulted in severe losses on both sides. In early 1945, President Roosevelt met with British Prime Minister **Winston Churchill** and Soviet director **Joseph Stalin** in Yalta, Crimea, known as the **Yalta Conference**, to plan their final assault on Germany and discuss postwar strategies. The Allies continued their attack, liberating Nazi death camps. A defeated Hitler eventually committed suicide, and Germany surrendered on May 7, 1945. However, Japan did not yield, even after the capture of Okinawa in June. As a result, the U.S. dropped atomic bombs on the Japanese cities of Hiroshima and then Nagasaki in August, forcing Japan to surrender on September 2, 1945.

Many factors contributed to the United States' success in World War II.

The United States was an economic powerhouse, providing a consistent supply of money, steel, weapons, and food to the Allied powers. Even with 16 million American soldiers fighting overseas, the production continually increased as a stream of women and people of color entered the industrial workforce. The Allied powers also made use of groundbreaking technological innovations, such as anti-aircraft radar and code-breaking computers.

The Allied powers jointly and cooperatively waged a multi-theater war. After a cooperative, daring D-Day amphibious invasion of Nazi-held beaches in Normandy by the American, British, and Canadian militaries, along with troops from a variety of other countries, American and British forces drove the Nazis out of Western Europe and North Africa. At the same time, the Soviet Union resiliently held the line against a Nazi onslaught and eventually turned the tide of the war.

The United States took the lead in the Pacific theater in an "island-hopping" strategy to create space for an aggressive air bombing campaign and clear a path to Japan. President Harry S. Truman authorized the first-ever use of atomic weapons on the Japanese cities of Nagasaki and Hiroshima in August 1945, effectively ending the war. Although many activists have criticized the use of nuclear weapons, and the decision remains controversial to this day, many argue that an invasion would have left many millions more people dead.

Postwar Diplomacy

Postwar Conditions for Various Nations

World War II had a devastating impact on Europe and Asia. Nearly all Asian and European states had death tolls in the millions, and entire urban centers lay in ruins. For example, an American firebombing campaign incinerated nearly 16 square miles of Tokyo. As a result, European and Asian countries struggled to find a footing in the conflict's immediate aftermath, relying heavily on American financial and military assistance to rebuild critical industries.

In contrast, the United States had escaped the conflict with minimal damage to domestic industries and exponentially fewer civilian casualties compared to all of the other major combatants. Furthermore, American economic production also dwarfed all of its competitors, and Western Europe functioned as an ideal export market for American goods. America's wartime loans and continued financial assistance also translated into durable political influence in Western Europe.

The United States' position in the global hierarchy was strong even compared to the Soviet Union, the only other remaining superpower. Somewhere between 13 million and 27 million Soviet citizens died in the fighting, which led all combatants by a wide margin. As such, the United States emerged from World War II as one of the most powerful states in modern history.

Toward the end of World War II, a group of fifty nations (including the U.S. and the Soviet Union) formed the **United Nations** as a peacekeeping group on October 24, 1945. However, Communism continued to spread throughout the world, including to Latin America, Africa, and Asia, which led to a variety of conflicts throughout the remainder of the twentieth century.

Practice Quiz

Questions 1–5 are based on the following poem. Read it carefully then answer the questions.

> I sit and sew—a useless task it seems,
> My hands grown tired, my head weighed down with dreams—
> The panoply of war, the martial tred of men,
> Grim-faced, stern-eyed, gazing beyond the ken
> Of lesser souls, whose eyes have not seen Death,   5
> Nor learned to hold their lives but as a breath—
> But—I must sit and sew.
>
> I sit and sew—my heart aches with desire—
> That pageant terrible, that fiercely pouring fire
> On wasted fields, and writhing grotesque things   10
> Once men. My soul in pity flings
> Appealing cries, yearning only to go
> There in that holocaust of hell, those fields of woe—
> But—I must sit and sew.
>
> The little useless seam, the idle patch;   15
> Why dream I here beneath my homely thatch,
> When there they lie in sodden mud and rain,
> Pitifully calling me, the quick ones and the slain?
> You need me, Christ! It is no roseate dream
> That beckons me—this pretty futile seam,   20
> It stifles me—God, must I sit and sew?
> Poem "I Sit and Sew" by Alice Moore Dunbar-Nelson, 1918

1. In line 9, the speaker mentions a "pageant." What is she referring to?
   a. A beauty pageant
   b. The current war
   c. A popular play
   d. A wedding celebration

2. In the first stanza, who are the "martial tred of men, / Grim-faced, stern-eyed" that the speaker mentions in lines 3 and 4?
   a. Children
   b. Enemies
   c. Soldiers
   d. Neighbors

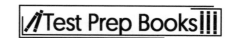
3. What idea does the speaker effectively contrast in this poem?
   a.   The idea between the usefulness of sewing and the uselessness of war, namely that men's bodies are literally being wasted on the battlefield while sewing gives the opportunity of creating clothes for those same bodies.
   b.   The idea between right and wrong, specifically that the war and everything relating to it is immoral, and the domestic side of life, including sewing, can be seen as doing good.
   c.   The idea between sacrifice and selfishness; the speaker is admitting that she is being selfish for wanting to pursue her passion of sewing rather than helping out with the war.
   d.   The idea between activeness and passiveness in the sense that the speaker views sewing as passiveness and longs to do something active in order to help out in the war.

4. What type of poetic lines are included in this poem?
   a.   English sonnets
   b.   Alternating tercets
   c.   Rhyming couplets
   d.   Syllabic haikus

5. How many stanzas does this poem have?
   a.   1
   b.   2
   c.   3
   d.   4

See answers on next page.

131

Answer Explanations

1. B: The speaker is referring to the current war, Choice B. The lines say: "I set and sew—my heart aches with desire— / That pageant terrible, that fiercely pouring fire / On wasted fields, and writhing grotesque things / Once men" (lines 8–11). Pageant is a metaphor for the battlefield in this poem. After she mentions the word "pageant," the speaker then goes on to describe the "pageant," or war, by describing the fire, fields, and dying men. Choices A, C, and D do not fit the description of "pageant" laid out in the poem and are therefore incorrect.

2. C: The speaker is referring to soldiers in these lines, so Choice C is correct. If we look at the surrounding context clues, the word "war" is mentioned before the description of these men. The word "tred" refers to a sort of weary marching. Choice A is incorrect because the poem refers to men, not children. Choice B is possible; however, there is nothing in the poem to indicate that these men are the enemies of the writer. In fact, the author's desire to join the men indicates that they are allies rather than enemies. Therefore, this choice is incorrect. Choice D is incorrect because, while the soldiers may in fact be the author's neighbors, there is nothing in the poem that indicates the author knows any of the soldiers personally.

3. D: The speaker effectively contrasts the idea between activeness and passiveness in the sense that the speaker views sewing as something passive and longs to do something active in order to help out in the war. In the first stanza, the dull act of sewing is set in contrast with the horror that happens in her dreams. In the second stanza, the massacre in the war is contrasted by her, again "sitting and sewing" and yearning to help. Finally, in the third stanza, her "useless seam" is contrasted with the soldiers dying in the mud.

The stark contrast of the comforts and ease of sewing to the pain and suffering of soldiers in active duty is a central theme in this poem. Choice A is incorrect because the author actually seems to indicate the opposite, that in the current situation sewing is less desirable (although perhaps not useless) than war and that she longs to join the war effort, which would be unlikely if she viewed it as useless. Choice B is incorrect because the author does not address the concepts of right and wrong in this poem. Choice C is incorrect because the author does not address sewing and soldiering in terms of selfishness. Additionally, she longs to join the war the war effort rather than sewing, indicating that she is not being selfish.

4. C: Poetic lines that can be seen in this poem are rhyming couplets. Rhyming couplets are two pairs of lines that end with rhyming words. We see this all the way through, except for the last line in each stanza, which ends with the word "sew." Here are some examples of the end rhymes of the rhyming couplets: "seems" and "dreams," "things" and "flings," "rain" and "slain." Choices A, B, and D do not describe the poetic lines included in this poem.

5. C: A stanza is a group of lines that make up a repeating metrical unit of a poem. We see that there are three stanzas, and each stanza consists of seven lines each. The seven lines have three rhyming couplets (six lines) and end with a seventh line that has no end rhyme. However, the last word in every unit is "sew," which makes a cohesive repetition in the poem. Because the poem has three stanzas, Choices A, B, and D are incorrect.

132

Period 8: 1945–1980

The Cold War from 1945 to 1980

War Against Communism

Within two years of World War II, the world was involved in a different kind of war—a **Cold War**—that pitted capitalism and Communism against each other. World War II left Europe on the brink of collapse, leaving the United States and Soviet Union as the world's undisputed remaining superpowers. The United States and its allies embarked on a campaign of containment in an attempt to keep Communism from spreading to other countries and to create a global free-market economy instead.

Postwar U.S. Foreign Policy

The United States developed a foreign policy after World War II that was based on international security and aid, as well as developing economic institutions and infrastructures that supported a free-market economy. In the 1940s, U.S. president Harry S. Truman, in an effort to contain Communism, offered U.S. military and economic support to any nation threatened by Communist takeover, whether from external or internal forces. This became known as the **Truman Doctrine** (1947). In 1949, the United States, Canada, and ten European nations developed an alliance known as the **North Atlantic Treaty Organization (NATO)** based on the principles of the Truman Doctrine and preventing the spread of Communism.

When West Germany was invited into NATO in 1955, the Soviet Union responded with a similar alliance known as the **Warsaw Pact**. The Warsaw Pact and NATO were vehicles for the United States and Soviet Union to flex their military might. In addition to conventional arms, the two superpowers competed in a nuclear arms race throughout the Cold War. The nuclear arms race resulted in a policy of deterrence known as **mutual assured destruction (MAD)** – the concept that, if one superpower detonated its nuclear missiles, the other would do the same and both would be destroyed. There were several close calls during the Cold War due to mixed signals, misunderstandings, or provocation—the most notorious being the **Cuban Missile Crisis** (October 1962) when the Soviet Union placed nuclear missiles in Cuba, ninety miles away from Florida.

Containing Communism

The United States fought a series of proxy wars against the Soviet Union to prevent the spread of Communism. The **Korean War** (1950–1953) was an attempt by Communist North Korea to take over nominally democratic, anti-Communist South Korea. Korea was part of the Japanese Empire until the end of World War II, when the Soviet Union and the United States divided it along the 38th Parallel into a northern zone, administered by the Soviets, and a southern zone, administered by the United States. North and South Korea became sovereign states during the Cold War, and each government claimed to be the only true government of Korea.

After North Korea invaded South Korea in 1950, China and the Soviet Union joined together to support North Korea while the United Nations, particularly the United States, supported South Korea until an armistice was signed in 1953. The armistice established the **Korean Demilitarized Zone (DMZ)** that once again divided Korea into a Communist North and a democratic South, although it now deviates from the

133

38th Parallel. The 38th Parallel was an important demarcation during the war itself, as America was reluctant to pursue the North Koreans across the parallel and risk escalating the proxy war into a conventional one against the Soviets.

The **Vietnam War** (1955–1975) was another proxy war pitting the United States against Communism. North Vietnam, supported by China and the Soviet Union, fought against South Vietnam, supported by the United States, South Korea, and other nations dedicated to preventing the spread of Communism. The North Vietnam military directed and supported the **Viet Cong** guerilla fighters, officially known as the National Liberation front of South Vietnam, who were a communist political organization in South Vietnam determined to overthrow the South Vietnamese government and unify Vietnam. Although the United States was the superior conventional military force, the American military struggled mightily against the guerilla tactics of the Viet Cong. As intense opposition to the war mounted in the United States, the United States withdrew (1973) and the North Vietnamese captured Saigon in April 1975. The war encompassed the Laotian Civil War and the Cambodian Civil war and ended with Vietnam, Laos, and Cambodia all falling to Communism.

The Soviet Union similarly struggled against guerilla forces backed by the United States during the **Soviet-Afghan War**, which lasted from 1979 to 1989. The United States provided military and financial support to the Afghans during the conflict, many of whom would later found al-Qaeda or join the Taliban to fight the United States, including Osama bin Laden.

Conflict and Détente

Tensions fluctuated between the United States and the Soviet Union during the Cold War (1947–1991), ranging from large-scale indirect hot wars to periods of easing hostilities (**détente**). The major hot wars, or conflicts in which the Americans and/or Soviets overtly committed substantial personnel and supplies to the fighting, were the Korean War (1950–1953), Vietnam War (1955–1975), and Soviet-Afghan War (1979–1989). Additionally, throughout the Cold War, the Soviets and Americans both covertly funded and supplied many dozens of proxy forces in armed conflicts.

Periods of détente typically featured more dialogue and less indirect fighting compared to overt hot wars. The longest period of détente occurred in the 1970s as American president Richard Nixon and Soviet general secretary Leonid Brezhnev sought to avert further nuclear escalation by establishing a stronger working dialogue. Several major treaties, including the **Anti-Ballistic Missile Treaty** (1972) and the nonbinding **Helsinki Accords** (1975), were signed in the 1970s in an attempt to improve relations and encourage disarmament. However, even at the best of times, both superpowers never fully stopped arming proxies and conducting a variety of disinformation campaigns and election interference in foreign countries. Détente officially ended when the Soviet Union invaded Afghanistan in 1979.

The Red Scare

Exposing Communists and Containing Communism

Red Scare refers to the widespread fear of Communism and of the spread of Communism throughout the United States. While there was a Red Scare after World War I, there was a Second Red Scare after World War II that was also called **McCarthyism** (1947–1957). Wisconsin senator Joseph McCarthy led the charge in a series of investigations and trials that sought to uncover communist agents and propagandists in the U.S. government, Hollywood, and other public institutions. Anti-communist

sentiment rose sharply in the U.S. after World War II as the Soviet Union began expanding its influence throughout Europe and establishing Communist governments in territory it acquired during the war.

The Soviet development of a nuclear bomb and the rise of Communism in China, both in 1949, and the invasion of South Korea by Communist North Korea in 1950 exacerbated the fears of U.S. citizens regarding Communism itself, and especially the concern of espionage in the United States. McCarthy was elected to the Senate in 1946, and in 1950, became famous when he claimed there were over 200 communists infiltrating the State Department. These claims led to a series of investigations and public hearings which reached their peak in 1954 with thirty-six days of televised hearings. Despite claims to the contrary, the Soviet messages intercepted and decoded by the **Venona Project** (1943–1980) proved that there were hundreds of Americans passing information to the Russians. However, McCarthy often put forward wild and unsubstantiated claims, which he then backed to the hilt. In 1954 he was censored by the Senate and by 1957 the Second Red Scare was largely over. McCarthyism is now a term that has become synonymous with Cold War fears and any type of public defamation or indiscriminate allegations.

Karl Marx (1818–1883), a philosopher, social scientist, historian, and revolutionary, is considered one of the most influential Socialist thinkers of the nineteenth century. His ideas became known as **Marxism**, and Marx heavily influenced powerful Socialist and Communist leaders, such as **Vladimir Lenin**, with his 1848 pamphlet *The Communist Manifesto*. In this pamphlet, he explained that, in a capitalist society, perpetual "class struggle" exists in which a ruling class (**bourgeois**) controls the means of production and exploits the working class (**proletariat**), who are forced to sell labor for wages. He advocated for the working class to rebel against the ruling class and establish a classless society with collective ownership of the means of production. He envisioned world history as a series of stages in which capitalism eventually collapses into Communism.

Economy After 1945

Economic Growth

The United States' annual **gross domestic product** (GDP) continually grew between 1950 and 1970 and, in some years, increased by as much as eight percent. Economists believe four factors played an outsized role in America's rapid economic expansion.

First, technological innovations increased the efficiency and profitability of commercial enterprises. The development of commercial airlines expedited long-distance travel times, and the invention of color television provided a new way for businesses to reach customers. In addition, some innovations created new economic sectors, especially in relation to computers.

Second, post-World War II euphoria and economic prosperity produced a baby boom. The resulting population increase drove up consumer spending and industrial productivity rates. The baby boomer generation was also incredibly productive due to the low costs of higher education and housing.

Third, heavy taxes on economic elites boosted government spending, which translated to more government services and infrastructure investments. For example, Congress passed the Federal Aid Highway Assistance Act (1956) to fund the construction of more than 40,000 miles of interconnected federal highways,

Fourth, the private sector experienced significant gains based on a virtuous cycle of increased consumer spending, mass manufacturing innovations, and strong demand for American products abroad.

Suburbs and a Migration to the Sun Belt

During the 1950s and 1960s, Americans enjoyed more social mobility than any other national population. The United States led the world in industrial production, manufacturing exports, and consumer spending. Telephones and televisions further broadened economic opportunities and tightened community bonds. Additionally, many American families were lifted into the middle class with assistance from the **GI Bill** (1944), which provided veterans with subsidized loans, unemployment benefits, and tuition assistance. Between 1944 and 1956, nearly eight million American veterans claimed tuition assistance under the GI Bill, which improved household incomes and expanded America's supply of skilled labor.

The explosive growth of the American middle class led to rapid suburbanization. Many factors influenced what has come to be known as "**white flight**," where white Americans migrated en masse to the suburbs and away from the more ethnically diverse city centers beginning in the 1950s and 1960s. While racism is one possible factor, others include decreasing home values and rising crime and tax rates in the cities, with corresponding increasing home values, less crime, and lower taxes in the suburbs, which also had the advantage of giving families more space. Some American families moved farther away than the nearby suburbs and relocated to the **Sun Belt**, which refers to the Southeastern and Southwestern regions of the United States. The Sun Belt offered a more appealing climate and lower tax rates than the Northeast and Midwest. In addition, the Sun Belt was also home to several economic sectors, such as the aerospace, defense, and oil industries, that experienced rapid growth in the 1960s and 1970s.

Culture after 1945

Mass Culture and the Counter-Culture Movement

In the postwar years, mass culture was more homogenized than it typically had been. This homogeny inspired many artists, intellectuals, and young people to challenge that conformity. The **counterculture movement** became popular during the 1960s as millions of children from the Baby Boomer generation entered into adulthood. Many of these young adults were disaffected and unhappy with the social norms of their parents' generation. In general, they rejected ideas such as segregation, support for the Vietnam war, traditional sexual mores, and traditional gender roles for women. The counterculture movement also included widespread experimentation with drugs. Many members of the counterculture movement inherited the beatnik's interest in African and Asian cultures, and many, often called hippies, adopted alternative lifestyles. One of the key elements of the movement was an emphasis on experimentation, artistry, and self-expression. As a result, the counter-culture movement produced many musicians and avant-garde artists.

The counterculture movement was also closely connected to other protest movements during the 1960s, including the Civil Rights movement and opposition to the war in Vietnam. In 1965, young men began burning their draft cards, which was a criminal offense, in protest of the war and, in particular, the **draft**, which frequently sent young men to fight in war they didn't believe in. Massive demonstrations against the war occurred around the country, especially on college campuses, but many other people also refused to support the war effort, including clergymen and even some veterans who

136

had fought in Vietnam. The counterculture movement had a lasting impact on the social and cultural history of the United States.

Early Steps in the Civil Rights Movement (1940s and 1950s)

Legal and Political Successes in Ending Segregation

Activists began organizing the civil rights movement in the 1940s to achieve racial equality by ending segregation and enfranchising African Americans. The general strategy was to build public support and pressure the federal government to enforce the Fourteenth and Fifteenth Amendments.

Many historians consider A. Philip Randolph and Bayard Rustin's **March on Washington Movement** (1941–1946) to be the beginning of the civil rights movement. Randolph and Rustin's nonviolent tactics heavily contributed to the desegregation of the military (1948) and inspired a new generation of civil rights activists, including Martin Luther King Jr. The civil rights movement then gained steam in the late 1940s and 1950s as activists developed new legal strategies such as boycotts, sit-ins, and litigation. Activists enjoyed considerable success in targeting specific businesses with boycotts. After Claudette Colvin and Rosa Parks courageously refused to give up their seats on Montgomery, Alabama, buses in 1955, King led a successful bus boycott. Similarly, in 1958, the **National Association for the Advancement of Colored People** (NAACP) Youth Council conducted sit-ins at a lunch counter in Kansas, and their victory sparked a nationwide movement.

Targeted litigation also propelled the civil rights movement, and the NAACP led several efforts to bring legal challenges against discriminatory laws. Five of these test cases were combined in the famous Supreme Court case **Brown v. Board of Education** (1954), in which the Supreme Court ultimately ruled that the segregation of public schools was unconstitutional. Three years later, President Dwight D. Eisenhower enforced the Supreme Court's decision by ordering the 101st Airborne Division to escort nine African American schoolchildren ("**Little Rock Nine**") into an illegally segregated school.

Despite these notable achievements, progress was a gradual process. An overwhelming majority of white Americans characterized the civil rights movement as the work of outside agitators and denounced King as a race baiter. Jim Crow laws remained in effect, as did unwritten and discriminatory rules of behavior, especially in the South, as evidenced by the brutal mutilation and murder of **Emmett Till**—a 14 year-old boy accused of whistling at a white woman in a Mississippi grocery store. Despite opposition, early civil rights activists' dedication and sacrifices paved the way for landmark victories in the 1960s.

Governmental Efforts to Promote Racial Equality

All three branches of the United States government implemented measures to desegregate the nation and promote racial equality. The armed services became desegregated in 1948 with Executive Order 9981 by President Harry S. Truman. When the Supreme Court ruled that school segregation was illegal in 1954 in the revolutionary case **Brown v. the Board of Education**, the **Civil Rights Movement** was set in motion. This movement continued throughout the 1950s and 1960s and included dozens of nonviolent protests such as the Montgomery bus boycott in Alabama. The boycott was organized after **Rosa Parks** was arrested because she refused to give up her seat on the bus to a white man.

The Southern Christian Leadership Conference (SCLC) was soon formed as a way to bring African Americans together to help fight segregation in a peaceful way. The Reverend **Dr. Martin Luther King, Jr.** was its first president. Dr. King and his supporters kept up the fight throughout the 1960s, staging sit-ins at segregated lunch counters, **Freedom Rides** on segregated buses, and marches and protests in segregated cities, such as Birmingham, Alabama. The demonstrations often ended in violence and police brutality, which served to aid the movement and led to the passage of the **Civil Rights Act** in 1964. As the broadest and arguably most impactful civil rights legislation since Reconstruction, the Civil Rights Act called for the desegregation of schools and public facilities and made it illegal for employers to discriminate based on race or ethnicity.

America as a World Power

Cold War Conflict in Latin America

The United States practiced a supercharged version of the Monroe Doctrine as it endeavored to keep Communism out of its proverbial backyard. While the United States publicly championed democracy and freedom, many policy decisions were based primarily on American commercial and geopolitical interests.

The United States backed proxy wars and coup attempts in more than a dozen Latin American countries between 1945 and 1980. Material support was most often provided to groups aligned against left-wing governments. Most infamously, in 1973, the United States backed the overthrow of the democratically elected Chilean president **Salvador Allende**. With help from his American allies, General **Augusto Pinochet** then seized control and instituted a military dictatorship. Pinochet is most remembered for zealously supporting free markets and brazenly ordering secret police to kidnap, imprison, and/or assassinate thousands of dissidents.

Long-standing American proxy forces, such as the Guatemalan White Hand and Nicaraguan Contras, also regularly deployed death squads to terrorize indigenous populations, socialist communes, and left-wing governments. Overall, American foreign policy was not successful at supporting freedom or developing democracy in Latin America.

Debates Over Military Activity

Although the American public generally supported massive military spending during the Cold War, some aspects of the United States military were incredibly controversial.

During his famous farewell address in 1961, President **Dwight D. Eisenhower** delivered a warning about how the growing military-industrial complex threatened American democracy by consolidating unwarranted power. Although antiwar activists continually condemned the military-industrial complex as it expanded throughout the Cold War, reform was never attempted due to strong anti-Communist sentiments, bureaucratic inertia, and the effect of arms manufacturers on domestic employment.

Antiwar activists also frequently protested against nuclear proliferation, arguing it was immoral to build weapons of mass destruction; however, nuclear stockpile reductions didn't occur until the end of the Cold War.

Americans debated the power of the executive branch, which had grown continuously since the 1930s. Additionally, antiwar activists accused the U.S. government of using its extensive enforcement powers to infiltrate, harass, and squash left-wing political movements in the United States. Some of those accusations turned out to be true. Under the leadership of **Edgar Hoover**, the Federal Bureau of Investigation (FBI) conducted an illegal covert program known as the Counter Intelligence Program (COINTELPRO) (1956–1971) to infiltrate, harass, discredit, and annihilate groups they deemed to be subversive, including the Black Panthers, the Chicano Movement, the American Indian Movement (AIM), the Communist Party USA, the Ku Klux Klan, and the National States' Rights Party, among others.

New International Allies

Following the end of World War II, decolonization and nationalist movements resulted in the formation of more than a hundred newly independent states in Africa, Asia, and the Middle East. An overwhelming number of these states attempted to remain as neutral as possible during the Cold War in an attempt to stabilize their economic and political development. In addition, most new states were reluctant to cede authority to global superpowers, particularly when they had just gained their independence.

During the 1960s, states joined the **Non-Aligned Movement** to collectively announce their neutrality and avoid being collateral damage in foreign ideological conflicts, particularly the various conflicts of the Cold War. According to Cuban leader Fidel Castro's **Havana Declaration** (1979), the Non-Aligned Movement stood in solidarity with all countries that experienced colonialism, imperialism, racism, and foreign intervention of any kind. Some of the member states also had powerful incentives to seek collective security and publicly declare neutrality, particularly those states with left-wing governments, such as Cuba and Yugoslavia. Despite the Non-Aligned Movement's efforts, American and Soviet policymakers gave little credence to foreign countries' proclamations of neutrality, especially if a country occupied valuable geopolitical space or possessed strategic assets. The superpowers were also effective at enlisting the help of client states through coercion, financial incentives, and military assistance. For example, Cuba was deeply in debt to the Soviet Union and, after voting against a statement condemning the Soviet Union for invading Afghanistan (another member of the Non-Aligned Movement) in 1979, Cuba lost its social standing as a leader of the Non-Aligned Movement.

The Vietnam War

During World War II, Vietnamese rebels worked with the Allied powers to overthrow Japanese Imperial Forces and, upon their victory, the rebels expected to receive independence from France, which had colonized Vietnam in the late nineteenth century as part of its French Indochina colony. France refused to free Vietnam and the United States provided France with an overwhelming amount of financial and material support to prevent the spread of Communism across Southeast Asia. In turn, the Soviet Union and China backed the Communist rebel faction, which sought independence for Vietnam.

Following the **Geneva Accords** of 1954, Vietnam split into Communist North Vietnam and capitalist South Vietnam, which resulted in the region becoming one of the active fronts in the Cold War. To deter the Soviet-backed North Vietnamese forces from invading, in 1955 the United States began providing more financial and military assistance to South Vietnam. One proven and one alleged naval skirmish collectively known as the **Gulf of Tonkin** incident (1964) provided President Lyndon B. Johnson with the justification for a full-scale American military intervention. Much of the fighting occurred in Vietnam's dense jungles, and both sides committed atrocities at an alarming rate. One of those atrocities, the **My**

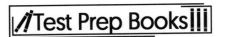
Lai massacre (1968), involved American forces murdering hundreds of Vietnamese villagers in cold blood, while the South Korean armed forces, the Viet Cong, and the North Vietnamese Army also committed multiple massacres.

The United States held a decisive advantage throughout the conflict due to its air superiority and massive bombing campaigns of North Vietnam and Laos. For example, the United States dropped more bombs on Laos alone than it did in the entirety of World War II. In addition, the United States conducted a secret bombing campaign against Cambodia to destroy Communist supply lines.

Despite its military victories, many Americans opposed the war, which caused anti-war protests and unrest. Anti-war opposition reached a fever pitch in the aftermath of North Vietnam's **Tet Offensive** (1968). Although the Tet Offensive was a military disaster, it was a public relations coup for North Vietnam because it thoroughly disproved President Johnson's claims that the conflict was nearly over. As a result, the United States dramatically reduced its combat forces, and a cease-fire was signed in 1973. North Vietnamese forces then steamrolled through South Vietnam, and the last U.S. forces pulled out in 1975 shortly before the fall of Saigon, which officially ended the Vietnam War.

The Great Society

Concern for Poverty

As Europe sifted through the ashes in the aftermath of World War II, the United States occupied a dominant economic position. A large supply of blue-collar manufacturing jobs lifted millions of Americans into the middle class, and the United States invested significant amounts of its newfound wealth on major infrastructure projects to support the surging birth rate. At the same time, tens of millions were locked out of this idyllic society.

The federal government provided minimal assistance to alleviate poverty. Slum-like housing was pervasive in urban areas. Additionally, many rural communities and urban neighborhoods lacked access to essential services. African Americans and people of color especially suffered in the postwar socioeconomic system due to the prevalence of segregation, racial discrimination, voting restrictions, and artificial limitations placed on economic pursuits.

President Lyndon B. Johnson took action to eliminate poverty through a set of policy initiatives called the **War on Poverty**. The War on Poverty was the second-largest expansion of America's social safety net after the New Deal, and many of its programs, including Medicaid, Medicare, and subsidies for food, have survived through the present day. Additionally, the War on Poverty dramatically increased federal funding for public education, job training, and community services.

Liberalism

Liberalism arguably peaked in the 1960s in terms of its control over the White House and both houses of Congress. A major part of liberals' emergence as the clear-cut electoral favorite was based on a combination of hawkish foreign policy and progressive domestic reform.

Liberal politicians supported a variety of military interventions to contain Communism. **President John F. Kennedy**, a New England liberal Democrat, authorized the failed **Bay of Pigs** invasion (1961) to covertly overthrow Cuba's Communist regime and took America further down the road to a full-fledged armed

conflict in Vietnam. His successor, liberal Democrat Lyndon B. Johnson, exploited the **Gulf of Tonkin incident** (1964) to justify the full-scale invasion of Vietnam.

Anti-Communist sentiment insulated liberals from conservative attacks, many of which characterized ending segregation and enfranchising people of color as a Soviet plot to destroy America to push through sweeping domestic reform.

Combined with his expertise in congressional procedures and penchant for coercion, President Johnson masterfully leveraged this liberal groundswell to pass a series of landmark legislation, including the Civil Rights Act (1964), the Food Stamp Act (1964), the Voting Rights Act (1965), and the Social Security Act (1965).

The Great Society

The **Great Society** was another major government program that the Democratic Party supported. President Lyndon B. Johnson sought to end poverty and improve education. For example, he raised the minimum wage and created programs to provide poor Americans with job training. The Great Society also implemented a number of Civil Rights laws to address racial discrimination.

The Immigration and Nationality Act of 1965

Immigrants flocked to the United States in the mid-twentieth century to gain political freedoms, pursue opportunities in the booming economy, and protect their families from social unrest.

During the early 1960s, the United States was still using the **National Origins Formula** to restrict immigration from outside Northwestern Europe and Latin America. The **Immigration and Nationality Act of 1965** abolished and repealed the restrictive quota system and established a foundation for contemporary immigration policy. However, Congress did include a provision to limit immigration from the Western Hemisphere for the first time in American history.

The Immigration and Nationality Act of 1965 ushered in many demographic changes. The lifting of restrictions on Asian immigrants led to sharp increases in Chinese, Japanese, Korean, and Vietnamese immigration. Likewise, immigration from most African countries reached record highs after 1965. At the same time, Hispanic immigration officially declined, although estimates of illegal border crossing steadily increased as the Cold War destabilized Latin America and forced families to flee for safety. Aside from changing immigrants' demographic composition, the removal of the National Origins Formula led to a steep rise in total immigration. For example, foreign-born people accounted for five percent of the United States' population in 1965, but by 2016 it had increased to 14 percent.

The African American Civil Rights Movement (1960s)

Civil Rights Activists

Martin Luther King, Jr. was a Civil Rights leader and activist as well as a Baptist minister. Dr. King argued for nonviolent resistance during the Civil Rights movement, for which he won the Nobel Peace Prize in 1964. Dr. King was assassinated on April 4, 1968, in Memphis, Tennessee.

Dr. Martin Luther King Jr. gave his speech "**I Have a Dream**" as part of the **1963 March on Washington**. Drawing on Lincoln's past speech at Gettysburg, Dr. King argued that America's journey to true equality

141

was not over. His references to biblical passages gave the speech a spiritual tone, but he also mentioned specific locations across the nation to emphasize that local struggles were tied with national consequences. Through its optimistic tone, Dr. King's speech reflects not only civil rights activism but also the American dream of freedom and progress.

Cesar Chavez was a labor union activist who organized transient Hispanic agricultural workers in an effort to obtain better working conditions in the 1960s and 1970s. He co-founded the National Farm Workers Association. Chavez became a historical icon after his death and is famous for popularizing the slogan "Sí, se puede," or "Yes, it can be done."

Betty Friedan was an American feminist and writer in the second wave of feminism in the 1960s who was elected the first president of the **Nation Organization for Women** (NOW). Her book, *The Feminine Mystique*, is widely regarded as the spark that began this second wave. Friedan aimed to empower women to be in an equal partnership with men. She also led the **Women's Strike for Equality** in 1970, which advocated for equal opportunities for women in jobs and education.

Debates Over Nonviolence

Much of America was still resistant toward desegregating the country and promoting racial equality. Racial tensions were at an all-time high in the early to mid-1960s. This led to social and political unrest within the country, which also slowed the progress of civil rights activists. Not all civil rights activists were united in their ideas and actions to advocate for change. Particularly after 1965, there was a marked rise in the debates between civil rights activists over violent versus nonviolent approaches toward the movement. An African American human rights activist and Muslim minister named **Malcolm X** advocated for the rights of African Americans and against nonviolence. He became a member of the Nation of Islam, and through that platform promoted the separation of black and white Americans and black supremacy (although he eventually left the Nation of Islam and founded Muslim Mosque, Inc., and the Organization of Afro-American Unity). Malcolm X rejected the Civil Rights movement for its emphasis on integration as well as passive resistance. Malcolm X is known to his admirers as a courageous and important figure in African American history.

Supreme Court Decisions Expanded Civil Rights

During the 1960s, the Supreme Court handed down a series of landmark decisions that greatly expanded civil rights and protected civil liberties.

The Supreme Court expanded civil rights through its prohibitions on racial discrimination. In **Bailey v. Patterson** (1962), the Supreme Court prohibited the segregation of interstate and intrastate transportation systems. Combined with the court's decision in **Brown v. Board of Education** (1954), this decision effectively ended the racial segregation of public places. In **Loving v. Virginia** (1967), the Supreme Court found Virginia's Racial Integrity Act (1924) to be unconstitutional and prohibited race-based restrictions on marriage. In **Jones v. Alfred H. Mayer Co.** (1968), the court reversed prior precedents and relied on the Civil Rights Act of 1886 to prohibit racial discrimination in both public and private commercial transactions.

Numerous landmark Supreme Court decisions strengthened civil liberties during the 1960s. In **Mapp v. Ohio** (1961), the Supreme Court ruled that the Fourth Amendment protected people from unreasonable searches and seizures conducted by state law enforcement as well as federal law enforcement. In **Engel**

v. Vitale (1962), the court reaffirmed the separation of church and state by invalidating a New York statute that forced schoolchildren to recite a prayer. In **Gideon v. Wainwright** (1963), the Supreme Court found that the government must provide criminal defendants with an attorney if they otherwise cannot afford legal representation. In **Griswold v. Connecticut** (1965), the court laid the foundation for a constitutional right to privacy in its finding that married people had the right to obtain and use contraception. In **Miranda v. Arizona** (1966), the Supreme Court threw out a defendant's confession because the police violated his Fifth Amendment protection from self-incrimination by failing to inform him of his right to remain silent. In **Tinker v. Des Moines** (1969), the court found the wearing of an anti-war armband in school to be permissible free speech under the First Amendment.

The Civil Rights Movement Expands

Latino, American Indian, and Asian American Civil Rights Movements

Asian Americans, American Indians, and Latinos had mixed results in advocating for greater equality and justice for past abuses.

Asian American political movements lobbied Congress to outlaw racial discrimination in employment and public settings. Additionally, Asian Americans pushed for the overturn of disproportionately restrictive immigration laws that targeted Asian migrants, such as the **Asian Exclusion Act of 1924**. They achieved a notable success through the passage of the significantly more liberal **Immigration and Nationality Act of 1965**, which removed significant obstacles for millions of Asian immigrants.

During the 1960s and 1970s, numerous American Indian and Latino activists founded political movements modeled after the civil rights and Black Power movements. The **Chicano Movement** formed around the desire to empower Mexican Americans to fight back against systematic racial discrimination and seek justice for the generation of Mexican Americans who were collectively deported during the Great Depression. Likewise, the **American Indian Movement** (AIM) and **Red Power Movement** encouraged American Indians to be proud of their heritage and collectively defend their historic homeland from the federal government. Both of these movements adopted many of the civil rights movement's use of civil disobedience; however, they also had more confrontational elements, particularly when organizing against antiwar actions.

Feminist and LGBT Activists

The women's rights and lesbian, gay, bisexual, and transgender (LGBT) movements gained steam in the mid-twentieth century, achieving some groundbreaking victories in the fight for legal and socioeconomic equality.

After World War II, although many women lost their factory jobs to soldiers returning home, the conflict marked a major turning point for women. As women continued to seek more advanced levels of educational and professional opportunities, feminists mobilized the women's rights movement to push for more societal equality, equal compensation, birth control access, and legal protection against sexual violence. The Supreme Court's decision to uphold the constitutionality of abortion in **Roe v. Wade** (1973) was a major victory for the budding feminist movement; however, they faced a fierce backlash from social conservatives and Christian evangelicals who condemned abortion and pushed back against gender equality.

143

Frequent police raids at the legendary Stonewall Inn, a Mafia-owned gay bar in Greenwich Village in New York City, led to the **Stonewall Riots** (1969), a series of spontaneous protests occurring over five days after a police raid turned violent. After the Riots, several LGBT activists formed the **Gay Liberation Movement** to forcibly resist police harassment and raise awareness of LGBT issues. During the 1970s and early 1980s, the LGBT Rights Movement formed to advocate for legal equality and support LGBT politicians, such as **Harvey Milk**, the first openly gay person to serve in the U.S. government.

Feminists in the Counterculture Movement

Although women had achieved political equality, they continued to demand reform throughout the twentieth century. In the early 1900s, **Margaret Sanger** provided women with information about birth control, which was illegal at the time. Women entered the industrial workforce in large numbers during World War II, but when the war ended, they were fired so that veterans would have jobs when they came home. Many women were frustrated when told they had to return to their domestic lives. **Simone de Beauvoir**, a French writer, published her book *The Second Sex* after World War II, and an English translation was published in 1953.

It highlighted the unequal treatment of women throughout history and sparked a feminist movement in the United States. In 1963, **Betty Friedan** published a book called *The Feminine Mystique*, which revealed how frustrated many suburban wives were with the social norms that kept them at home. During the 1960s, women participated in the sexual revolution and exerted more control over their own sexuality. In 1972, Congress passed **Title IX**, which prohibited sexual discrimination in education and expanded women's sports programs. In the 1970s, women's rights activists also pushed for greater access to birth control, and in 1973 the Supreme Court issued the controversial decision **Roe v. Wade**, which removed many barriers to abortion services. Women also demanded greater protection from domestic abuse and greater access to divorce.

During the twentieth century, many American women made notable achievements, including Amelia Earhart, who was the first woman to cross the Atlantic in an airplane in 1928. In 1981, Sandra Day O'Connor became the first woman to serve on the Supreme Court. In 1983, Sally Ride became the first female astronaut. In 1984, Geraldine Ferraro became the first woman to run for vice-president, although she was unsuccessful. However, many activists continue to demand reform in the twenty-first century. For example, women only account for 20 percent of the U.S. Senate and House of Representatives. Furthermore, women earn approximately 82 percent of what men in similar jobs are paid. In 1980, President Jimmy Carter declared March to be Women's History Month.

Youth Culture of the 1960s

Anti-War Protests

Following the end of World War II, Americans broadly supported anti-Communist policies and believed they were necessary to win the Cold War. The United States' intervention in the Korean War caused minimal backlash among the public. In addition, the vast majority of Americans were concerned about Communist espionage activity, and nearly all Americans either supported or ignored their country's continual involvement in regime change all over the world. However, once the United States escalated its involvement in the Vietnam War in 1964, public support quickly eroded. Various factors contributed to the public's antagonism toward the war, including the unprecedented coverage of a military conflict

on color television and the organizational experience many protest leaders gained in the civil rights movement.

Anti-war demonstrations were overwhelmingly peaceful and incredibly diverse in terms of race, ethnicity, gender, age, religion, educational attainment, and profession. However, protestors increasingly took more radical action after reporters uncovered covert bombing campaigns and mass atrocities during the late 1960s. As a result, protests occasionally erupted in violence. For example, National Guardsmen killed four protestors at Kent State University in 1970, which led to renewed calls for more aggressive protest tactics. Increasing antagonism for the war at home, combined with poor morale in the U.S. armed forces and the difficulty of pursuing the war, led the United States to pull combat forces out of Vietnam in 1973 and fully withdraw in 1975 as the North Vietnamese captured Saigon and completed their takeover of South Vietnam.

The New Left

Some groups on the Left also rejected liberal policies, arguing that political leaders did too little to transform the racial and economic status quo at home and pursued immoral policies abroad.

These left-wing Americans went further than liberal Democrats in demanding more racial, economic, and gender equality. During the 1960s and 1970s, activists founded thousands of influential grassroots political institutions and movements. Although these groups never formed a cohesive movement, they're commonly classified as the **New Left** based on their shared criticism of capitalism, imperialism, and other hierarchical power structures. Most New Left groups called for the merging of labor organizations and social activism to oppose America's authoritarian and antidemocratic elements. Rather than participating in liberal efforts to reform economic and political systems, the New Left favored more radical direct action to eradicate poverty and achieve justice.

New Left groups differed wildly in their chosen causes and approaches. The **Students for a Democratic Society** (SDS) was one of the largest New Left groups, and its student leadership cadre organized a number of actions to support the antiwar movement before it splintered in the late 1960s. The **Youth International Party** was most well known for its anarchist political leanings and satirical street theater protests. The **Weather Underground** led the militant and hyper-revolutionary wing of the New Left, and its members engaged in a variety of unlawful acts ranging from jailbreaks to bombing campaigns.

The Environment and Natural Resources from 1968 to 1980

U.S. Involvement in the Middle East and a National Energy Policy

The United States vigorously sought to maximize its commercial interests in the Middle East as the region decolonized during the aftermath of World War II. The region was especially critical because it contained an overwhelming majority of the world's proven oil deposits. In addition to functioning as a vehicular and industrial power source, petroleum was a necessary component of several emergent economic sectors including plastics and agricultural petrochemicals. Furthermore, the Middle East held immense geopolitical value because it functioned as a land bridge between the communist East and capitalist West.

The United States worked closely with its chief ally, the United Kingdom, to protect their mutual corporate interests in the Middle East, including oil-rich Bahrain, Iraq, Iran, Kuwait, and Qatar, as British

145

colonies gained independence. When independence movements threatened to nationalize their country's oil supply, the United States and United Kingdom responded with extreme measures. For example, in 1953, American and British foreign policymakers backed a successful coup d'état in Iran.

During the 1970s, oil crises wracked the global market, particularly after the **Iranian Revolution** (1978–1979) ousted the American-backed Shah from power. The Iranian takeover of the U.S. Embassy and capture of 52 Americans resulted in the **Iran Hostage Crisis** (November 4, 1979–January 20, 1981), which lasted 444 days and led to an embargo on Iranian oil. In response to the oil crisis of 1979, the United States invested in alternative sources of foreign oil production as well as its own domestic capabilities, and also began looking into developing alternatives to fossil fuels.

Environmental Legislation

America's manufacturing boom unleashed a host of environmental problems. During the postwar era, nearly all American cities suffered from chronic smog, and many communities completely lost access to locally sourced clean drinking water due to agricultural and industrial chemical runoff. Furthermore, commercial developers bulldozed vast stretches of American wilderness, and industrialists exploited natural resources at unsustainable rates. As environmental issues mounted in the 1960s, environmental activism surged, especially after the publication of Rachel Carson's *Silent Spring* (1962).

The environmental movement's first major achievement was securing the passage of the **Clean Air Act** (1963). The Clean Air Act was the first environmental law in American history with a national scope, and its air quality regulations were some of the strongest in the world. Growing support for environmentalism later motivated President Nixon to establish the **Environmental Protection Agency** (EPA) in 1970. The EPA enjoys the power to promulgate regulations, and it can also conduct enforcement operations when Congress provides specific statutory authorizations. The **Clean Water Act** (1972) was another landmark piece of environmental legislation. Among other initiatives, the Clean Water Act provided funding for wastewater treatment, created a framework to help states regulate pollution, and protected wetland ecosystems.

Society in Transition

Conservatives Challenge Liberal Laws

Conservatives did their best to thwart the rising tide of liberalism in the 1960s.

During the 1960s, conservatives called for tax cuts, federal budget cuts, and more emphasis on states' rights. Unfortunately, one effect of the emphasis on states' rights was to energize southern conservatives who wanted to obstruct integration. For example, during the early 1960s, several southern states refused to fully comply with the Supreme Court's landmark decision in **Brown v. Board of Education** (1954), which found segregated public schools to be unconstitutional. Likewise, conservatives consistently worked to undermine the civil rights movement and the War on Poverty. In addition to limited government and segregation, conservatives supported more radical action to contain Communism. For example, the 1964 Republican presidential candidate, Barry Goldwater, openly discussed the possibility of limited nuclear strikes in Vietnam.

Conservatives regularly condemned many liberal policies in stark moral terms. Under this view, conservatives portrayed integration and gender equality as evidence of moral decay. The nexus between

146

Christian morality and conservative policies merged during the 1960s as states attempted to outlaw abortion and diminish birth control access, culminating with conservatives' outrage over the Supreme Court's decision to uphold women's right to abortion as constitutional in **Roe v. Wade** (1973).

Waning Trust in the Government

The U.S. government struggled to maintain its legitimacy and project its authority during the 1970s.

The **Watergate scandal** (1972–1974) infamously eroded American confidence and trust in government. **Richard Nixon** won the presidential election of 1972 in a historic landslide victory, but members of his re-election committee had broken into the headquarters of the Democratic National Committee in the Watergate Office Building on June 17, 1972, in an attempt to steal information and bug phone lines. President Nixon initially attempted to cover up his involvement but, faced with impeachment in the House for obstruction of justice, abuse of power, and contempt of Congress, with a likely conviction in the Senate, he resigned in 1974. President **Gerald Ford** pardoned Nixon to help the country heal; however, it only served to ignite a storm of protests and disillusionment.

The anti-Vietnam War movement reached a fever pitch in the 1970s and heavily influenced President Nixon's decision to withdraw American forces. Furthermore, several Middle Eastern crises challenged the United States. Arab states responded to American support for Israel in the **Yom Kippur War** (1973) with an oil embargo, which intensified a global economic downturn. From 1973 to 1980, the United States struggled to break out of a deep recession that featured both high unemployment and high inflation. The **Iranian Revolution** (1978–1979) added to the turmoil as the victorious nationalists held Americans hostage in the **Iran Hostage Crisis** and threatened the global oil supply.

Clashes Between Conservatives and Liberals

Conservatives and liberals spent the 1970s locked in a culture war over numerous political, cultural, and social issues.

The **Sexual Revolution** (1960–1980) horrified social conservatives, particularly the Christian fundamentalist wing of the rising conservative movement. Conservatives denounced everything from unmarried cohabitation to family planning. The debate over abortion was perhaps the most controversial because it amounted to a zero-sum game, arguing between women's rights to have control over their own bodies and Christian beliefs of life beginning at conception.

Race was another divisive topic. Conservatives generally believed that federal intervention interfered with their individual rights. On the other side, many African American political groups condemned budget cuts as thinly veiled class warfare, and there were frequent protests over racial injustices in urban areas.

Given the popularity of liberal landmark legislation passed in the 1960s, conservatives generally pursued a strategy known as "starving the beast." Rather than attempting to overturn the legislation, Republicans advocated for shrinking the federal budgets and slashing taxes to decrease government revenue. Although liberal Democrats generally succeeded in protecting national social programs, they were less successful at the local level. For example, California conservatives successfully enacted **Proposition 13** (1978)—a state constitutional amendment that capped property taxes, resulting in massive state budget cuts.

Evangelicals and Religious Conservatives

The Christian evangelical movement experienced a major revival after World War II. During the 1950s, American evangelical leaders deemphasized strict biblical interpretations and prioritized personal spiritual connections. In addition, many evangelicals attempted to develop more interfaith dialogue and promote more tolerance. However, evangelicalism made a sharp turn toward fundamentalism in the late 1960s and 1970s as church leaders increasingly demanded followers abide by the leaders' strict gospel interpretations. Evangelicals also frequently adopted television as an effective method of proselytizing. Many Christian theologians have criticized Christian fundamentalists and televangelists for espousing the prosperity gospel, which ties divine blessings to wealth accumulation.

Evangelicals regularly engaged in social activism to protest acts they found immoral, such as premarital sex and abortion, and they became more politically conscious during the Goldwater and Nixon presidential campaigns. During the late 1970s, **Jerry Falwell, Sr.**, organized a powerful evangelical-led political advocacy group known as the **Moral Majority** (1979). The Moral Majority worked closely with both of Ronald Reagan's presidential campaigns as he crafted a coalition based on elite business interests, foreign policy hawks, social conservatives, and evangelicals. Ever since the Moral Majority group formed, evangelicals have remained a permanent fixture in the modern-day Republican party.

Practice Quiz

Questions 1–3 are based on the following passage:

When researchers and engineers undertake a large-scale scientific project, they may end up making discoveries and developing technologies that have far wider uses than originally intended. This is especially true in NASA, one of the most influential and innovative scientific organizations in America. NASA spinoff technology refers to innovations originally developed for NASA space projects that are now used in a wide range of different commercial fields. Many consumers are unaware that products they are buying are based on NASA research! Spinoff technology proves that it is worthwhile to invest in science research because it could enrich people's lives in unexpected ways.

The first spinoff technology worth mentioning is baby food. In space, where astronauts have limited access to fresh food and fewer options with their daily meals, malnutrition is a serious concern. Consequently, NASA researchers were looking for ways to enhance the nutritional value of astronauts' food. Scientists found that a certain type of algae could be added to food, improving the food's neurological benefits. When experts in the commercial food industry learned of this algae's potential to boost brain health, they were quick to begin their own research. The nutritional substance from algae then developed into a product called life's DHA, which can be found in over 90 percent of infant food sold in America.

Another intriguing example of a spinoff technology can be found in fashion. People who are always dropping their sunglasses may have invested in a pair of sunglasses with scratch-resistant lenses—that is, it's impossible to scratch the glass, even if the glasses are dropped on an abrasive surface. This innovation is incredibly advantageous for people who are clumsy, but most shoppers don't know that this technology was originally developed by NASA. Scientists first created scratch-resistant glass to help protect costly and crucial equipment from getting scratched in space, especially the helmet visors in space suits. However, sunglass companies later realized that this technology could be profitable for their products, and they licensed the technology from NASA.

1. What is the main purpose of this article?
   a. To advise consumers to do more research before making a purchase
   b. To persuade readers to support NASA research
   c. To tell a narrative about the history of space technology
   d. To define and describe instances of spinoff technology

2. What is the organizational structure of this article?
   a. A general definition followed by more specific examples
   b. A general opinion followed by supporting evidence
   c. An important moment in history followed by chronological details
   d. A popular misconception followed by counterevidence

3. Why did NASA scientists research algae?
   a. They already knew algae was healthy for babies.
   b. They were interested in how to grow food in space.
   c. They were looking for ways to add health benefits to food.
   d. They hoped to use it to protect expensive research equipment.

4. Which of the following was NOT a movement that was going on in the 1960s?
   a. Civil Rights Movement
   b. End the War Movement
   c. Women's Rights Movement
   d. LGBTQ Rights Movement

5. The case of Brown v. Board of Education reversed what landmark Supreme Court doctrine?
   a. Judicial review doctrine
   b. Public safety exception
   c. Due process doctrine
   d. Separate but equal doctrine

See answers on next page.

Answer Explanations

1. D: This is an example of a purpose question—*why* did the author write this? The article contains facts, definitions, and other objective information without telling a story or arguing an opinion. In this case, the purpose of the article is to inform the reader. Choices *A* and *B* are incorrect because they argue for an opinion or present a position. Choice *C* is incorrect because the focus of the article is spinoff technology, not the history of space technology.

2. B: A general opinion followed by supporting evidence. This organization question asks readers to analyze the structure of the essay. The topic of the essay is about spinoff technology, and the thesis statement at the end of the first paragraph offers the opinion, "Spinoff technology proves that it is worthwhile to invest in science research because it could enrich people's lives in unexpected ways." The next two paragraphs provide evidence to support this opinion. Choice *A* is the second-best option because the first paragraph gives a general definition of spinoff technology, while the following two paragraphs offer more detailed examples to help illustrate this idea. However, it is not the best answer because the main idea of the essay is that spinoff technology enriches people's lives in unexpected ways. Choice *C* is incorrect because the essay does not provide details of any specific moment in history. Choice *D* is incorrect because the essay does not discuss a popular misconception.

3. C: This reading comprehension question can be answered based on the second paragraph—scientists were concerned about astronauts' nutrition and began researching useful nutritional supplements. Choice *A* in particular is not true because it reverses the order of discovery (first NASA identified algae for astronaut use, and then it was further developed for use in baby food). Choices *B* and *D* are not uses of algae discussed in the article.

4. B: End the War Movement. The 1960s were a time of growth for the United States. Everyone was pushing for rights and for changes to the system, and people were beginning to challenge the government. End the War was still a decade off, however, with Vietnam still around the corner. Choice *A* is incorrect because the Civil Rights Movement, led by leaders like Martin Luther King Jr., dominated the 1960s leading up to the Civil Rights Act. Choices *C* and *D* are incorrect because women's rights were also key throughout the decade, as well as the movement for LGBTQ rights.

5. D: Separate but equal doctrine. Brown v. Board of Education set the stage for the fight for civil rights throughout the United States and was the first true rebuff to segregation. It overturned the separate but equal doctrine laid out in the Plessy v. Ferguson Supreme Court case. Choice *A* is incorrect because the doctrine of judicial review was established one hundred years earlier and has never been overturned. Choice *B* is incorrect because the public safety exception has to do with Miranda Rights. Choice *C* is incorrect because the due process doctrine doesn't apply here.

Reagan and Conservatism

Ronald Reagan's Presidential Victory

In the presidential election of 1980, Republican nominee **Ronald Reagan** carried forty-four states and the Republicans won a majority in the U.S. Senate after twenty-eight years of Democratic control. Reagan presented an optimistic message and broadcast a television advertisement that proclaimed, "It's morning again in America." He promised to restore America's military power, cut government regulations for many industries, and reduce taxes. Reagan enjoyed the support of resurgent conservative Christian evangelicals, who wanted to restore morality to American society. They were particularly concerned about issues such as abortion. The **Moral Majority**, founded by Baptist minister Jerry Falwell in 1979, was one key group that helped Reagan win the election. This coalition helped realign party loyalties as more liberal Republicans and conservative Democrats shifted their allegiance to support Reagan's platform.

Conservative Efforts to Counteract Liberal Programs

Conservatives' demands to shrink the size and scope of the government reached new heights with Ronald Reagan's election in 1980. They argued that programs championed by liberal administrations were counterproductive in stimulating economic growth and reducing poverty. In general, conservatives believe the free market fights poverty more efficiently and effectively than government programs; therefore, they often singularly focus on ways to spur economic growth. According to free-market theories, a rising tide of economic prosperity would lift American households into the middle class and beyond. However, this has not worked in practice. Despite the unprecedented generation of wealth during the late twentieth and early twenty-first centuries, Americans' real wages did not meaningfully increase, and the United States has plummeted down global ranks of economic mobility.

From 1980 through the present, Republican politicians have been more successful at cutting taxes and reducing government revenue than drastically cutting the largest social programs, such as Social Security and Medicare. Entitlement programs are extremely popular among constituents, including those who might otherwise oppose government spending, and the law of inertia weighs against making massive structural changes to long-running programs. The budgets for these programs are also often protected by law, making them even more difficult to change. Although liberal voters have consistently rejected spending cuts, the Democratic establishment is far more flexible. For example, the Democratic Clinton administration supported and secured more aggressive social safety net cuts than most of his Republican counterparts.

Policy Debates

American policymakers have continuously debated free-trade agreements, social programs, and financial regulation since 1980.

Free-trade agreements, such as the **North American Free Trade Agreement** (1994), have come under heavy scrutiny as more corporations outsource positions to reduce labor costs. Despite devastating job losses, there's elite bipartisan agreement that free trade reduces consumer costs and generates

economic growth. However, the administration of President **Donald Trump** (2017–2021) placed unprecedented scrutiny on free trade as it sought to revive American manufacturing.

The scope of America's social safety net has faced existential challenges since the early 1980s. Both political establishments categorically reject European-style cradle-to-grave social service systems; however, there's fierce debate over whether programs should exist at all. Some liberals have fought to expand existing programs, whereas Republicans have often demanded privatization and balanced budgets.

Debate continues to rage regarding financial regulation. Many argue that deregulation has worsened the severity of bust cycles, which routinely impoverish American households and enrich financial elites. Additionally, they claim that the system is highly unstable and would have entirely collapsed during the **Great Recession** (2007–2009) without government intervention. However, others argue that government regulation and policies actually created the Great Recession. Although there seems to be broad public support for reform, only nominal and piecemeal legislation has ever been implemented.

Conservative Beliefs Advanced After 1980

Ronald Reagan's landslide victories in the 1980 and 1984 presidential elections birthed the modern Republican Party. President Reagan crafted a coalition consisting of elite business interests, middle-class households, social conservatives, and Christian evangelicals. The combination of pro-growth economic policies and social conservatism is still the driving force behind American conservatism today.

Pro-growth policies seek to limit the government's role in the economy. President Reagan pursued a distinct economic agenda that's commonly referred to as **Reaganomics**, which included slashing taxes, eliminating social programs, repealing business regulations, removing government oversight, and restraining labor unions. Modern conservatives have adopted Reaganomics with few exceptions. When out of power, Republican politicians vehemently resist the expansion of social services based on concerns over national debt.

Similarly, social conservatism seeks to protect the private sphere from government intrusion and defend traditional values, such as two-parent households and abstinence before marriage. Ronald Reagan fostered a tight relationship with evangelical leaders, which led to the Republican Party elevating its rejection of abortion and same-sex marriage to high-profile policy positions. Modern-day conservatives have continued to fiercely oppose abortion, but after **Obergefell v. Hodges** (2015) legalized same-sex marriage, conservatives have shifted toward upholding the concept of two genders in opposition to transgenderism, which they often claim is detrimental to women and girls, particularly in competitive sports. In addition, present-day conservative values often come into conflict with wide-spread conceptions of multiculturalism and political correctness.

Debates Over Social Issues

Heated debates have erupted throughout the United States over a wide range of social issues, including immigration, diversity, and gender.

In relatively recent history, immigration has become the single most divisive political issue since slavery. Conservatives in general support severe restrictions on immigration, which can include rejecting amnesty for undocumented immigrants. Immigration reform has become an incredibly hot button issue

for politicians on both the left and the right and likely had an effect on the losses of Republican House majority leader Eric Cantor in 2014 and House speaker John Boehner in 2015.

Diversity, gender, and family issues have similarly fueled long-term culture wars in recent times. Conservatives have consistently and systematically opposed the expanded application of civil rights-era legislation. Although liberals generally champion diversity, conservatives protect traditional American values and culture, such as Christianity and European heritage. Similar sides exist in the debate over sexuality, with liberals defending tolerance and conservatives holding to traditional interpretations of sex. Likewise, gender issues have escalated as more women entered the workforce in the 1980s and then climbed the corporate ladder. Enduring controversies related to gender include the gender wage gap, sexual harassment, sexual violence, and the transition away from traditional family roles.

The End of the Cold War

Reagan's Anti-Communist Efforts

President Ronald Reagan pursued an aggressive anti-Communist policy program and conveyed his anti-Communist objectives through speeches, diplomatic efforts, and military decisions.

First, the Reagan administration demanded and secured the largest peacetime buildup of conventional and nuclear weapons in American history. During his first term alone, officially declared American military spending doubled.

Second, the Reagan administration was more covert in its application of raw American military power, particularly in avoiding large-scale confrontations with the Soviet Union. However, that's not to say President Reagan was a peacenik. One of the Reagan administration's more successful proxy wars was financing and arming the *mujahideen* in the **Afghan-Soviet War** (1979–1989). On the other end of the spectrum, the **Iran-Contra Affair** (1985–1987) involved serial violations of a federal embargo on weapon sales to Iran and Reagan officials using the cash payments to illegally arm right-wing Nicaraguan rebel groups (*Contras*), who systematically committed human rights violations.

Third, President Reagan artfully delivered high-profile speeches to strengthen diplomatic initiatives. Most famously, Reagan's **"Evil Empire"** speech (1983) framed the Cold War as an existential struggle between good and evil that solidified America's capitalist coalition. Likewise, President Reagan famously implored Soviet leaders to tear down the **Berlin Wall** in 1987, which occurred two years later.

Ending the Cold War

The Reagan administration placed maximum pressure on the Soviet Union in the hopes of further destabilizing the Soviet system as it teetered toward an outright collapse. Most broadly, President Reagan pursued a policy of peace through strength. In practice, this involved an aggressive expansion of America's nuclear stockpile and massive public investments in military preparedness.

President Reagan understood that the Soviet Union couldn't afford to keep pace with American defense spending due to its many financial and political issues. Combined with a decade of stagnant economic growth, the political situation was in turmoil as Eastern European nationalist movements began to increasingly seek independence. As a result, Soviet leaders were forced to decide between falling behind in the arms race or suffering a deadly blow to their economic system.

With military pressure serving as the proverbial stick, President Reagan treated diplomacy as the carrot to entice Soviet leaders into negotiating nuclear weapon reductions, reducing tensions with the West, and implementing liberal economic and political reforms. Between 1985 and 1988, President Reagan held four diplomatic summits with Soviet leader **Mikhail Gorbachev**, and they formed an unlikely but fruitful working relationship that produced several important treaties, including the **Intermediate-Range Nuclear Forces (INF) Treaty** (1987).

The Cold War ended in 1991 after the Berlin Wall fell (1989) and the Soviet Union dissolved (1991).

Post-War Position

The end of the Cold War left the United States in a delicate but powerful position as the sole remaining global superpower. In the absence of Soviet pushback, the United States rushed to open diplomatic channels and integrate former Soviet states in Eastern Europe into the global capitalist system. Along with free-trade agreements, the United States was eager to expand the membership of international organizations it largely controlled, including the North Atlantic Treaty Organization (NATO), the International Monetary Fund (IMF), and the World Trade Organization (WTO).

Unlike other historical imperial projects, American hegemony is unique in its reliance on soft power, particularly consumer culture and entertainment, to popularize its free-trade and corporate agenda. Still, the American imperial regime has faced a barrage of geopolitical challenges in defending the international system it largely dominates. This has forced American policymakers to decide whether and how the United States should function as a world police, either by authorizing UN peacekeeping missions or conducting military interventions. Some of these interventions have been disastrous for the United States' reputation. More specifically, the **War on Terror** (2001–present) has dealt a serious blow to America's standing within the global community as a good faith actor and worthy leader.

A Changing Economy

Digital Communication Advancements Increase Economic Productivity

Despite the recurring cycles of financial busts and soaring wealth inequality, digital communication innovations have spurred unbelievable gains in productivity since 1980. In fact, even when controlling for inflation, American productivity nearly tripled between 1980 and 2019, as measured by the difference in real gross domestic product (GDP). Digital communications first elevated production in the 1980s when television established itself as an essential platform for mass marketing. The internet and mobile phones have since further expedited commercial interactions and accelerated industrial automation. Finally, some digital communication companies, such as Google and Facebook, now rank among the most profitable corporations in the world.

Unlike previous communication innovations, the internet allows users to exchange libraries of information and audiovisual content with lightning speed. As such, digital communications increased the efficiency of global economic relationships like never before, and Americans were in the strongest position to consolidate market control given the United States' disproportionate influence within the global capitalist system it crafted after the end of the Cold War. From the comfort of their homes, enterprising Americans could source and manufacture products overseas, create global marketing campaigns, provide technological assistance, and pursue a host of other economic opportunities in the newly integrated global market.

Technological Innovations and Social Networks

Technological innovations have completely transformed American daily life and culture. Computing power has produced exponential increases in production efficiencies, fueling the economic sprint toward mechanical automation. For example, the iPhone X from Apple® has approximately 100,000 times more computing power than the computer that was used to send the Apollo 11 mission to the moon in 1969. Enhanced computing power has been a continual driver of growth and opened myriad employment opportunities in digital-based economic sectors. In addition, the internet constructed and organized a network of shocking complexity and scope. Social networks have created digital platforms with billions of members.

Mobile phones possibly had the most dynamic and transformative impact on daily life by bringing the power of a laptop computer in the pocket of nearly every American citizen, streamlining communication on all fronts. With mobile phones, Americans could reliably and immediately communicate with their contacts in endless ways, ranging from phone calls to social media platforms. This was a major breakthrough for businesses looking to directly engage with customers, and the development of location services such as geographic information systems (GIS) and global positioning systems (GPS) resulted in mobile phones functioning like interactive maps. Along with processing power, mobile phones are equipped with high-end cameras, adding an audiovisual component to social and commercial interactions.

Employment Changes

The American economy has radically shifted from industrial-oriented to service-oriented sectors over the last several decades. As free trade expanded after the Cold War, American manufacturing declined so rapidly that the industrial Midwest became commonly known as the **Rust Belt**. With steady blue-collar employment increasingly difficult to find, many former factory workers were forced to make do in the hospitality sector and gig economy, or with short-term contractual work. Many economists and politicians have pushed for funding to provide for a smooth transition; however, companies in the emergent technological sectors have led the transition toward a workforce full of independent contractors instead of employees to save money and boost profits.

President Reagan's privatization blitz pushed American unions to the edge of a cliff, and globalization has threatened to deliver the death stroke. Union membership consistently declined for decades as American companies continue to scramble for cheaper sources of labor. The decline of union membership has coincided with the stagnation of working and middle-class wages. Free market enthusiasts contend that American unions aren't viable under the prevailing market conditions because businesses cannot compete in the hypercompetitive global marketplace without remaining flexible.

Stagnation of Real Wages

Ever since the country's founding, the **American Dream** has served as a beacon of hope for people aspiring to reach the middle class as embodied by home ownership, self-sufficiency, and disposable income. Given the vast amounts of undeveloped land within its territories, the American Dream remained a more achievable reality than the socioeconomic mobility on offer anywhere else in the world for centuries. However, automation, globalization, and privatization have taken a hatchet to working and middle-class families' **real wages**, or wages after adjustments for inflation. At the same time, most white-collar positions have experienced significant real wage growth, particularly at the

executive level. The resulting record-breaking economic inequality has since threatened to unravel American economic, political, and social systems.

The **millennial generation**, consisting of those born between 1980 and 1995, has been hit the hardest by wage stagnation and economic inequality. For example, millennials account for approximately 25 percent of the population while holding an estimated three percent of the country's wealth. They earn less in real wages than their grandparents' generations because the real costs for housing, education, and health care have all skyrocketed. On top of their middling economic prospects, young generations of Americans will be forced to assume and manage the mountain of debt amassed by earlier generations.

Migration and Immigration in the 1990s and 2000s

Southern and Western Influences

Although all of American society has rapidly evolved since 1980, nowhere is the transformation more self-evident than in the American South and West.

Like the rest of the United States, the economy in the American South has become more service oriented and urbanized. For the first time in history, several southern states have grown to become some of the wealthiest in the United States. Texas boasts the second-highest GDP, and Florida ranks fourth. In terms of politics and culture, the ascendance of African American communities has challenged traditional southern conservatism. Many southern states have majority African American populations, and those communities have gained more independence and cultural influence in relatively recent history.

The American West has experienced a staggering amount of development since 1980. California is the center of American entertainment as well as a cradle of technological innovation. Economic prosperity has led to California becoming the most populous state by a wide margin, and its GDP is the fifth highest in the entire world. Compared with most other regions in the country, the politics in the West feature a broader ideological range, and Western culture tends to place more emphasis on tolerance and acceptance than anywhere else in the country.

Latin American and Asian Immigration

Immigrants' country of origin has shifted toward Asia, the Caribbean, Central America, and South America since 1980. As executive-level and academic interactions have increased throughout the global economy, American-based multinational corporations have helped skilled workers obtain visas to work in sensitive and critical industries, such as technology and energy. On average, such workers have been arriving from China, India, Japan, South Korea, and South America since 1980. In addition, many immigrants continue to embark for the traditional purpose of pursuing the American Dream. Asian immigrants often seek to establish small businesses in the United States, enter the middle class, and help their children obtain a quality education. Most Asian and South American immigrants settle in metropolitan areas with sizable immigrant populations, such as Chinatowns and Koreatowns.

Central American and Caribbean immigrant groups differ markedly from their contemporaries. Compared to Asian and South American immigrants, they are significantly more likely to be refugees fleeing from abject poverty, societal chaos, and perpetual violence. Although many of these immigrants

find safe havens in large cities, they also commonly work as migrant laborers in rural area, serving as a critical source of cheap agricultural labor.

Challenges of the 21st Century

The War on Terror

On **September 11, 2001 (9/11)**, members of the al-Qaeda terrorist organization hijacked American airliners and successfully crashed two planes into the Twin Towers of the World Trade Center in New York and one plane into the Pentagon in Arlington, VA. A fourth plane crashed in a field in Pennsylvania when the passengers fought the terrorists who hijacked the plane. There were roughly 3,000 deaths caused by these attacks; most of them were civilians. In response, President **George W. Bush** leveraged public anger to launch large-scale invasions of Afghanistan and Iraq.

The **War in Afghanistan** (2001–2021) is the longest war in American history. The Taliban, a fundamentalist Islamic organization that controlled Afghanistan from 1996–2001, sheltered and provided material aid to al-Qaeda's leader, **Osama bin Laden**. The American invasion forced the Taliban into a strategic retreat; however, as time passed, the United States began prioritizing other conflicts. Both the Obama and Trump administrations considered the idea of a full withdrawal of U.S. troops; however, they feared the consequences of abandoning Afghanistan's new and relatively democratic government. As it turns out, they were right to do so. The Biden administration pulled out of Afghanistan in 2021, with 95% of troops out of the county by July 31, 2021. By August 15, 2021, the Taliban captured the capital, Kabul, and the Afghan government fell. The last American evacuation flight left Kabul on August 30, 2021.

The **Iraq War** (2003–2011) began with the Bush administration receiving incorrect intelligence information tying Iraqi dictator **Saddam Hussein** to weapons of mass destruction and presenting that information to Congress, the United Nations, and the mainstream media. Although the American military quickly annihilated the Iraqi state, Iraqis' resistance to the occupation led to a sectarian insurrection that undermined all hopes of building a stable and self-sufficient government. The conflict is widely considered to be one of the greatest strategic foreign blunders in American history.

Activists challenged whether the **War on Terror** (2001–present) was worth its costs to human rights and civil liberties. In the immediate aftermath of the 9/11 terrorist attacks, Congress rushed to pass the **Authorization for Use of Military Force** (AUMF) of 2001, and only Barbara Lee (D-CA) voted against the bill that became law on September 18, 2001. A second AUMF, "Authorization for the Use of Military Force Against Iraq," became law on October 16, 2002. Human rights activists feared this broad delegation of executive power essentially gave the White House blanket permission to wage a global war. The AUMFs remain law in 2022, although as of June 2021 a bill has passed the House of Representatives to repeal them.

Shortly after the 2001 AUMF, conservative Congress led the charge to introduce legislation known as the **Patriot Act** to expand the War on Terror into digital spaces. Congress believed monitoring the conversations of suspected terrorists was critical for protecting the homeland. During the Bush and Obama administrations, cabinet-level public officials repeatedly and adamantly denied under oath that all American citizens were subject to widespread surveillance. **Edward Snowden**, a National Security Agency (NSA) contractor, proved these denials to be categorically false when he leaked evidence of

domestic surveillance networks to the press in 2013. No government official was ever charged with perjury, and little has been done to reform the system.

Climate Change and the Dependence on Fossil Fuels

American policymakers and activists have raised concerns over the United States' dependence on fossil fuels and the resulting damage inflicted on the environment. Although the primary proximate cause of the War on Terror was inarguably the 9/11 terrorist attacks, American interests in the Middle East date back to at least World War II.

The United States and its Western European allies have long sought to maximize their influence and control over the region's oil production. Saddam Hussein had previously challenged American oil interests in Kuwait, and American policymakers were eager to prevent any future meddling. Overall, the United States' dependence on the global oil trade was a major contributing factor behind American invasions and occupations in the Middle East.

Aside from seeking to reduce American military commitments, concerns about climate change have raised questions about oil and resource consumption in the United States. Global temperatures have increased for decades, and some scientific experts have concluded that economic activity is driving this trend. Although green energy has gained significant popular support in recent years, questions remain regarding what actions the United States can and should take unilaterally or in coalition with other nations in light of global concerns over pollution and climate change.

The United States as a Superpower

For over twenty years after the terrorist attacks on the World Trade Center in New York City, the United States was entangled in the politics of the Middle East, and to this day the United States is still working to find ways to cope with the ongoing threat of global terrorism. The events of September 11, 2011—often referred to simply as **9/11**—galvanized the United States of America into a self-declared war on terrorism. These events have challenged and changed many relationships between the United States and the world. Some scholars, for instance, saw the war on terrorism as the final blow to old Cold War politics. However, recent military events in Eastern Europe, Syria, and the broader Middle East indicate that the Cold War may be "heating up" again on the geopolitical stage.

The United States' economy remains the largest in the world, making it a strong contender to continue its role as "Leader of the Free World." Although U.S. economic hegemony has declined, relatively, in an era of globalization and **North American Free Trade Agreement** (NAFTA), the United States is poised to remain an economic player in the coming decades.

Practice Quiz

Questions 1–3 refer to the map below.

Map Depicting Population of the United States of America (2011)

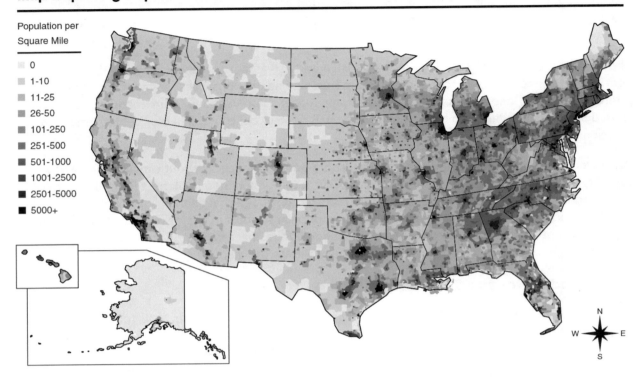

1. Which measurement does the data on the map primarily illustrate?
   a. Agricultural density
   b. Arithmetic density
   c. Physiological density
   d. Population distribution

2. Which technique does the map use to plot the relevant information?
   a. Area patterns
   b. Clustering
   c. Dispersal
   d. Line patterns

3. Based on the map, which region is most likely to have the highest population density?
   a. Northeast
   b. Northwest
   c. Central
   d. Southeast

Please use the map below to answer Questions 4 and 5:

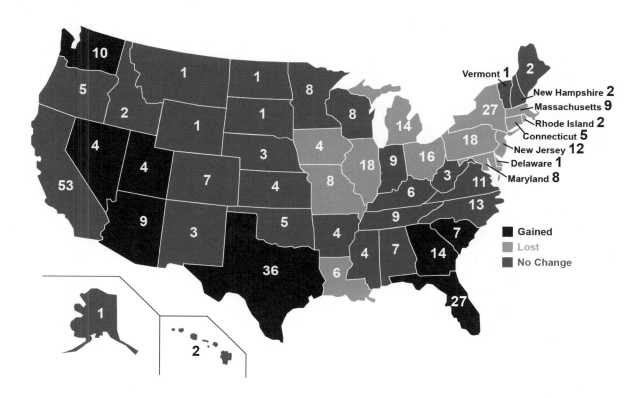

4. How many total electoral votes are accounted for by the states that gained representatives as a result of the 2010 U.S. census?
   a. 123
   b. 111
   c. 97
   d. 88

5. Which of the following statements is reflected in the map?
   a. More states gained or lost representatives than experienced no change at all.
   b. Most states that gained representatives were concentrated in the Pacific Northwest and Great Plains regions.
   c. Most states that lost representatives were concentrated in the Midwest and Northeast.
   d. More less-populous states lost representatives than more-populous states.

See answers on next page.

Answer Explanations

1. B: The map depicts "Population per Square Mile," and this data is represented in the shading pattern. Arithmetic density is calculated by dividing a population by some unit of measure. Given the information contained in the title and legend, the map is depicting the arithmetic density of the United States. Thus, Choice *B* is the correct answer. Agricultural density is calculated by dividing the number of farmers by the amount of arable land. Nothing in this map suggests it relates to agriculture, so Choice *A* is incorrect. Physiological density is calculated by dividing the total population by the amount of arable land. The legend doesn't refer to arable land, so Choice *C* is incorrect. Population distribution relates to the patterns of movement and settlement for a group. The map only shows the current population per square mile, not where the population has previously been, so Choice *D* is incorrect.

2. A: The map plots information through slight differences in shading patterns, which symbolize various levels of arithmetic density. Area patterns plot data based on differences in the pattern. Thus, Choice *A* is the correct answer. While clustering is often used to analyze population density, the map is using shading. The defining characteristic of clustering patterns is a series of points with tight clusters of points illustrating areas with high population density. Therefore, Choice *B* is incorrect. Dispersal patterns are used to plot population distribution, so Choice *C* is incorrect. Line patterns illustrate relationships based on the space between lines, and the map doesn't contain this type of line. Therefore, Choice *D* is incorrect.

3. A: The legend indicates that the areas with the darkest shading have the highest population density. Compared to the rest of the country, the entire Northeast region is a much darker shade of gray, with some areas appearing almost black. Thus, Choice *A* is the correct answer. The Northwest region has an area of high population density on the coast, but it doesn't match the Northeast region. Therefore, Choice *B* is incorrect. The Central region has a fairly high population density compared to the Northwest region and the Southwest region, but the shading isn't as dark as it is in the Northeast region. Therefore, Choice *C* is incorrect. The Southeast region has the second highest population density on the map. Although the Florida coasts have incredibly dark shading, the rest of the Southeast region doesn't match the Northeast region, so Choice *D* is incorrect.

4. B: If you add up the representatives in states that gained representatives (South Carolina, Georgia, Florida, Texas, Arizona, Utah, Nevada, and Washington), the total is 111. Therefore, Choices *A, C,* and *D* are incorrect.

5. C: Most states that lost representatives are located in the Rust Belt—the Midwest and Northeast—as illustrated by the light grey states on the map. Choice *A* is incorrect because more states remained unchanged than lost or grained representation. Choice *B* is incorrect because most states that gained representation were scattered in the South and the West, not the Pacific Northwest and Great Plains. Choice *D* is incorrect because this map does not provide information on population levels in the various states.

Practice Test

Multiple-Choice Questions

Questions 1–5 are based on the following passage:

Christopher Columbus is often credited for discovering America. This is incorrect. First, it is impossible to "discover" somewhere where people already live; however, Christopher Columbus did explore places in the New World that were previously untouched by Europe, so the term "explorer" would be more accurate. Another correction must be made, as well: Christopher Columbus was not the first European explorer to reach the present-day Americas! Rather, it was Leif Erikson who first came to the New World and contacted the natives, nearly five hundred years before Christopher Columbus.

Leif Erikson, the son of Erik the Red (a famous Viking outlaw and explorer in his own right), was born in either 970 or 980, depending on which historian you believe. His own family, though, did not raise Leif, which was a Viking tradition. Instead, one of Erik's prisoners taught Leif reading and writing, languages, sailing, and weaponry. At age 12, Leif was considered a man and returned to his family. He killed a man during a dispute shortly after his return, and the council banished the Erikson clan to Greenland.

In 999, Leif left Greenland and traveled to Norway, where he would serve as a guard to King Olaf Tryggvason. It was there that he became a convert to Christianity. Leif later tried to return home with the intention of taking supplies and spreading Christianity to Greenland, however his ship was blown off course and he arrived in a strange new land: present day Newfoundland, Canada.

When he finally returned to his adopted homeland, Greenland, Leif consulted with a merchant who had also seen the shores of this previously unknown land we now know as Canada. The son of the legendary Viking explorer then gathered a crew of 35 men and set sail. Leif became the first European to set foot in the New World as he explored present-day Baffin Island and Labrador, Canada. His crew called the land "Vinland," since it was plentiful with grapes.

During their time in present-day Newfoundland, Leif's expedition made contact with the natives, whom they referred to as Skraelings (which translates to "wretched ones" in Norse). There are several secondhand accounts of their meetings. Some contemporaries described trade between the peoples. Other accounts describe clashes where the Skraelings defeated the Viking explorers with long spears, while still others claim the Vikings dominated the natives. Regardless of the circumstances, it seems that the

This material is provided for exam preparation purposes only and does not indicate an endorsement of any specific scientific, political, or religious point of view. © TPB Publishing. You have been licensed one copy of this document for personal use only. Any other reproduction or redistribution is strictly prohibited. All rights reserved.

Vikings made contact of some kind. This happened around 1000, nearly five hundred years before Columbus famously sailed the ocean blue.

Eventually, in 1003, Leif set sail for home and arrived at Greenland with a ship full of timber. In 1020, seventeen years later, the legendary Viking died. Many believe that Leif Erikson should receive more credit for his contributions in exploring the New World.

1. Which of the following best describes how the author generally presents the information?
   a. Chronological order
   b. Comparison-contrast
   c. Cause-effect
   d. Conclusion-premises

2. Which of the following is an opinion, rather than a historical fact, expressed by the author?
   a. Leif Erikson was definitely the son of Erik the Red; however, historians debate the year of his birth.
   b. Leif Erikson's crew called the land "Vinland," since it was plentiful with grapes.
   c. Leif Erikson deserves more credit for his contributions in exploring the New World.
   d. Leif Erikson explored the Americas nearly five hundred years before Christopher Columbus.

3. Which of the following most accurately describes the author's main conclusion?
   a. Leif Erikson is a legendary Viking explorer.
   b. Leif Erikson deserves more credit for exploring America hundreds of years before Columbus.
   c. Spreading Christianity motivated Leif Erikson's expeditions more than any other factor.
   d. Leif Erikson contacted the natives nearly five hundred years before Columbus.

4. Which of the following best describes the author's intent in the passage?
   a. To entertain
   b. To inform
   c. To alert
   d. To suggest

5. Which of the following can be logically inferred from the passage?
   a. The Vikings disliked exploring the New World.
   b. Leif Erikson's banishment from Iceland led to his exploration of present-day Canada.
   c. Leif Erikson never shared his stories of exploration with the King of Norway.
   d. Historians have difficulty definitively pinpointing events in the Vikings' history.

Questions 6 and 7 are based on the graphic that follows a brief introduction to the topic:

The United States Constitution directs Congress to conduct periodic censuses to determine the country's population. The United States Census Bureau carries out the surveys and collects both population numbers and demographic information. In 1790, then Secretary of State Thomas Jefferson conducted the first census, and the most recent U.S. census was in 2010. The next U.S. census will be the first to be issued primarily through the Internet.

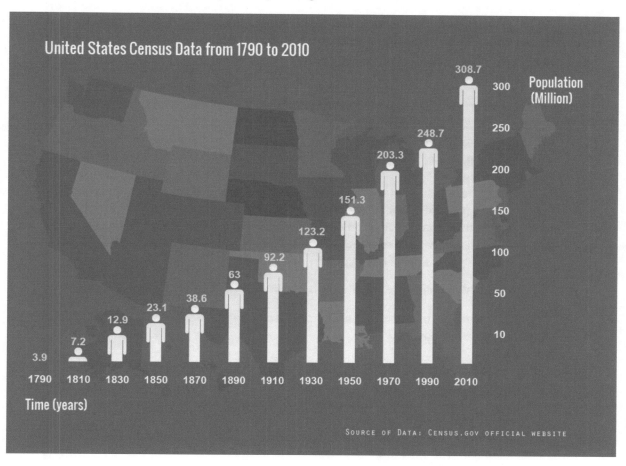

6. In which of the following years was the United States population less than it was in 1930?
    a. 1950
    b. 1970
    c. 1910
    d. 1990

7. In what twenty-year interval did the population increase the most?
    a. From 1930 to 1950
    b. From 1950 to 1970
    c. From 1970 to 1990
    d. From 1990 to 2010

Questions 8–12 are based on the following passage:

Four score and seven years ago our fathers brought forth on this continent, a new nation, conceived in Liberty, and dedicated to the proposition that all men are created equal.

Now we are engaged in a great civil war, testing whether that nation, or any nation so conceived and so dedicated, can long endure. We are met on a great battle-field of that war. We have come to dedicate a portion of that field, as a final resting place for those who here gave their lives that that nation might live. It is altogether fitting and proper that we should do this.

But, in a larger sense, we can not dedicate—we can not consecrate—we cannot hallow—this ground. The brave men, living and dead, who struggled here, have consecrated it, far above our poor power to add or detract. The world will little note, nor long remember what we say here, but it can never forget what they did here. It is for us the living, rather, to be dedicated here to the unfinished work which they who fought here have thus far so nobly advanced. It is rather for us to be here dedicated to the great task remaining before us—that from these honored dead we take increased devotion to that cause for which they gave the last full measure of devotion—that we here highly resolve that these dead shall not have died in vain—that this nation, under God, shall have a new birth of freedom—and that government of the people, by the people, for the people, shall not perish from the earth.

Abraham Lincoln's "Address Delivered at the Dedication of the Cemetery at Gettysburg," 1863

8. Which of the following is the best description for the phrase *four score and seven years ago*?
    a.   A unit of measurement
    b.   A period of time
    c.   A literary movement
    d.   A statement of political reform

9. What is the setting of this text?
    a.   A battleship off of the coast of France
    b.   A desert plain on the Sahara Desert
    c.   A battlefield in North America
    d.   The residence of Abraham Lincoln

10. What message is the author trying to convey through this address?
    a.   The audience should perpetuate the ideals of freedom that the soldiers died fighting for.
    b.   The audience should honor the dead by establishing an annual memorial service.
    c.   The audience should form a militia that would overturn the current political structure.
    d.   The audience should forget the lives that were lost and discredit the soldiers.

166

11. In the following selection, what does the word *resolve* mean?

... we here highly resolve that these dead shall not have died in vain—that this nation, under God, shall have a new birth of freedom—and that government of the people, by the people, for the people, shall not perish from the earth.

a. Foresee
b. Request
c. Prescribe
d. Decide

12. What is the effect of Lincoln's statement in the following excerpt from the passage?

But, in a larger sense, we can not dedicate—we can not consecrate—we can not hallow—this ground. The brave men, living and dead, who struggled here, have consecrated it, far above our poor power to add or detract.

a. His comparison emphasizes the great sacrifice of the soldiers who fought in the war.
b. His comparison serves as a reminder of the inadequacies of his audience.
c. His comparison serves as a catalyst for guilt and shame among audience members.
d. His comparison attempts to illuminate the great differences between soldiers and civilians.

Questions 13–14 are based on the following passage:

In general, the orientations on the left emphasize social and economic equality and advocate for government intervention to achieve it. Orientations on the right of the spectrum generally value the existing and historical political institutions and oppose government intervention, especially in regard to the economy.

Communism is a radical political ideology that seeks to establish common ownership over production and abolish social status and money. Communists believe that the world is split between two social classes—capitalists and the working class (often referred to as the proletariat). Communist politics assert that conflict arises from the inequality between the ruling class and the working class; thus, communism favors a classless society.

Conservatism is a political ideology that prioritizes traditional institutions within a culture and civilization. Conservatives, in general, oppose modern developments and value stability. Since conservatism depends on the traditional institution, this ideology differs greatly from country to country. Conservatives often emphasize the traditional family structure and the importance of individual self-reliance. Fiscal conservatism is one of the most common variants, and in general, the proponents of fiscal conservatism oppose government spending and public debt.

Progressivism maintains that progress in the form of scientific and technological advancement, social change, and economic development improve the quality of human life. Progressive ideals include the view that the political and economic interests of the ruling class suppress progress, which results in perpetual social and economic inequality.

Libertarianism opposes state intervention on society and the economy. Libertarians advocate for a weak central government, favoring more local rule, and seek to maximize personal

autonomy and protect personal freedom. Libertarians often follow a conservative approach to government, especially in the context of power and intervention, but favor a progressive approach to rights and freedom, especially those tied to personal liberty, like freedom of speech.

Liberalism was developed during the Age of Enlightenment in opposition to absolute monarchy, royal privilege, and state religion. In general, liberalism emphasizes liberty and equality, and liberals support freedom of speech, freedom of religion, free markets, civil rights, gender equality, and secular governance. Liberals support government intervention into private matters to further social justice and fight inequality; thus, liberals often favor social welfare organizations and economic safety nets to combat income inequality.

Fascism is a form of totalitarianism that became popular in Europe after World War I. Fascists advocate for a centralized government led by an all-powerful dictator, tasked with preparing for total war and mobilizing all resources to benefit the state. The concept of hierarchy (the ruler above the ruled, the ruling class over all others, the fascist nation above other nations, etc.) is a key element of fascist ideology. It vehemently opposes all forms of egalitarianism. This orientation's distinguishing features include a consolidated and centralized government.

Socialism is closely tied to an economic system. Socialists prioritize the health of the community over the rights of individuals, seeking collective and equitable ownership over the means of production. Socialists tend to be willing to work to enact Socialist policies, like social security, universal health care, unemployment benefits, and other programs related to building a societal safety net.

13. Using the information from the passage above and the introduction about left-axis and right-axis political orientations, which of the following correctly categorizes the orientations mentioned in the passage?
    a.   Left-axis ideologies: Socialism, Progressivism, Liberalism; Right-axis ideologies: Fascism, Libertarianism, Communism, Conservatism
    b.   Left-axis ideologies: Socialism, Progressivism, Liberalism, Communism; Right-axis ideologies: Fascism, Libertarianism, Conservatism
    c.   Left-axis ideologies: Socialism, Progressivism, Libertarianism, Liberalism; Right-axis ideologies: Fascism, Communism, Conservatism
    d.   Left-axis ideologies: Socialism, Progressivism, Libertarianism, Communism; Right-axis ideologies: Fascism, Liberalism, Conservatism

14. Which of the following correctly states the main difference between Fascism and Libertarianism?
    a.   Fascists favor a powerful, centralized government, whereas Libertarians favor individual liberty.
    b.   Fascists prioritize governmental spending on strengthening the military, whereas Libertarians prioritize government spending on societal safety nets.
    c.   Fascists favor progressive social structures, whereas Libertarians are only progressive in adopting new technology.
    d.   Fascists believe governmental involvement in terms of power and intervention should be minimal, whereas Libertarians prioritize governmental spending on strengthening the military.

Questions 15–18 are based on the following passage:

Immigrants and emigrants move for physical, cultural, economic, and political reasons. An immigrant is a person who comes from another country to the one currently being discussed, while an emigrant is a person who leaves their home country to settle elsewhere. Geographers traditionally separate reasons for migration into push and pull factors. Political push factors include war, government-induced violence and intimidation, genocide, or oppression. Economic push factors include economic depressions or panics, among other factors. Political pull factors include things like the lure of democracy, safety, and liberty. Economic pull factors include job creation, higher wages, and low unemployment rates. Environmental push factors include flooding, natural disasters, droughts, nuclear contamination, and water contamination. Environmental pull factors include more hospitable climates, low chances of natural disasters, and outdoor aesthetics.

15. Using the information from the passage, as well as your knowledge of social studies concepts, which of the following statements is correct?
    a. Refugees may immigrate from their country because of political push factors.
    b. Refugees may emigrate from their country because of political push factors.
    c. Refugees may immigrate from their country because of political pull factors.
    d. Refugees may emigrate from their country because of political pull factors.

16. During the 1960s–1980s, deindustrialization in cities in the Industrial North (now called the "Rust Belt"), including hubs like Buffalo, Cleveland, Chicago, and Milwaukee, would be considered an example of which of the following?
    a. Political push factor
    b. Political pull factor
    c. Economic push factor
    d. Economic pull factor

17. In the late 19th and early 20th centuries, millions of people immigrated to the United States from Europe because they were enamored by the purported freedoms in the United States. This would be an example of which of the following?
    a. Political push factor
    b. Political pull factor
    c. Economic push factor
    d. Economic pull factor

18. The relocation of many people from the Sahel region of North Africa to other areas because of intense droughts is an example of which of the following?
    a. Political push factor
    b. Political pull factor
    c. Environmental push factor
    d. Environmental pull factor

Question 19 is based on the following map:

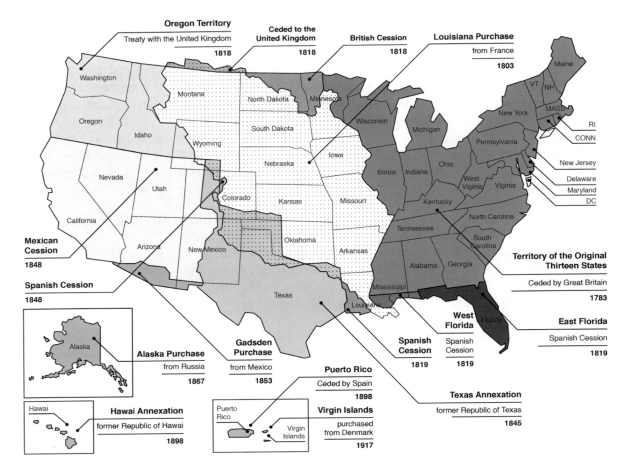

19. What current state did the United States gain through military force against a non-native nation-state?
    a. Nebraska
    b. Missouri
    c. Alaska
    d. Nevada

20. Which of these choices BEST describes a participatory democracy?
    a. A system in which only the educated and wealthy members of society vote and decide upon the leaders of the country
    b. A system in which groups come together to advance certain select interests
    c. A system that emphasizes everyone contributing to the political system
    d. A system in which one group makes decisions for the population at large

Questions 21 and 22 are based on the following table:

Branch	Role	Checks & Balances on Other Branches	
Executive	Carries out the laws	**Legislative Branch** • Proposes laws • Vetoes laws • Calls special sessions of Congress • Makes appointments • Negotiates foreign treaties	**Judicial Branch** • Appoints federal judges • Grants pardons to federal offenders
Legislative	Makes the laws	**Executive Branch** • Has the ability to override a President's veto • Confirms executive appointments • Ratifies treaties • Has the ability to declare war • Appropriates money • Has the ability to impeach and remove President	**Judicial Branch** • Creates lower federal courts • Has the ability to impeach and remove judges • Has the ability to propose amendments to overrule judicial decisions • Approves appointments of federal judges
Judicial	Interprets the laws	**Executive Branch** • Has the ability to declare executive actions unconstitutional	**Legislative Branch** • Has the ability to declare acts of Congress unconstitutional

21. Using the table provided and your understanding of checks and balances, which of the following is true regarding legislation?

a. Members of Congress debate and vote on legislation, although the president may request that legislators consider a certain proposal. The legislation will pass through Congress if it receives a three-quarters majority in both chambers, but the president can veto legislation that he or she disagrees with. The Supreme Court may review legislation and declare it unconstitutional.

b. Members of Congress debate and vote on legislation, although the president may request that legislators consider a certain proposal. The legislation will pass through Congress if it receives a two-thirds majority in both chambers, but the president can veto legislation that he or she disagrees with. The Supreme Court may review legislation and declare it unconstitutional.

c. Members of Congress debate and vote on legislation, although the president may request that legislators consider a certain proposal. The president may veto legislation that he or she disagrees with, but Congress can override the veto with a three-quarters majority in both chambers. The Supreme Court may review legislation and declare it unconstitutional.

d. Members of Congress debate and vote on legislation, although the president may request that legislators consider a certain proposal. The president may veto legislation that he or she disagrees with, but Congress can override the veto with a two-thirds majority in both chambers. The Supreme Court may review legislation and declare it unconstitutional.

22. Using the table provided and your understanding of checks and balances, which of the following is true regarding federal judges?

a. The legislative branch appoints federal judges, but the executive branch can impeach and remove judges.

b. The executive branch appoints federal judges, but the legislative branch can impeach and remove judges.

c. The judicial branch appoints federal judges, but the executive branch can impeach and remove judges.

d. The judicial branch appoints federal judges, but the legislative branch can impeach and remove judges.

Questions 23 and 24 are based on the following passage:

> The creed which accepts as the foundation of morals, Utility, or the Greatest Happiness Principle, holds that actions are right in proportion as they tend to promote happiness, wrong as they tend to produce the reverse of happiness. By happiness is intended pleasure, and the absence of pain; by unhappiness, pain, and the privation of pleasure....
>
> The utilitarian morality does recognise in human beings the power of sacrificing their own greatest good for the good of others. It only refuses to admit that the sacrifice is itself a good. A sacrifice which does not increase, or tend to increase, the sum total of happiness, it considers as wasted.
>
> Excerpt from John Stuart Mill's Utilitarianism, 1861

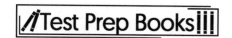

23. What is the meaning of "Utility"?
    a. Actions should be judged based on the net total of pleasure they tend to promote.
    b. Actions requiring sacrifice can never be valuable.
    c. Actions that promote sacrifice and increase happiness are more valuable than actions that only increase happiness.
    d. Actions can be valuable even if the pain outweighs the pleasure.

24. What is John Stuart Mill best known for?
    a. For being a social justice advocate during the Civil Rights Movement.
    b. For being the fifth Vice President of the United States.
    c. For being the second member of Parliament to advocate for women's right to vote.
    d. For making the call to counterattack after the Japanese attack on Pearl Harbor on December 7, 1941.

Questions 25 and 26 are based on the following passage:

The history of all hitherto existing society is the history of class struggles.

Freeman and slave, patrician and plebeian, lord and serf, guild-master and journeyman, in a word, oppressor and oppressed, stood in constant opposition to one another, carried on an uninterrupted, now hidden, now open fight, that each time ended, either in a revolutionary reconstitution of society at large, or in the common ruin of the contending classes....

Let the ruling classes tremble at a Communistic revolution. The proletarians have nothing to lose but their chains. They have a world to win.

Working Men of All Countries, Unite!

Karl Marx and Friedrich Engels, *The Communist Manifesto*, 1848

25. What's the main idea presented in the passage?
    a. Working men are morally superior to the ruling class.
    b. Every society will come to an end at some point.
    c. History is defined by class struggle and working men must now unite and fight the ruling class to gain freedom.
    d. Working men are in the same position as the slave, plebeian, serf, and journeyman.

26. Which of the following identities did Karl Marx NOT adhere to?
    a. Revolutionary
    b. Fascist
    c. Social scientist
    d. Historian

Questions 27 and 28 are based on the following image:

Spectrum of Political Ideologies

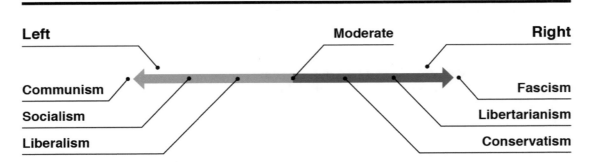

27. Of the following ideologies, which one advocates for the most radical government intervention to achieve social and economic equality?
    a. Socialism
    b. Liberalism
    c. Libertarianism
    d. Fascism

28. Of the following ideologies, which one prioritizes stability and traditional institutions within a culture?
    a. Socialism
    b. Liberalism
    c. Conservatism
    d. Libertarianism

Questions 29 and 30 are based on the following diagram:

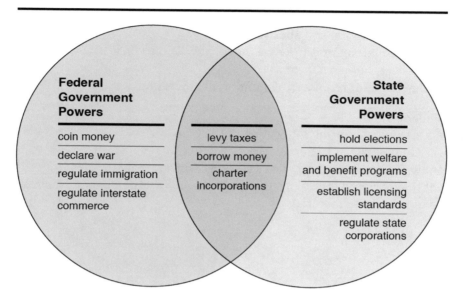

Separation of Powers

Federal Government Powers
- coin money
- declare war
- regulate immigration
- regulate interstate commerce

(overlap)
- levy taxes
- borrow money
- charter incorporations

State Government Powers
- hold elections
- implement welfare and benefit programs
- establish licensing standards
- regulate state corporations

29. Which of the following terms best describes the missing title in the circles?
   a. Reserved powers
   b. Implied powers
   c. Delegated powers
   d. Concurrent powers

30. Although not shown in the diagram, implied powers do what?
   a. Implied powers are the specific powers granted to the federal government by the Constitution.
   b. Implied powers are the unwritten powers that can be reasonably inferred from the powers specifically granted to the federal government in the Constitution.
   c. Implied powers are the reasonable powers required by the government to manage the nation's affairs and maintain sovereignty.
   d. Implied powers are the unspecified powers belonging to the state that are not expressly granted to the federal government or denied to the state by the Constitution.

Questions 31 and 32 are based on the following passage:

Ambition must be made to counteract ambition. The interest of the man, must be connected with the constitutional rights of the place. It may be a reflection on human nature, that such devices should be necessary to control the abuses of government. But what is government itself, but the greatest of all reflections on human nature? If men were angels, no government would be necessary. If angels were to govern men, neither external nor internal controls on government would be necessary. In framing a government which is to be administered by men

175

over men, the great difficulty lies in this: you must first enable the government to control the governed; and in the next place oblige it to control itself.

James Madison, writing as Publius, "Federalist No. 51," 1788

31. What is the main idea presented in the excerpt?
   a.   Men are inherently immoral and abusive.
   b.   The best form of government is the type that angels would construct.
   c.   Government reflects human nature.
   d.   An effective government requires a separation of powers to regulate itself.

32. What are *The Federalist Papers*?
   a.   Anonymous articles supporting ratification of the Constitution.
   b.   A document identifying basic liberties.
   c.   A document which articulated America's system of government.
   d.   A document that required the colonists to pay a tax on legal documents, newspapers, magazines, and other printed materials.

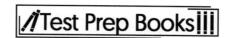

Questions 33 and 34 are based on the following diagram:

Checks and Balances

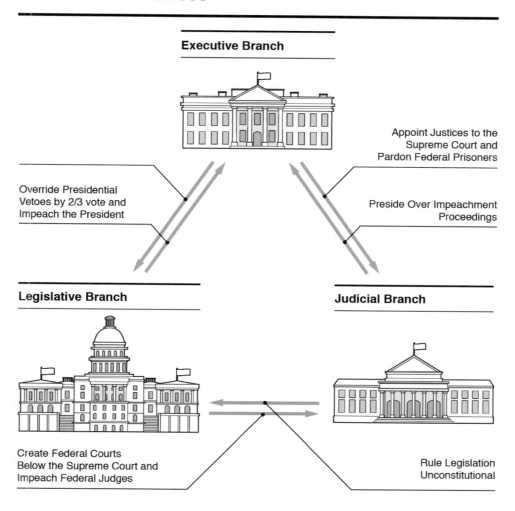

Executive Branch

Appoint Justices to the Supreme Court and Pardon Federal Prisoners

Override Presidential Vetoes by 2/3 vote and Impeach the President

Preside Over Impeachment Proceedings

Legislative Branch

Judicial Branch

Create Federal Courts Below the Supreme Court and Impeach Federal Judges

Rule Legislation Unconstitutional

33. Which of the following answer choices best completes the diagram?
    a. Impeach members of Congress and veto legislation
    b. Call special sessions of Congress and refuse to enforce laws
    c. Call special sessions of Congress and veto legislation
    d. Impeach members of Congress and refuse to enforce laws

34. What amendment guarantees American citizens the right to keep and bear arms?
    a. First Amendment
    b. Second Amendment
    c. Third Amendment
    d. Fourth Amendment

177

Questions 35 and 36 are based on the following table:

Presidential Election of 1824			
Candidate	Electoral Votes	Popular Votes	State Votes in the House of Representatives
Andrew Jackson	99	153,544	7
John Quincy Adams	84	108,740	13
William H. Crawford	41	46,618	4
Henry Clay	37	47,136	0

35. Who won the presidential election of 1824?
    a. Andrew Jackson
    b. John Quincy Adams
    c. William H. Crawford
    d. Henry Clay

36. What electoral system can result in a second round of voting, commonly referred to as a runoff?
    a. Majority systems
    b. Plurality systems
    c. Single transferable systems
    d. Party list systems

Questions 37–42 are based upon the following passage:

Fellow-citizens, pardon me, allow me to ask, why am I called upon to speak here to-day? What have I, or those I represent, to do with your national independence? Are the great principles of political freedom and of natural justice, embodied in that Declaration of Independence, extended to us? and am I, therefore, called upon to bring our humble offering to the national altar, and to confess the benefits and express devout gratitude for the blessings resulting from your independence to us?

Would to God, both for your sakes and ours, ours that an affirmative answer could be truthfully returned to these questions! Then would my task be light, and my burden easy and delightful. For who is there so cold, that a nation's sympathy could not warm him? Who so obdurate and dead to the claims of gratitude, that would not thankfully acknowledge such priceless benefits? Who so stolid and selfish, that would not give his voice to swell the hallelujahs of a nation's jubilee, when the chains of servitude had been torn from his limbs? I am not that man. In a case like that, the dumb might eloquently speak, and the "lame man leap as an hart."

But, such is not the state of the case. I say it with a sad sense of the disparity between us. I am not included within the pale of this glorious and anniversary! Your high independence only reveals the immeasurable distance between us. The blessings in which you, this day, rejoice, are not enjoyed in common. – The rich inheritance of justice, liberty, prosperity and independence, bequeathed by your fathers, is shared by you, not by me. The sunlight that brought life and healing to you, as brought stripes and death to me. This Fourth [of] July is *yours,* not *mine. You* may rejoice, *I* must mourn. To

178

drag a man in fetters into the grand illuminated temple of liberty, and call upon him to join you in joyous anthems, were inhuman mockery and sacrilegious irony. Do you mean, citizens, to mock me, by asking me to speak to-day? If so, there is a parallel to your conduct. And let me warn you that it is dangerous to copy the example of a nation whose crimes, lowering up to heaven, were thrown down by the breath of the Almighty, burying that nation in irrecoverable ruin! I can to-day take up the plaintive lament of a peeled and woe-smitten people!

"By the rivers of Babylon, there we sat down. Yea! we wept when we remembered Zion. We hanged our harps upon the willows in the midst thereof. For there, they that carried us away captive, required of us a song; and they who wasted us required of us mirth, saying, Sing us one of the songs of Zion. How can we sing the Lord's song in a strange land? If I forget thee, O Jerusalem, let my right hand forget her cunning. If I do not remember thee, let my tongue cleave to the roof of my mouth."

Excerpt from speech "What to the Slave is the Fourth of July?" by Frederick Douglass, 1852

37. What is the tone of the first paragraph of this passage?
    a. Incredulous
    b. Inclusive
    c. Contemplative
    d. Nonchalant

38. Which word CANNOT be used synonymously with the term *obdurate* as it is conveyed in the sentence below?

    Who so obdurate and dead to the claims of gratitude, that would not thankfully acknowledge such priceless benefits?

    a. Steadfast
    b. Stubborn
    c. Contented
    d. Unwavering

39. What is the central purpose of this text?
    a. To demonstrate the author's extensive knowledge of the Bible
    b. To highlight the disparity between slaves and free men and protest slavery in a nation supposedly devoted to liberty
    c. To convince wealthy landowners to adopt new holiday rituals
    d. To explain why minorities often relished the notion of segregation in government institutions

40. Which statement serves as evidence for the answer to question 39 above?
    a. By the rivers of Babylon, there we sat down.
    b. Fellow-citizens, pardon me, allow me to ask, why am I called upon to speak here to-day?
    c. I can to-day take up the plaintive lament of a peeled and woe-smitten people!
    d. The rich inheritance of justice, liberty, prosperity and independence, bequeathed by your fathers, is shared by you, not by me.

41. The statement below features an example of which of the following literary devices?

> Your high independence only reveals the immeasurable distance between us.

a. Assonance
b. Parallelism
c. Amplification
d. Hyperbole

42. The speaker's use of biblical references, such as "rivers of Babylon" and the "songs of Zion," helps the reader to do all EXCEPT which of the following?
a. Identify with the speaker using common text
b. Draw a connection between another group of people who have been affected by slavery and American slaves
c. Recognize the equivocation of the speaker and those that he represents
d. Appeal to the listener's sense of humanity

Questions 43–48 are based upon the following passage:

MANKIND being originally equals in the order of creation, the equality could only be destroyed by some subsequent circumstance; the distinctions of rich, and poor, may in a great measure be accounted for, and that without having recourse to the harsh, ill-sounding names of oppression and avarice. Oppression is often the CONSEQUENCE, but seldom or never the MEANS of riches; and though avarice will preserve a man from being necessitously poor, it generally makes him too timorous to be wealthy.

But there is another and greater distinction, for which no truly natural or religious reason can be assigned, and that is, the distinction of men into KINGS and SUBJECTS. Male and female are the distinctions of nature, good and bad the distinctions of heaven; but how a race of men came into the world so exalted above the rest, and distinguished like some new species, is worth enquiring into, and whether they are the means of happiness or of misery to mankind.

In the early ages of the world, according to the scripture chronology, there were no kings; the consequence of which was, there were no wars; it is the pride of kings which throw mankind into confusion. Holland without a king hath enjoyed more peace for this last century than any of the monarchical governments in Europe. Antiquity favors the same remark; for the quiet and rural lives of the first patriarchs hath a happy something in them, which vanishes away when we come to the history of Jewish royalty.

Government by kings was first introduced into the world by the Heathens, from whom the children of Israel copied the custom. It was the most prosperous invention the Devil ever set on foot for the promotion of idolatry. The Heathens paid divine honors to their deceased kings, and the Christian world hath improved on the plan, by doing the same to their living ones. How impious is the title of sacred majesty applied to a worm, who in the midst of his splendor is crumbling into dust!

As the exalting one man so greatly above the rest cannot be justified on the equal rights of nature, so neither can it be defended on the authority of scripture; for the will of the

180

Almighty, as declared by Gideon and the prophet Samuel, expressly disapproves of government by kings. All anti-monarchical parts of scripture have been very smoothly glossed over in monarchical governments, but they undoubtedly merit the attention of countries which have their governments yet to form. RENDER UNTO CAESAR THE THINGS WHICH ARE CAESAR'S is the scripture doctrine of courts, yet it is no support of monarchical government, for the Jews at that time were without a king, and in a state of vassalage to the Romans.

Now three thousand years passed away from the Mosaic account of the creation, till the Jews under a national delusion requested a king. Till then their form of government (except in extraordinary cases, where the Almighty interposed) was a kind of republic administered by a judge and the elders of the tribes. Kings they had none, and it was held sinful to acknowledge any being under that title but the Lord of Hosts. And when a man seriously reflects on the idolatrous homage which is paid to the persons of kings, he need not wonder that the Almighty, ever jealous of his honor, should disapprove of a form of government which so impiously invades the prerogative of heaven.

Excerpt from "Common Sense" by Thomas Paine, 1776

43. According to the passage, what role does avarice, or greed, play in poverty?
    a. Avarice makes a man poor.
    b. Avarice is the consequence of wealth.
    c. Avarice prevents a man from being poor but makes him too fearful to be wealthy.
    d. Avarice is what drives a person to be wealthy.

44. Of these distinctions, which does the author believe to be beyond natural or religious reason?
    a. Good and bad
    b. Male and female
    c. Human and animal
    d. King and subjects

45. According to the passage, what are the Heathens responsible for?
    a. Government by kings
    b. Quiet and rural lives of patriarchs
    c. Paying divine honors to their living kings
    d. Equal rights of nature

46. Which of the following best states Paine's rationale for denouncing monarchy?
    a. It is against the laws of nature.
    b. It is against the equal rights of nature and is denounced in scripture.
    c. Despite scripture, a monarchal government is unlawful.
    d. Neither the law nor scripture denounce monarchy.

47. Based on the passage, what is the best definition of the word *idolatrous*?
    a. Worshipping kings
    b. Being deceitful
    c. Sinfulness
    d. Engaging in illegal activities

181

48. What is the essential meaning of the following lines?

> And when a man seriously reflects on the idolatrous homage which is paid to the persons of kings, he need not wonder that the Almighty, ever jealous of his honor, should disapprove of a form of government which so impiously invades the prerogative of heaven.

  a. God disapproves of the irreverence of a monarchical government.
  b. With careful reflection, men should realize that heaven is not promised.
  c. God will punish those that follow a monarchical government.
  d. Belief in a monarchical government cannot coexist with belief in God.

Question 49 is based on the following passage:

> Hand in hand with this we must frankly recognize the overbalance of population in our industrial centers and, by engaging on a national scale in a redistribution, endeavor to provide a better use of the land for those best fitted for the land. The task can be helped by definite efforts to raise the values of agricultural products and with this the power to purchase the output of our cities. It can be helped by preventing realistically the tragedy of the growing loss through foreclosure of our small homes and our farms. It can be helped by insistence that the Federal, State, and local governments act forthwith on the demand that their cost be drastically reduced. It can be helped by the unifying of relief activities which today are often scattered, uneconomical, and unequal. It can be helped by national planning for and supervision of all forms of transportation and of communications and other utilities which have a definitely public character. There are many ways in which it can be helped, but it can never be helped merely by talking about it. We must act and act quickly.
>
> Finally, in our progress toward a resumption of work we require two safeguards against a return of the evils of the old order; there must be a strict supervision of all banking and credits and investments; there must be an end to speculation with other people's money, and there must be provision for an adequate but sound currency.
>
> President Franklin D. Roosevelt, Inaugural Address, March 4, 1933

49. Which of the following best describes President Roosevelt's underlying approach to government?
  a. Government must be focused on redistribution of land.
  b. Government must "act and act quickly" to intervene and regulate the economy.
  c. Government must exercise "strict supervision of all banking."
  d. Government must prevent the "growing loss through foreclosure."

Question 50 is based on the following passage:

> What, to the American slave, is your 4th of July? I answer: a day that reveals to him, more than all other days in the year, the gross injustice and cruelty to which he is the constant victim. To him, your celebration is a sham; your boasted liberty, an unholy license; your national greatness, swelling vanity; your sounds of rejoicing are empty and heartless; your denunciations of tyrants, brass fronted impudence; your shouts of liberty and equality, hollow mockery; your prayers and hymns, your sermons and thanksgivings, with all your religious parade, and solemnity, are, to him, mere bombast, fraud, deception, impiety, and hypocrisy—a thin veil to cover up crimes

which would disgrace a nation of savages. There is not a nation on the earth guilty of practices, more shocking and bloody, than are the people of these United States, at this very hour.

Excerpt from "What to the Slave is the Fourth of July?" by Frederick Douglass, 1852

50. What is the specific hypocrisy that Douglass repudiates?
a. The Declaration of Independence declared that all men are created equal, but Thomas Jefferson owned slaves.
b. Americans are free, but they do not value their freedom.
c. The Fourth of July is a celebration about freedom, and slavery remained legal in the United States.
d. The United States is a Christian nation, but American traditions contradict their faith.

Question 51 is based on the following passage:

May it please your honor, I shall never pay a dollar of your unjust penalty. All the stock in trade I possess is a $10,000 debt, incurred by publishing my paper—*The Revolution*—four years ago, the sole object of which was to educate all women to do precisely as I have done, rebel against your man-made, unjust, unconstitutional forms of law, that tax, fine, imprison and hang women, while they deny them the right of representation in the government; and I shall work on with might and main to pay every dollar of that honest debt, but not a penny shall go to this unjust claim. And I shall earnestly and persistently continue to urge all women to the practical recognition of the old revolutionary maxim, that "Resistance to tyranny is obedience to God."

An Account of the Proceedings on the Trial of Susan B. Anthony on the Charge of Illegal Voting, 1874.

51. What is the main idea presented in the excerpt?
a. Taxation without representation is tyranny.
b. Domestic abuse and violence against women is the cause of tyranny.
c. Anthony cannot pay her fine due to debt accumulated from fighting for women's rights.
d. Denying women the right to vote is tyranny and must be resisted.

52. Which of the following most accurately describes the platform of Ronald Reagan?
a. Christianity, optimism, and preserving social safety nets
b. Increased defense spending, deregulation, and tax cuts
c. Moral majority, international cooperation, and compromise
d. Conservatism, opposition to abortion, and organized labor

Question 53 is based on the following graph:

History of Unemployment in the United States

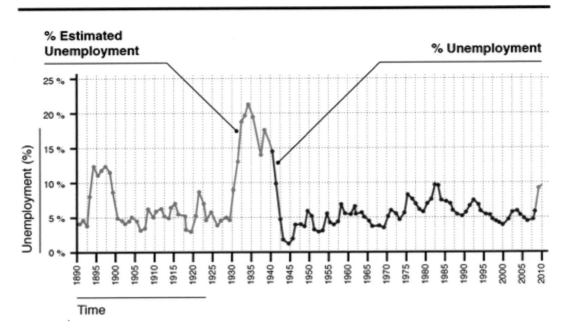

53. Which event caused the second-largest increase in unemployment in American history?
    a. Panic of 1893
    b. Depression of 1920
    c. Depression of 1929
    d. Great Recession of 2007

Questions 54–55 are based on the following passage:

I heartily accept the motto, "That government is best which governs least"; and I should like to see it acted up to more rapidly and systematically. Carried out, it finally amounts to this, which also I believe—"That government is best which governs not at all"; and when men are prepared for it, that will be the kind of government which they will have. Government is at best but an expedient; but most governments are usually, and all governments are sometimes, inexpedient. The objections which have been brought against a standing army, and they are many and weighty, and deserve to prevail, may also at last be brought against a standing government. The standing army is only an arm of the standing government. The government itself, which is only the mode which the people have chosen to execute their will, is equally liable to be abused and perverted before the people can act through it. Witness the present Mexican war, the work of comparatively a few individuals using the standing government as their tool; for, in the outset, the people would not have consented to this measure.

This American government—what is it but a tradition, though a recent one, endeavoring to transmit itself unimpaired to posterity, but each instant losing some of its integrity? It has not the vitality and force of a single living man; for a single man can bend it to his will. It is a sort of wooden gun to the people themselves. But it is not the less necessary for this; for the people

184

must have some complicated machinery or other, and hear its din, to satisfy that idea of government which they have. Governments show thus how successfully men can be imposed on, even impose on themselves, for their own advantage. It is excellent, we must all allow. Yet this government never of itself furthered any enterprise, but by the alacrity with which it got out of its way. It does not keep the country free. It does not settle the West. It does not educate. The character inherent in the American people has done all that has been accomplished; and it would have done somewhat more, if the government had not sometimes got in its way. For government is an expedient by which men would fain succeed in letting one another alone; and, as has been said, when it is most expedient, the governed are most let alone by it. Trade and commerce, if they were not made of india-rubber, would never manage to bounce over the obstacles which legislators are continually putting in their way; and, if one were to judge these men wholly by the effects of their actions and not partly by their intentions, they would deserve to be classed and punished with those mischievous persons who put obstructions on the railroads.

But, to speak practically and as a citizen, unlike those who call themselves no-government men, I ask for, not at once no government, but at once a better government. Let every man make known what kind of government would command his respect, and that will be one step toward obtaining it.

Excerpt from *Civil Disobedience* by Henry David Thoreau, 1847

54. Which phrase best encapsulates Thoreau's use of the term *expedient* in the first paragraph?
   a. A dead end
   b. A state of order
   c. A means to an end
   d. Rushed construction

55. Which best describes Thoreau's view on the Mexican War?
   a. Government is inherently corrupt because it must wage war.
   b. Government can easily be manipulated by a few individuals for their own agenda.
   c. Government is a tool for the people, but it can also act against their interest.
   d. The Mexican War was a necessary action, but not all the people believed this.

Short-Answer Questions

Read the following passage and then answer the question that follows.

In recent years there have been many signs of improvement, but only in proportion as the principles and practices that the white people of the state understand are those of Reconstruction are rejected or superseded. To the northern man Reconstruction probably meant and still means something quite different from what the white man of Alabama understands by the term. But as the latter understands it, he has accepted none of its essential principles and intends to accept none of its so-called successes.

In destroying all that was old, Reconstruction probably removed some abuses; from the new order some permanent good must have resulted. But credit for neither can rightfully be claimed until it can be shown that those results were impossible under the régime destroyed.

Excerpt from *Civil War and Reconstruction in Alabama* (1905) by Walter L. Fleming, American historian

1. Based on the excerpt above, answer the following:

   a) Briefly explain how ONE historical event or development undermined traditional Southern power structures during Reconstruction.

   b) Briefly provide ONE historical example supporting the author's claim that Southern whites never accepted Reconstruction's "so-called successes."

   c) Briefly provide ONE historical event or development to explain how the end of Reconstruction impacted African Americans' economic opportunities.

"The Gin House" (1879), unknown artist, published in "Cotton," *The American Cyclopædia*, v. 5, 1879, p. 405

2. Based on the image above, answer the following:

   a) Briefly describe ONE characteristic of late nineteenth-century agricultural production based on the image.

   b) Briefly provide ONE example of how this method of agricultural production impacted the South's economic development.

   c) Briefly explain ONE historical event or development triggered by the invention of the agricultural system expressed in the image.

186

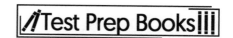
3. Answer the following:

a) Briefly describe ONE specific historical difference between the American independence movement in the period 1750 to 1763 and in the period 1763 to 1776.

b) Briefly explain ONE specific historical consequence of British expansion on the American independence movement between 1750 and 1770.

c) Briefly provide ONE specific historical example of mass media contributing to the American independence movement during the 1770s.

4. Answer the following:

a) Briefly describe ONE specific historical similarity between American global power in the aftermath of World War I compared to American global power in the aftermath of World War II.

b) Briefly describe ONE specific historical difference between American global power in the aftermath of World War I and American global power in the aftermath of World War II.

c) Briefly describe ONE specific historical effect of American global power in either the aftermath of World War I or in the aftermath of World War II.

Document-Based Question

Evaluate and distinguish between the different perspectives on the causes of the American Civil War (1861–1865).

Document 1

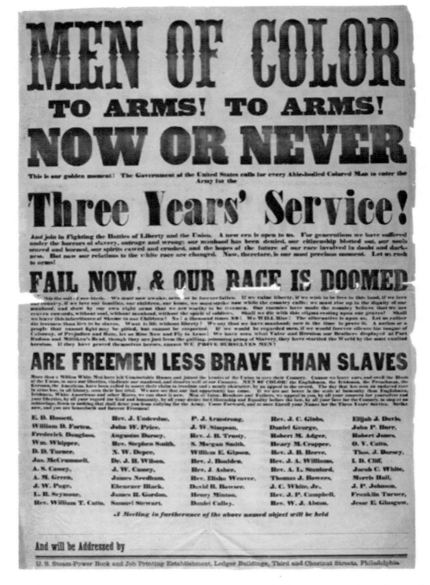

The image above is titled "Men of Color Civil War Recruitment Broadside" (1863), written by Frederick Douglass and signed by 54 African American community leaders

Document 2

States which claimed a sovereign right to secede from the Union naturally claimed the corresponding right to resume possession of all the land they had ceded to that Union's Government for the use of its naval and military posts. So South Carolina, after leading the way to secession on December 20, 1860, at once began to work for the retrocession of the forts defending her famous cotton port of Charleston. These defenses, being of vital consequence to both sides, were soon to attract the strained attention of the whole country...

The situation, here as elsewhere, was complicated by Floyd, President Buchanan's Secretary of War, soon to be forced out of office on a charge of misapplying public funds. Floyd, as an ardent

188

Southerner, was using the last lax days of the Buchanan Government to get the army posts ready for capitulation whenever secession should have become an accomplished fact. He urged on construction, repairs, and armament at Charleston, while refusing to strengthen the garrison, in order, as he said, not to provoke Carolina. Moreover, in November he had replaced old Colonel Gardner, a Northern veteran of "1812," by Anderson the Southerner, in whom he hoped to find a good capitulator. But this time Floyd was wrong.

Excerpt from *Captains of the Civil War: A Chronicle of the Blue and Gray*, 1921, by William Wood, American historian

Document 3

Charleston, S. C., *November 8, 1860.*—Yesterday on the train, just before we reached Fernandina, a woman called out: "That settles the hash." Tanny touched me on the shoulder and said: "Lincoln's elected." "How do you know?" "The man over there has a telegram."

The excitement was very great. Everybody was talking at the same time. One, a little more moved than the others, stood up and said despondently: "The die is cast; no more vain regrets; sad forebodings are useless; the stake is life or death." "Did you ever!" was the prevailing exclamation, and some one cried out: "Now that the black radical Republicans have the power I suppose they will Brown[1] us all." No doubt of it.

[1] A Reference to John Brown of Harper's Ferry.

Excerpt from *A Diary from Dixie*, 1906, by May Boykin Chestnut, Southern author and wife of influential Confederate leader James Chestnut, Jr.

Document 4

There were two political parties, it is true, in all the States, both strong in numbers and respectability, but both equally loyal to the institution which stood paramount in Southern eyes to all other institutions in state or nation. The slave-owners were the minority, but governed both parties. Had politics ever divided the slave-holders and the non-slave-holders, the majority would have been obliged to yield, or internecine war would have been the consequence. I do not know that the Southern people were to blame for this condition of affairs. There was a time when slavery was not profitable, and the discussion of the merits of the institution was confined almost exclusively to the territory where it existed. The States of Virginia and Kentucky came near abolishing slavery by their own acts, one State defeating the measure by a tie vote and the other only lacking one. But when the institution became profitable, all talk of its abolition ceased where it existed; and naturally, as human nature is constituted, arguments were adduced in its support. The cotton-gin probably had much to do with the justification of slavery.

Excerpt from *Personal Memoirs of U.S. Grant*, Volume 1, 1885, by Ulysses S. Grant, Commanding General of the United States Army during the American Civil War and President of the United States during Reconstruction

Document 5

Our reliance is in the *love of liberty* which God has planted in our bosoms. Our defense is in the preservation of the spirit which prizes liberty as the heritage of all men, in all lands, every where. Destroy this spirit, and you have planted the seeds of despotism around your own doors. Familiarize yourselves with the chains of bondage, and you are preparing your own limbs to wear them. Accustomed to trample on the rights of those around you, you have lost the genius

of your own independence, and become the fit subjects of the first cunning tyrant who rises. And let me tell you, that all these things are prepared for you with the logic of history, if the elections shall promise that the next Dred Scott decision and all future decisions will be quietly acquiesced in by the people.

Excerpt of "Speech at Edwardsville, Illinois," by Abraham Lincoln on September 13, 1858, published in *The Papers and Writings of Abraham Lincoln*, Volume 5 (1865)

Document 6

As a mere historical fact, we have seen that African servitude among us—confessedly the mildest and most humane of all institutions to which the name "slavery" has ever been applied—existed in all the original States, and that it was recognized and protected in the fourth article of the Constitution. Subsequently, for climatic, industrial, and economical—not moral or sentimental—reasons, it was abolished in the Northern, while it continued to exist in the Southern States. Men differed in their views as to the abstract question of its right or wrong, but for two generations after the Revolution there was no geographical line of demarcation for such differences. The African slave-trade was carried on almost exclusively by New England merchants and Northern ships. Mr. Jefferson—a Southern man, the founder of the Democratic party, and the vindicator of State rights—was in theory a consistent enemy to every form of slavery....

The truth remains intact and incontrovertible, that the existence of African servitude was in no wise the cause of the conflict, but only an incident. In the later controversies that arose, however, its effect in operating as a lever upon the passions, prejudices, or sympathies of mankind, was so potent that it has been spread, like a thick cloud, over the whole horizon of historic truth.

Excerpt from *The Rise and Fall of the Confederate Government*, Volume 1, 1881, by Jefferson Davis, President of the Confederate States

Document 7

Charleston was then a proud, aristocratic city, and assumed a leadership in the public opinion of the South far out of proportion to her population, wealth, or commerce. On more than one occasion previously, the inhabitants had almost inaugurated civil war, by their assertion and professed belief that each State had, in the original compact of government, reserved to itself the right to withdraw from the Union at its own option, whenever the people supposed they had sufficient cause. We used to discuss these things at our own mess-tables, vehemently and sometimes quite angrily; but I am sure that I never feared it would go further than it had already gone in the winter of 1832-'33, when the attempt at "nullification" was promptly suppressed by President Jackson's famous declaration, "The Union must and shall be preserved!" and by the judicious management of General Scott.

Still, civil war was to be; and, now that it has come and gone, we can rest secure in the knowledge that as the chief cause, slavery, has been eradicated forever, it is not likely to come again.

Excerpt from *Memoirs of General W. T. Sherman*, Volume 1, 1875, by William Tecumseh Sherman, General in the United States Army during the American Civil War

Long Essay Questions

1. Assess the extent to which the Spanish–American War (1899) transformed American foreign policy between 1890 and 1945.

2. Compare the similarities and differences between European colonizers' labor systems as practiced in the Americas between 1492 and 1800.

3. Evaluate the stances of American political parties and political movements in relation to civil rights during the Cold War (1947–1991).

Answer Explanations

Multiple-Choice Explanations

1. D: The passage does not proceed in chronological order since it begins by pointing out Leif Erikson's explorations in America, so Choice *A* does not work. Although the author compares and contrasts Erikson with Christopher Columbus, this is not the main way in which the information is presented; therefore, Choice *B* does not work. Neither does Choice *C* because there is no mention of or reference to cause and effect in the passage. However, the passage does offer a conclusion (Leif Erikson deserves more credit) and premises (first European to set foot in the New World and first to contact the natives) to substantiate Erikson's historical importance. Thus, Choice *D* is correct.

2. C: Choice *C* is the correct answer because it is the author's opinion that Erikson deserves more credit. That, in fact, is the conclusion in the piece, but another person could argue that Columbus or another explorer deserves more credit for opening up the New World to exploration. Rather than being an indisputable fact, it is a subjective value claim. Choice *A* is incorrect because it describes facts: Leif Erikson was the son of Erik the Red and historians debate Leif's date of birth. These are not opinions. Choice *B* is incorrect; that Erikson called the land "Vinland" is a verifiable fact, as is Choice *D* because he did contact the natives almost 500 years before Columbus.

3. B: Choice *B* is correct because, as stated in the previous answer, it accurately identifies the author's statement that Erikson deserves more credit than he has received for being the first European to explore the New World. Choice *A* is incorrect because the author aims to go beyond describing Erikson as a mere legendary Viking. Choice *C* is incorrect because the author does not focus on Erikson's motivations, let alone name the spreading of Christianity as his primary objective. Choice *D* is incorrect because it is a premise that Erikson contacted the natives 500 years before Columbus, which is simply a part of supporting the author's conclusion.

4. B: Choice *B* is correct because the author wants the reader to be informed about Leif Erikson's contribution to exploring the new world. While several other answers are possible options, Choice *B* is the strongest. Choice *A* is incorrect because the author is not in any way trying to entertain the reader. Choice *C* is incorrect because the nature of the writing does not indicate the author would be satisfied with the reader merely being alerted to Erikson's exploration; instead, the author is making an argument about the credit he should receive. Choice *D* is incorrect because the author goes beyond a mere suggestion; "suggest" is too vague.

5. D: Choice *D* is correct because there are two examples of historians having trouble pinning down important dates in Viking history: Leif Erikson's date of birth the results of his encounter with the natives of Vinland. Choice *A* is incorrect because the author never addresses the Vikings' state of mind or emotions. Choice *B* is incorrect because the author does not elaborate on Erikson's exile and whether he would have become an explorer if not for his banishment. Choice *C* is incorrect because there is not enough information to support this premise. It is unclear whether Erikson informed the King of Norway of his finding. Although it is true that the king did not send a follow-up expedition, he could have simply chosen not to expend the resources after receiving Erikson's news. It is not possible to logically infer whether Erikson told him.

6. C: The correct answer is Choice C, 1910. There are two ways to arrive at the correct answer. You could find the four answer choices on the graph and compare them, or you could identify that the population never decreases from one census to the next. Thus, the correct answer needs to be the only answer choice that is earlier in time than the others, Choice C. Choices A, B, and D are incorrect because they are later in time, and thus have a greater population, than the 1930 census.

7. D: The population increased the most between 1990 and 2010. The question is asking you to identify the rate of change for each interval. Between 1990 and 2010, the population increased by approximately 60 million. Thus, Choice D is the correct answer. The slope of the graph is also the steepest in this interval, which represents its higher increase. Choice A is incorrect because between 1930 and 1950, the population increased by approximately 28 million. Choice B is incorrect because between 1950 and 1970, the population increased by approximately 52 million. Choice C is incorrect because between 1970 and 1990, the population increased by approximately 45 million.

8. B: It is apparent that Lincoln is referring to a period of time within the context of the passage because the sentence contains the words *years* and *ago*. Choices A, C, and D do not fit the language or context of the sentence and are therefore incorrect.

9. C: Lincoln's reference to *the brave men, living and dead, who struggled here,* proves that he is referring to a battlefield. Choices A and B are incorrect, as a *civil war* is mentioned and not a war with France or a war in the Sahara Desert. Choice D is incorrect because it does not make sense to consecrate a President's ground instead of a battlefield ground for soldiers who died during the American Civil War.

10. A: The audience should perpetuate the ideals of freedom that the soldiers died fighting for. Lincoln doesn't address any of the topics outlined in Choices B, C, or D. Therefore, Choice A is the correct answer.

11. D: The word *resolve* means to make up one's mind or decide on something. Choices A, B, and C are incorrect because they do not fit the meaning and context of the sentence.

12. A: Choice A is correct because Lincoln's intention was to memorialize the soldiers who had fallen as a result of war as well as celebrate those who had put their lives in danger for the sake of their country. Choices B and C are incorrect because Lincoln's speech was supposed to foster a sense of pride among the members of the audience while connecting them to the soldiers' experiences. Choice D is incorrect because Lincoln does not a distinction between soldiers and civilians but rather pointing his audience toward the sacrifices made by the soldiers on the battlefield at Gettysburg.

13. B: As stated in the passage, left-axis political orientations typically favor social and economic equality and advocate for government intervention to achieve these goals. Communism, socialism, liberalism, and progressivism are examples of political orientations on the left side of the spectrum that are discussed in the passage. Right-axis political orientations generally value the existing and historical political institutions and oppose government intervention, especially in regard to the economy. Libertarianism, conservatism, and fascism are the three orientations from the passage that are considered right-axis orientations. It is true that libertarians have some progressive ideals; however, libertarianism is still usually considered a right-axis orientation because it opposes government intervention. Libertarianism, Conservatism, and Fascism are the three orientations from the passage that are considered right-axis orientations. It is true that Libertarians have some progressive ideals; however, Libertarianism is still usually considered a right-axis orientation because the political ideals are

conservative. Fascism is considered a right-axis orientation because of its emphasis on hierarchy and traditional political structures, particularly in opposition to egalitarianism.

14. A: Choice *A* is correct because Fascists advocate for a strong, consolidated, centralized government led by an all-powerful dictator. They believe a key role of this centralized government is to prepare for war. While Libertarians still tend to maintain a conservative approach to government, especially in the context of power and military intervention, they favor a weaker central government and emphasize individual liberty above all else. Choice *B* is incorrect because Libertarians do not prioritize government spending. Choice *C* is incorrect because Fascists favor a powerful, centralized government whereas Libertarians favor a weaker central government. Choice *D* is incorrect because Fascists believe in government intervention at every level and Libertarians do not prioritize governmental spending at all.

15. B: Choice *B* is correct because refugees emigrate from (leave) their country because of push factors. Emigration occurs when a person or entire group of people move *from* a location. Immigration occurs when a person or entire group of people move *to* a location. Push factors encourage (or force) people to move from their homes. Pull factors attract people to a location. As the passage mentioned, political push factors include war, government-induced violence and intimidation, genocide, or oppression. Refugees are those pushed from their home country because of such political factors. Refugees are often forcefully expunged from their home states when new countries are formed or when national boundaries are redrawn. For example, the unification of North Vietnam and South Vietnam after the Vietnam War brought hundreds of thousands of Vietnamese refugees to the United States during the 1970s. Choices *A* and *C* are incorrect because refugees *leave* their country, i.e., they emigrate *from* their country. Refugees immigrate *to* a different country. Choice *D* is incorrect because refugees leave their country because of push factors, not pull factors.

16. C: Deindustrialization in cities in the Industrial North during the 1960s–1980s pushed many residents away from industrial hubs like Buffalo, Cleveland, Chicago, and Milwaukee because the number of jobs dropped significantly. Thus, people needed to move elsewhere to find employment. This is an example of an economic push factor—pushing people out of the area because of an economic downturn. Choice *A* is incorrect because the situation described is an economic factor, not a political factor. Choice *B* is incorrect because the situation described is an economic factor, not a political factor, and because economic downturn is a push factor rather than a pull factor. Choice *D* is incorrect because an economic downturn is a push factor rather than a pull factor.

17. B: This scenario describes a political pull factor because it involves people moving to capitalize on the hopes of a better political situation; this enticement "pulls" them to the new location. Choice *A* is incorrect because a better political situation is pull factor rather than a push factor. Choices *C* and *D* are incorrect because the situation describes a political factor rather than an economic factor.

18. C: This scenario describes an environmental push factor. Environmental push factors include flooding, natural disasters, droughts, nuclear contamination, and water contamination, among others. In the Sahel region of North Africa, many people have been forced to find new lands due to the intense droughts. As another example, after Hurricane Katrina, many New Orleans residents had to relocate to Houston, Baton Rouge, or other cities to find refuge from the environmental and economic devastation. Choices *A* and *B* are incorrect because the scenario describes an environmental factor rather than a political factor. Choice *D* is incorrect because drought is an example of a push factor rather than a pull factor.

19. D: Choice *D* is correct. Mexico ceded Nevada as part of the peace agreement ending the Mexican-American War. Choices *A*, *B*, and *C* are incorrect because they are territories gained via purchase when the question asks about military force. Missouri and Nebraska became American territories through the Louisiana Purchase, and the United States purchased Alaska from Russia.

20. C: A participatory democracy in its truest form is a system in which everyone participates in the political system. Choice *A* describes an elite democracy, which was advocated by some of the Founders like James Madison. Choice *B* is a pluralist democracy—one where interest groups and advocacy for certain issues dominate the government. Choice *D* describes an aristocracy or an oligarchy rather than a participatory democracy.

21. D: According to the system of checks and balances outlined in the Constitution, members of Congress debate and vote on legislation, although the president may request that legislators consider a certain proposal. The president may veto legislation that he or she disagrees with, but Congress can override the veto with a two-thirds majority in both chambers. The Supreme Court may review legislation and declare it unconstitutional. Choices *A* and *B* are incorrect because legislation requires a simple majority of both chambers to become a law. These options also do not mention the ability of Congress to override the President's veto, thus missing an important element of the checks and balances between the branches of government. Choice *C* is incorrect because Congress can override the President's veto with a two-thirds majority in both chambers, not a three-quarters majority.

22. B: According to the system of checks and balances, the executive branch appoints federal judges, but the legislative branch can impeach and remove judges. The legislative branch must also approve the appointment of federal judges. Choice *A* is incorrect because it is the opposite of the correct answer. Choice *C* is incorrect because the Judicial branch does not appoint federal judges and the executive branch does not have the power of impeachment. Choice *D* is incorrect because the judicial branch does not appoint federal judges.

23. A: Choice *A* is correct. John Stuart Mill was an English philosopher and political economist who advocated for utilitarianism and women's rights. In the excerpt, "utility" is defined as actions that are "right in proportion as they tend to promote happiness, wrong as they tend to produce the reverse of happiness." The excerpt then explains that happiness is measured by pleasure, and the reverse is pain. Therefore, Mill calls for actions to be evaluated based on the net total of pleasure. Choice *B* is incorrect because sacrifice can still be valuable if it leads to more pleasure than pain. The excerpt doesn't support Choice *C*, as there's no evidence that pleasure-generating sacrifices merit special status. Choice *D* contradicts the definition provided in the excerpt.

24. C: John Stuart Mill is best known for advocating for women's right to vote in Parliament in Great Britain. Mill believed in the philosophy of Utilitarianism, which suggests that whatever brings about the most positive effects is always the moral thing to do. He strongly believed that equality between the sexes would promote moral and intellectual advancement in humanity as a whole. Choices *A*, *B*, and *D* are incorrect because they address political situations in the United States rather than Great Britain.

25. C: Choice *C* is correct. Karl Marx, a philosopher, social scientist, historian, and revolutionary, is considered the father of communism. All the answer choices contain true statements or reasonable assumptions based on the passage; however, Choice *C* best articulates the main idea—society is the history of class struggle and working men must unite and fight a revolutionary battle like their historical ancestors.

26. B: Karl Marx was NOT considered a fascist. A fascist regime is necessarily an authoritarian form of government, whereas Marx argued for the end of hierarchical rule. Choices *A*, *C*, and *D* are incorrect because Karl Marx was a revolutionary, social scientist, historian, and philosopher, whose ideas contributed to the rise of Communism.

27. A: Choice *A* is correct. On the political spectrum, ideologies on the left side of the axis emphasize socioeconomic equality and advocate for government intervention, while ideologies on the right side of the axis seek to preserve society's existing institutions or structures. Therefore, the correct answer will be the farthest left on the axis, making Choice *A* correct. Choice *B* is incorrect because Liberalism supports less government intervention than Socialism. Choice *C* is incorrect because Libertarianism strongly opposes government intervention. Choice *D* is incorrect because, while Fascism advocates for strong government intervention, it supports a hierarchical structure and opposes equality.

28. C: Choice *C* is correct, as it most closely corresponds to the provided definition. Conservatism prioritizes traditional institutions. In general, conservatives oppose modern developments and value stability. Choices *A* and *B* are incorrect because socialism and liberalism both feature the desire to change the government to increase equality. Choice *D* is incorrect because libertarianism is more concerned with establishing a limited government to maximize personal autonomy rather than prioritizing stability and traditional institutions.

29. D: Choice *D* is correct. The missing title is in the overlap between federal and state government powers. Concurrent powers are shared between federal and state governments. Choice *A* is incorrect because reserved powers are the unspecified powers of the states not expressly granted to the federal government or denied to the state by the Constitution and left to the states by the Tenth Amendment. Choice *B* is incorrect because implied powers are the unstated powers that can be reasonably inferred from the specific powers outlined in the Constitution. Choice *C* is incorrect because delegated powers are the specific powers granted to the federal government by the Constitution.

30. B: Implied powers are the unwritten powers that can be reasonably inferred from the powers specifically granted to the federal government in the Constitution. Choice *A* refers to delegated powers: the specific powers granted to the federal government by the Constitution. Choice *C* refers to inherent powers: the reasonable powers required by the government to manage the nation's affairs and maintain sovereignty. Choice *D* refers to reserved powers: the unspecified powers belonging to the state that are not expressly granted to the federal government or denied to the state by the Constitution.

31. D: Choice *D* is correct. The Federalists supported the expansion of the federal government compared to the Articles of Confederation, and the anti-Federalists feared that a stronger central government would weaken the states. *The Federalist Papers* argued for the ratification of the Constitution to establish a more powerful central government. The main idea of this excerpt is to argue that the Constitution establishes a central government powerful enough to rule, while also providing checks and balances to ensure the government doesn't abuse its power. Separation of powers is the concept behind checks and balances, so Choice *D* is the correct answer. Choices *A* and *C* may be true statements, but they don't identify the main idea. Choice *B* references a theoretical assertion from the excerpt, but it's not the main idea.

32. A: *The Federalist Papers* were articles written anonymously under the pseudonym Publius that supported ratification of the U.S. Constitution . Choice *B*, a document identifying basic liberties, is the bill of rights. Choice *C*, a document which articulated America's system of government at the time of the

Constitutional Convention, is the Articles of Confederation. After the Constitution was ratified, it would be the document described by this answer choice. Choice *D*, a document that required the colonists to pay a tax on legal documents, newspapers, magazines, and other printed materials, is known as the Stamp Act.

33. C: Choice *C* is the correct answer. Checks and balances are the powers granted to ensure none of the three branches of government overstep their authority. Because the blank line connects to the checks from the executive branch to the legislative branch, the correct answer is the executive branch's checks and balances on the legislative branch. The executive branch can call special sessions of Congress and veto legislation, so Choice *C* is correct. Choice *A* is incorrect because, unlike the judicial and executive branches, members of the legislative branch cannot be impeached by another branch, though the legislative branch can expel its own members. Choices *B* and *D* are incorrect because the executive branch cannot refuse to enforce laws.

34. B: Choice *B* is correct. The Second Amendment states, "A well regulated Militia, being necessary to the security of a free State, the right of the people to keep and bear Arms, shall not be infringed." Choice *A* is incorrect because the First Amendment provides freedom of religion, speech, and the press, the right to assemble, and the right to petition the government. Choice *C* is incorrect because the Third Amendment establishes the right to refuse to house soldiers in times of war. Choice *D* is incorrect because the Fourth Amendment establishes a series of protections for citizens accused and charged with crimes.

35. B: Choice *B* is correct. The Electoral College determines the winner of presidential races, but if a candidate doesn't win a majority of electoral votes, the Twelfth Amendment requires the House of Representatives to decide the presidency, with each state delegation voting as a single bloc. The candidate with the most votes in the House wins the election. The total number of Electoral Votes in the table provided is 261; because no candidate has a majority of the votes (131), the vote went to the House of Representatives. Choice *A* is incorrect because the table shows that Andrew Jackson won a plurality of electoral and popular votes, but he didn't receive a majority. Choices *C* and *D* are incorrect because John Quincy Adams received the most votes in the House of Representatives, so he won the presidency.

36. A: Choice *A* is correct. Electoral systems dictate how the members of the ruling body are selected, how votes translate into positions, and how seats are filled in the political offices at each level of government. In a majority system, a candidate must receive a majority of the total votes in order to be awarded a seat, but if none of the candidates reach a majority, a second round of voting occurs, commonly referred to as a runoff. Choice *B* is incorrect because in a plurality system the candidate with the most votes, regardless of the total number, wins the election. Choice *C* is incorrect because in a single transferable system the voters each only have one ballot and rank the available candidates from most to least preferred. If a candidate is eliminated, the ballots that included him/her as the voter's first choice are transferred to each voter's second choice candidate rather than being wasted or lost because the first choice candidate is no longer eligible for election. Choice *D* is incorrect because in a party list system a political party makes a list of candidates and divides available electoral seats between the candidates on the list based on a variety of voting systems. There would be no need for a runoff election in any of these three types of electoral system.

37. A: The tone is incredulous. While contemplative is an option because of the inquisitive nature of the text, Choice *A* is correct because Frederick Douglass is astonished that he, a former slave, would be called upon to celebrate liberty that was not extended to him or to others of his race. Choice *B* is incorrect because Frederick Douglass is drawing contrasts between two groups of people rather than being inclusive. Choice *C* is incorrect because Frederick Douglass is expressing strong emotion, incredulity, rather than contemplation. Choice *D* is incorrect because Frederick Douglass is not nonchalant, nor accepting of the circumstances which he describes.

38. C: Choice *C*, *contented*, is the only word that has the opposite meaning of obdurate. Therefore, Choices *A*, *B*, and *D* are incorrect.

39. B: The main focus is to highlight the disparity between slaves and free men and protest slavery in a nation supposedly devoted to liberty. Frederick Douglass does make biblical references, it is not the main focus of the passage; therefore, Choice *A* is incorrect. The passage also makes no mention of wealthy landowners and doesn't speak of any positive response to the historical events, so Choices *C* and *D* are incorrect.

40: D: Choice *D* is the correct answer because it clearly references the disparity between slaves and free men in the United States. Choice *A* is incorrect because it demonstrates Frederick Douglass's knowledge of the Bible. Choice *B* is incorrect because it demonstrates his incredulity at his invitation to speak. Choice *C* is incorrect because Frederick Douglass is highlighting the terrible situation of slaves, but he is not highlighting the disparity between slaves and free men.

41: D: It is an example of hyperbole; the physical distance between Frederick Douglass and his audience was not, in fact, immeasurable. However, it clearly demonstrated the differences in the lives and situations of free men and slaves in the United States. Choice *A* is incorrect because assonance is the repetition of sounds and commonly occurs in poetry. Choice *B* is incorrect because parallelism refers to two statements that correlate, or parallel each other, in some manner. Choice *C* is incorrect because amplification normally refers to clarification of meaning by broadening the sentence structure, while hyperbole refers to a phrase or statement that is being exaggerated.

42: C: Recognize the equivocation of the speaker and those that he represents. Choice *C* is correct because the speaker is clear about his intention and stance throughout the text; he does not equivocate, so this answer choice is the only one that biblical references do not help the reader to do. Choice *A* is incorrect because quotations from the Bible would have been common at the time, creating a common ground between Frederick Douglass and his audience. Choice *B* is incorrect because another group of people affected by slavery are being referenced, and Frederick Douglass is clearly drawing a connection between that group of people and American slaves. Choice *D* is incorrect because Frederick Douglass's speech is designed to appeal to the listener's sense of humanity and create an abhorrence for slavery.

43. C: In lines 6 and 7, it is stated that avarice can prevent a man from being necessitously poor, but it also makes him too timorous, or fearful, to be wealthy. Choice *A* is incorrect because avarice prevents a man from being poor. Choice *B* is incorrect because the passage states that oppression, not avarice, is the consequence of wealth. Choice *D* is incorrect because the passage does not state that avarice drives a person's desire to be wealthy.

44. D: Paine believes that the distinction that is beyond a natural or religious reason is between king and subjects. Choice *A* is incorrect because he states that the distinction between good and bad is made in

198

heaven. Choice *B* is incorrect because he states that the distinction between male and female is natural. Choice *C* is incorrect because he does not mention anything about the distinction between humans and animals.

45. A: The passage states that the Heathens were the first to introduce government by kings into the world. Choice *B* is incorrect because the quiet lives of patriarchs came before the Heathens introduced this type of government and Paine puts it in opposition to government by kings. Choice *C* is incorrect because it was Christians, not Heathens, who paid divine honors to living kings. Heathens honored deceased kings. Choice *D* is incorrect because, while equal rights of nature are mentioned in the paragraph, they are not mentioned in relation to the Heathens.

46. B: Paine asserts that a monarchy is against the equal rights of nature and cites several parts of scripture that also denounce it. He doesn't say it is against the laws of nature, so Choice *A* is incorrect. Because he uses scripture to further his argument, it is not despite scripture that he denounces the monarchy. Therefore, Choice *C* is incorrect. Paine addresses the scripture doctrine of courts, which he claims does not support monarchy, and also clearly claims that scripture denounces a monarchical government; thus, Choice *D* is incorrect.

47. A: To be *idolatrous* is to worship someone or something other than God, in this case, kings. Choice *B* is incorrect because it is not defined as being deceitful. Choice *C* is incorrect because, while idolatry is considered a sin, it is an example of a sin, not a synonym for it. Choice *D* is incorrect because, while idolatry may have been considered illegal in some cultures, it is not a definition for the term.

48. A: The essential meaning of the passage is that the Almighty, God, disapproves of this type of government. Choice *B* is incorrect because, while heaven is mentioned, it is done so to suggest that the monarchical government is irreverent, not that heaven isn't promised. Choice *C* is incorrect because God's disapproval is mentioned, not his punishment. Choice *D* is incorrect because the passage refers to the Jewish monarchy, which required both belief in God and kings, and the tendency of monarchies to gloss over the anti-monarchical passages of scripture to support their form of government.

49. B: Choice *B* is correct. President Franklin D. Roosevelt introduced the New Deal, a series of executive orders and laws passed by Congress in response to the Great Depression. The excerpt describes how President Roosevelt intended to fight poverty by using the government's power to intervene and regulate the economy. Although Choices *A*, *C*, and *D* correctly identify specific activities referenced in the excerpt, they are specific examples of the underlying philosophy in action. The underlying philosophy is an active role for government in the nation's economic affairs.

50. C: Choice *C* is correct. Frederick Douglass escaped from slavery and worked as an abolitionist for the rest of his life. The excerpt references the hypocrisy of the Fourth of July, as the holiday celebrates freedom in a country with millions of slaves. Choices *A*, *B*, and *D* identify hypocritical aspects surrounding the slavery debate, but Choice *C* directly states the specific hypocrisy attacked in the excerpt.

51. D: Choice *D* is correct. Along with Lucy Stone and Elizabeth Cady Stanton, Susan B. Anthony was one of the most outspoken advocates for women's suffrage. Women couldn't vote in the United States until the Nineteenth Amendment was ratified in 1920. Choice *D* accurately expresses the main idea of the excerpt. Denying women the right to vote is tyranny, so Anthony will not pay a fine for voting illegally. Choice *A* is the second-best answer, but it's too general to be the main idea of an excerpt specifically

about women's suffrage. Choice *B* is incorrect because domestic abuse is not a topic addressed in this passage. Choice *C* is incorrect because Anthony is refusing to pay a fine because it is unjust, not claiming she can't pay it because of other debt.

52. B: Choice *B* is correct. Ronald Reagan won the presidential election of 1980 and promised to restore America's military power through defense spending, cutting government regulations, and reducing taxes. Evangelical Christians and the Moral Majority fiercely supported President Reagan's agenda, particularly his opposition to abortion and his conservative approach to social issues. The other answer choices include at least one mischaracterization. Choice *A* is incorrect because President Reagan generally opposed social programs. Choice *C* is incorrect because President Reagan valued American leadership more than international cooperation. In addition, his platform was far more radically conservative than compromising. Choice *D* is incorrect because President Reagan fought labor unions on several fronts, most notably when he broke a strike organized by an air traffic controllers' union.

53. A: Choice *A* is correct. The Depression of 1929, commonly referred to as the Great Depression, is the largest increase to unemployment, but the question asks for the second-largest increase. According to the graph, the Panic of 1893 increased unemployment by approximately ten percent; the Depression of 1920 increased unemployment by approximately six percent; the Depression of 1929 increased unemployment by approximately fifteen percent; and the Great Recession of 2007 increased unemployment by approximately four percent. Thus, the Panic of 1893 marks the second-largest increase to unemployment. As a result, Choices *B*, *C*, and *D* are incorrect.

54. C: This is a tricky question, but it can be solved through careful context analysis and vocabulary knowledge. One can infer that the use of "expedient," while not necessarily very positive, isn't inherently bad in this context either. Note how in the next line, he says, "but most governments are usually, and all governments are sometimes, inexpedient." This use of "inexpedient" indicates that a government becomes a hindrance rather than a solution; it slows progress rather than helps facilitate progress. Thus, Choice *A* and Choice *D* can be ruled out because they are hindrances or problems and would work better with *inexpedient* rather than *expedient*. Choice *B* makes no logical sense. Therefore, Choice *C* is the best description of *expedient*.

55. B: Choice *B* is the most accurate representation of Thoreau's views. Essentially, Thoreau brings to light the fact that the few people in power can twist government and policy for their own needs. Choices *A* and *C* are also correct to a degree, but the answer asks for the best description, which is Choice *B*. While Choice *D* is the only answer that mentions the Mexican War directly, Thoreau clearly thinks the war is unnecessary because the people generally didn't consent to the war.

Short-Answer Explanations

1.

a) The author remarks that Reconstruction destroyed the former Southern regime, and few things did more to disrupt those traditional power structures than the Reconstruction Amendments to the United States Constitution (Amendments 13, 14, and 15). Prior to Reconstruction, the Southern economic and political systems had been extremely hierarchical and dependent on a large supply of the free labor forcibly taken from African slaves. The Reconstruction Amendments brought an end to the institution of slavery and provided former slaves with political rights and civil liberty protections for the first time.

While the South did ultimately move to roll back the Reconstruction Amendments, the Reconstruction Amendments permanently eliminated a major pillar of traditional Southern power structures.

b) Southern whites' dissatisfaction with Reconstruction was clearly illustrated by their fervent support of undermining and thwarting racial equality after the withdrawal of federal troops in 1877. Immediately after the end of Reconstruction, Southern states passed a series of laws known collectively as Jim Crow laws to prevent people of color from exercising their new constitutional rights. Because Southern white men continued to dominate the racial caste system of the post-Civil War South, they were able to revive and sustain systemic white supremacy in economic, political, and social systems until the Civil Rights Movement in the 1960s.

c) Following the end of Reconstruction, Southern states passed Jim Crow laws to legally enforce white supremacy, and as a result, African Americans had extremely limited economic opportunities. The rise of the sharecropping industry underscores the economic plight of newly freed slaves. Without meaningful property rights and access to capital, most African Americans worked as sharecroppers, farming small parcels of land and paying white landowners a substantial share of the harvest. The system was highly exploitative due to the limited opportunities for advancement, and it deepened the generational poverty that dated back to slavery.

2.

a) The image depicts a complex cotton gin being operated by relatively few laborers. During the late eighteenth and early nineteenth centuries, the cotton gin greatly increased the efficiency and output of the cotton industry. Unlike earlier methods, the cotton gin offered a mechanical solution for cleaning and preparing cotton for export. Ever-increasing mechanization was a major characteristic of late nineteenth century agricultural production, and this trend accelerated as the North continued to industrialize, increasing the production of agricultural machinery and spare parts.

b) The cotton gin and other forms of mechanized agriculture contributed to the Southern states' continued dependence on agriculture. Many Southern leaders had hoped to build a New South after Reconstruction, largely based on mirroring Northern states' industrialization and urbanization. However, increasing yields sustained high profit margins, so plantation owners pursued large-scale production and sharecropping. Without the support of their wealthiest and most powerful citizens, the plans for a New South came to a halt.

c) The invention of the cotton gin increased sectionalism in the United States. Because the cotton gin increased the profitability of large-scale agriculture, it greatly strengthened Southern states' economic systems. This first occurred at a massive scale during the early nineteenth century when the Northern states were rapidly industrializing; in fact, the cotton gin spurred Northern industrialization because the larger supply of cotton led to the establishment of more factories and higher levels of textile production. While the economic differences between the North and South dated back to the era of the Thirteen Colonies, the cotton gin exponentially widened the economic divide.

3.

a) The American independence movement was significantly more aggressive in the period 1763 to 1776 as compared to the period 1750 to 1763. More Americans began discussing the need for greater unification in the early 1750s, but colonial leaders primarily lobbied for greater autonomy rather than independence. For example, Benjamin Franklin's Plan of Union (1754) called for a united colonial

201

government, but it didn't renounce the authority of the British Crown. The French and Indian War (1756–1763) marked a major turning point for the independence movement. Americans believed they would be rewarded for their service, but instead the British Crown raised taxes to recover what it had spent on protecting the colonies. Between 1763 and 1776, Britain passed a series of punitive measures intended to quash the growing rebellion, which only served to further fuel the American independence movement.

b) Britain acquired a staggering amount of North American territory after its victory in the Seven Years' War (1756–1763), annexing part of Spanish Florida and all of French Canada. While the new territory presented incredible profit potential, Britain faced issues balancing its conflicting problems with American Indian allies and American colonists. The British Crown decided to keep its agreement with the Iroquois, issuing the Royal Proclamation of 1763 to prohibit Americans from settling west of the Appalachian Mountains. Americans perceived this as a betrayal and increasingly sought to undermine British colonial rule. Over the next decade, the American independence movement rapidly gained popular support, allowing it to consolidate political and military power in the run-up to the American Revolutionary War (1775–1783).

c) During the 1770s, the most popular form of mass media was the publishing industry, particularly the widespread distribution of pamphlets. Thomas Paine's *Common Sense* (1776) was by far the most popular pamphlet of this period, and it was quickly distributed within the American independence movement. *Common Sense* denounced King George III for a variety of abuses, and it praised representative government for its emphasis on civic virtue. Overall, the American colonies' robust publishing industry represented the Patriots' best method of disseminating their revolutionary ideology and organizing mass actions against the British.

4.

a) The United States enjoyed a sizable boost in its relative global power in the aftermath of both World War I and World War II. Prior to World War I, the United States was an economic superpower, but European powers dwarfed America in terms of imperialism, military spending, and global influence. Afterward, the United States achieved parity with most global powers as reflected in its larger role in negotiating the Treaty of Versailles, arbitrating international disputes between major powers, and launching aggressive imperial interventions all over the world. World War II marked a similarly transformative movement for American power because the United States first established itself as one of two global superpowers in its aftermath.

b) The United States was significantly more powerful relative to other global powers in the aftermath of World War II as compared to its relative hierarchical position after World War I. The United States had developed from a powerful country to one of the most powerful countries in the world. European states suffered considerable devastation after World War I, but most maintained their status as global powers with control over extensive amounts of foreign territory. In contrast, the United States was one of two remaining superpowers after World War II. No country could compete with American manufacturing and financial military power, and only the Soviet Union could pose any type of deterrent to the projection of American power overseas.

c) The United States' disproportionate amount of global power after the end of World War II resulted in the systematic destruction of Latin America. During the Cold War, the United States covertly and overtly provided material support to regime change in more than a dozen Latin American countries. This

sometimes involved merely financing right-wing political movements, but material assistance was sometimes extended to known violators of human rights and death squads. American policymakers' fear of communism also led to the overthrow of democratically elected leaders, such as Chilean President Salvador Allende in 1973. Overall, the ascendance of American power at the end of World War II crippled the economic and political development of many Latin American states, particularly in regard to their long-term stability and self-sufficiency.

Index

Dear AP History Test Taker,

We would like to start by thanking you for purchasing this study guide for your AP History exam. We hope that we exceeded your expectations.

Our goal in creating this study guide was to cover all of the topics that you will see on the test. We also strove to make our practice questions as similar as possible to what you will encounter on test day. With that being said, if you found something that you feel was not up to your standards, please send us an email and let us know.

We would also like to let you know about other books in our catalog that may interest you.

AP Biology	**AP Chemistry**	**AP US Government**
amazon.com/dp/1628456221	amazon.com/dp/1628456914	amazon.com/dp/1637753616
(paid link)	(paid link)	(paid link)

As an Amazon Associate TPB Publishing earns from qualifying purchases.

We have study guides in a wide variety of fields. If the one you are looking for isn't listed above, then try searching for it on Amazon or send us an email.

Thanks Again and Happy Testing!
Product Development Team
info@studyguideteam.com

FREE Test Taking Tips Video/DVD Offer

To better serve you, we created videos covering test taking tips that we want to give you for FREE. **These videos cover world-class tips that will help you succeed on your test.**

We just ask that you send us feedback about this product. Please let us know what you thought about it—whether good, bad, or indifferent.

To get your **FREE videos**, you can use the QR code below or email freevideos@studyguideteam.com with "Free Videos" in the subject line and the following information in the body of the email:

    a. The title of your product

    b. Your product rating on a scale of 1-5, with 5 being the highest

    c. Your feedback about the product

If you have any questions or concerns, please don't hesitate to contact us at info@studyguideteam.com.

Thank you!

Made in the USA
Thornton, CO
02/06/23 22:48:38